BARRY JOHN THE KING

BARRY JOHN

The King

Barry John with Paul Abbandonato

MAINSTREAM
PUBLISHING

EDINBURGH AND LONDON

First published in Great Britain in 2000 by
MAINSTREAM PUBLISHING COMPANY (EDINBURGH) LTD
7 Albany Street
Edinburgh EH1 3UG

ISBN 1 84018 341 1

Jacket photographs © Allsport, except inset © Glenn Edwards

A catalogue record for this book is available from the British Library

Typeset in Futurist and Giovanni Book
Printed and bound in Great Britain by Butler and Tanner Ltd, Frome and London

CONTENTS

PREFACE

Over the past ten years or so several people have asked me to put pen to paper and reflect upon my story – not just my time in rugby, but what has happened to me off the pitch too.

I always took it with a pinch of salt. It was only when I came out of journalistic 'retirement' to write a rugby column for *Wales on Sunday* – having previously spent twenty-five years working for the *Daily Express* and the BBC – that my interest was rekindled. The paper's sports editor, Paul Abbandonato, was seconded to look after me and he quickly made me realise that there *was* still so much to say – an unwritten, untold and unusual story.

I could see Paul was fascinated by the anecdotes and the stories that I reeled off, and equally I was really enjoying doing my column with him. Thus, when the subject of writing a book cropped up, this time I replied, 'Why not?'

I know Paul has had opportunities to write sports books before, particularly in the field of football, but he tells me he declined the offers because the subject matter did not interest him enough. Isn't that strange? He always said 'no', I always said 'no' – and yet we met each other for the first time in the build-up to the 1999 Rugby World Cup and together we immediately said 'yes'.

Paul certainly took my response as an affirmative, because by the time we next met he had drawn up a synopsis of what he thought the book should involve – and even had an immediate commitment from the publishers!

So, here we are. It has been fascinating to say the least, although Paul will confirm that after the one-and-a-half-hour mark, my interest in the day's proceedings would tend to wane a little. He would not have any of that, though, and his unbelievable enthusiasm, expertise and the ease with which he has done this book, have certainly helped drive me along.

I want to say thank you to him because Paul made it possible. I only had to yap away – and most of my friends will tell you that comes very easily to me! I like the way he interpreted my words and I hope you will see my character emerging with the passing of every chapter.

I'm sure that after this book Paul will become even more sought after for future projects. He has become a good journalistic colleague and, more importantly, a good friend of mine. Hey, he even lent me a tenner the other day!

I would also like to thank Paul's wife Paula who, I'm told, was nine months pregnant with their third child, Joseph, when, on a cold November night, she sat up until midnight to write letters to the publisher on behalf of Paul and myself. My thanks also go to Jamie Bartlett for his I.T. expertise (not a subject either Paul or myself are particularly strong at); Howard Evans for facts and figures; Julian Cooper for his advice and help; my good friends Shaun and Carole Ellery and David and Lil Jones. A debt of gratitude also goes to the management of the Cardiff Bay Hotel and their waiter Owen Brewer, who kept us copiously supplied with refreshments – particularly the biscuits, which Paul devoured!

My thanks also go to *you* for reading this book. I hope you enjoy my story as much as I've enjoyed telling it to Paul.

Barry John
October 2000

FOREWORD BY GEORGE BEST

Not many people are aware of this, but rugby union was the first sport I played as a youngster – and as you would imagine, my position was the glamour one of fly-half. I do not think I would have made it on to the international stage and in any case, once I got a round ball, I was playing football day and night. But I never lost my early love of rugby, either union or league, and when I was playing for Manchester United I was a great fan of Salford.

I have watched lots of top rugby over the years and on a few memorable occasions I managed to watch Wales and Barry John in their pomp. That was probably the greatest Welsh side to have taken the field in the history of the sport. Yet even though it was full of legendary players, Barry still stood out.

Even in a truly great team you need a jewel, someone who stands out above everyone else, and he was that jewel. If you put it in football terms, Barry was the Welsh team's Diego Maradona or Pelé, and he was exactly the same when he swapped the red of Wales for the red of the British Lions. I can pay him no higher compliment.

The word that springs to mind when I think of Barry as a player is 'unpredictable'. So many times you would see him with ball in hand and opponents bearing down on him, thinking he was surely about to get caught. And, in an instant, he was gone – leaving his pursuers on their backsides. That is the most valuable asset in either code of football, the eleven-a-side or fifteen-a-side game.

What is more, Barry was always one of the lads. There were no airs about Barry. He just got on with his job and he never thought of himself as a superstar. But believe me, he was – very much so.

I used to bump into Barry on the circuit and you were always aware that he was that little bit special. He was revered by the public, his friends and his team-mates and his decision to retire early – like mine from football – took a few people aback, although I could understand the reasons.

It was only after we had hung up our boots that I got to know him really well. We frequently met up on the after-dinner speaking scene and I discovered what a truly great guy he is. One thing I quickly learned was that you did not want to follow him as a guest speaker, because it was impossible to top his fantastic stories.

Not that he has to say a word to have the audience in the palm of his hand. He gets a standing ovation as soon as his name is announced and he simply has to walk into a room for you to see the enormous respect people have for him. I have mixed with some of the biggest sporting celebrities in the world and, believe me, very, very few people have that special quality. The man is a 24-carat gem. The best.

TRIBUTES TO THE KING

The most vivid memory I have of my first visit to Cardiff Arms Park was of Barry John's performance. It was superb, though for an Englishman very frightening. He was always ready for the ball, taking it cleanly, putting it precisely where it was wanted and at times moving brilliantly himself down the field, running at the opposition to either score or set up wonderful tries.

He was an inspiration to his own side and Wales were the ones who took advantage most as a result whenever he was in the game.

We spectators should be grateful to Barry as well as to his team-mates. We just wish he had gone on playing for a few more years.

Rt Hon. Sir Edward Heath MBE
(Prime Minister, 1970–74)

———————————

Among the most lasting and pleasurable experiences of my many years in this world is to have watched Barry John play rugby for Wales and the British Lions. His consummate skills, coupled with unbelievable self-confidence, took him beyond the reach of ordinary people and prompted him to create opportunities on the field that no one else would have had the effrontery to attempt.

When under pressure, he had a rare quality of effortlessly creating time and space for himself and for his partner, that great scrum-half Gareth Edwards.

Another memorable player, W.B. (Billy) Cleaver, who turned out for Wales in the backs many times in the 1940s and 1950s, has said to me that Barry John's attitude to friends and foes alike on the field was, 'I can do it on my own. Stop me if you can.' Very few could. No wonder he was called The King.

Barry had the unconscious arrogance of great artists and this communicated itself to the rest of the Welsh and Lions side, who raised their game accordingly. If he had played in the modern game, I can picture in my thoughts how well he would have timed those beautifully handled runs which end with a try under the goalpost.

I plead guilty to writing about Barry John in superlatives, but how else do you describe rugby genius?

Rt Hon. James Callaghan
(Prime Minister, 1976–79)

ONE

WHY I QUIT – THE TRUTH

As I leaned over to lace up my boots, a tear came into my eye. I did my best to keep my feelings hidden from my mates in the dressing-room, but deep inside the emotions were churning me up. I was twenty-seven and at the peak of my powers, I was said to have the rugby world at my feet and had just scored a record number of points for the British Lions and for Wales – but this was the last time I was going to play a rugby match.

Only a handful of very close confidants shared my secret, including my wife Jan, of course, and my regular scrum-half partner Gareth Edwards. They knew I had simply had enough of being stuck inside a goldfish bowl as the most talked-about rugby player in the world. Seeing my name in newspaper headlines every single day; being pulled from pillar to post by being continually requested to attend functions, dinners, parties, receptions and awards ceremonies . . . I had become too far detached from ordinary people and I did not like it. Retiring was my only escape.

Perhaps only George Best, who was going through a similar experience as the most famous footballer of his generation with Manchester United, could fully understand my feelings. I loved playing rugby, George loved playing football, but in the end we shared a common bond, for neither of us could handle the circus act surrounding our fame as it spiralled totally out of control. George and I became good friends and met up many times during that period to discuss, among other things, the huge pressures we were each being put under. He of course, was to retire early himself shortly afterwards. I can sympathise greatly with someone like David Beckham today. As a Manchester United megastar he's become big enough in his own right – but throw his wife Victoria Adams, alias Posh Spice, into the equation and no wonder Beckham feels as if everything he does is being scrutinised under a microscope.

Let's get something into perspective straight away – what Bestie had to put up with, as the tall, dark and handsome Irish football genius dubbed the 'Fifth Beatle', was on a much grander scale than anything I encountered. But George was able to score brilliant goals on a Saturday afternoon and could then mingle with fellow superstars like Bobby Charlton and Denis Law at training on Monday morning.

Because rugby union was then an amateur game I did not have that luxury. In fact I had to fulfil three different roles and there were times when I felt like a dolly mixture sweet – 'Which one am I supposed to be today, then?' Role one was the breadwinner who worked as a finance representative to pay the mortgage. Role two was international rugby player, which meant I had to ensure I was at my sharpest mentally and physically. Role three was as a supposed superstar, required to attend functions at the poshest of London hotels next to grand names like George himself, Tom Jones and even the Prime Minister of the day, Sir Edward Heath. One of those roles is pressure enough; put the three together and you have, as I discovered, an impossible situation.

As I sat in the dressing-room, slightly misty-eyed, lacing my boots for the very last time that April day in 1972, I knew I had reached the point of no return. My decision to quit was going to hurt me and shock the sporting world, but I was going through with it. I had no alternative.

At least I was going out on a good cause. My final game was between a star-studded Barry John XV and a side selected by Carwyn James, coach to our victorious 1971 British Lions side in New Zealand nine months earlier. Its purpose was to raise money for the Urdd Gobaith Cymru (Welsh League of Youth), which was celebrating its fiftieth anniversary. Such was the quality of player on show at Cardiff Arms Park that night that, in effect, there were two Lions teams opposing each other. More than 36,000 turned up to watch us.

Fittingly, I scored a try in the last minute to win the game for my team, but I pointedly refused to take the conversion and threw the ball to Gareth Edwards instead. As I did so, everyone in the crowd must have wondered what was going on. Just a few months earlier my goal-kicking had enabled me to score 188 points in 17 matches on that Lions tour to New Zealand – a record which, incidentally, still stands today – and four weeks previously I had broken a fifty-eight-year-old landmark to become the top points scorer in Welsh rugby history.

I knew I was retiring, though, and as rugby to me has always been a game about scoring tries, I did not want to leave the stage by kicking the ball over the crossbar. I just told Gareth, 'You kick it.' He didn't say anything, slotted over the conversion and the final whistle was blown immediately afterwards.

After shaking the hands of the opposition I took one last look around the stadium as a player before walking off slowly. Physically I was leaving the pitch for the last time. Mentally the spark had gone from me four months earlier. When I reached the dressing-room I took off my boots, kissed them, put them down on the floor and thought quietly to myself, 'Well, this is it, Barry.' It suddenly dawned on me that I really would never wear them again.

Three decades on, hardly a day has passed when I'm not asked, 'Barry, why did you finish so early?' Yes, that still happens today when I'm in my mid-fifties. I know there is a whole new generation of people who have grown up aware of the name Barry John, without knowing my reasons for quitting so suddenly.

Over the years I have devised a perfect answer to the question which I give to everyone, young and old. I shrug my shoulders and reply, 'What's half an hour?' By this I mean that I had the rest of my adulthood to be getting on with and could not worry about missing a few years of rugby. My answer is not meant to be flippant – it is just a way, perhaps, of justifying my decision to myself.

If someone wants a more in-depth reply, wondering if I regret my decision, I will say: 'Circumstances were . . .' and very briefly explain a couple of things. If they persist, I stop the conversation there and then.

So do I regret it? I have never spoken about this in great detail in print, but the answer is yes, of course I have regrets – big regrets – and I've probably thought about them most days since. I suppose people expect me to say, 'No, I've no worries about what happened', but that would be untruthful on my part. Any top sportsman will tell you that you should carry on playing, particularly at the highest level, until the moment your body tells you that you simply cannot do it any more. I had already savoured unforgettable moments – including victory for the Lions in that rugby hotbed of New Zealand, and Grand Slam and Triple Crown wins for Wales. I knew I had a good few years left at the top and many more memorable victories to come.

But while I was reluctant to pack in a game that had given me so much, I had no option but to go through with my decision. Once made, it was irrevocable. When I sign autographs or give youngsters advice on how to play, I always say 'Enjoy your sport' – I was not enjoying mine any more. Off the pitch, people said circumstances meant I had stopped being a normal human being. But I *am* perfectly normal, proud of my west Wales working-class background, someone who still makes great play of saying 'please' and 'thank you' and opening doors for ladies. On the pitch, while I like to think I was a bit of an artist, the level of expectation was becoming way over the top with people anticipating wonder tries in every match. It was almost as if, to satisfy their desire, I had to dig a hole in the pitch and suddenly pop up at the other end behind the opposition defence to score a try!

Fame can be a great thing at first. It opens restaurant doors for you and gives you privileges others do not have. But by the end I began to feel as uncomfortable with it as George did. He had come over to Manchester as a raw fifteen-year-old from working-class roots in Belfast. I had a similar upbringing, but unlike George, had the advantage of a college education. However, that did nothing to prepare me for, or help me cope with, a situation that became so ridiculously out of hand that, during a refuelling stop on the way back from New Zealand with the Lions, I found myself on the front page of the *New York Times*! Had the world gone mad? I didn't think they had even heard of rugby in the United States, yet here I was staring hard at a picture of myself holding a can of Coca-Cola and reading about myself in one of their premier newspapers.

It was that Lions tour, when we became the first and only British side to beat the New Zealanders on their own patch, which took rugby into a new stratosphere as far as the media were concerned. British sport was, at best, average in those days, with little else to hit the column inches with any force. So the newspaper, magazine, television and radio people latched on to our success story: for the first time rugby was not only on the back pages, but also on the front pages, and even in non-sporting magazines.

As the fly-half who had scored most points in our 2–1 Test victory, I was the one attracting most of the attention. For example, after our victory in the third Test in Wellington, the London *Evening Standard* had the banner headline, 'JOHN THE KING HAS DONE IT' plastered across its front page in huge type.

One of my great friends, Clem Thomas (himself a former Lion), travelled out for the last two Test matches to tell me: 'Barry, you are being treated like a pop star back home. You are in every newspaper and magazine, they are selling posters of you, everyone is talking about you and they are even writing songs about you.' I remember then thinking this was a bit over the top, but I was soon to discover it was true.

When we flew home, the television stations changed their entire broadcasting schedules so that the news bulletins could cover our arrival direct from Heathrow. We were met by thousands of well-wishers at the airport – the pilot telling us it was a bigger reception than for any event he had known – and I even remember, in order to get away from the bustle and noise, having to conduct an interview with Kate Adie in the ladies' toilet.

Then the fame monster just grew and grew. Suddenly rugby players were being asked to attend functions at Buckingham Palace and Downing Street for the first time. I found myself in the top ten of a number of sports polls, previously uncharted territory for a rugby player. Up to a hundred letters a day began arriving by the sack-load at my Cardiff home, Cardiff Rugby Club and the Cardiff-based Forward Trust finance house where I used to work. Bestie, as I have pointed out, could mingle with Charlton and Law; I would go straight from playing for Wales on the Saturday to mixing with the same members of the public who had been cheering me on thirty-six hours earlier. Inevitably they just wanted to talk about the game – I wanted to forget it.

Every single day I was asked to attend a function, appear at a charity event, open a shop or do something else. There was a system to deal with the mail, but no system can really help if your presence is required at these functions every single time. From the moment we landed back at Heathrow to the day I actually retired, I do not think I had an average of even one meal a week with Jan in my own house. There was always an awards ceremony to attend, whether I was collecting a trophy or handing them out as guest of honour. Even on my rare days off I found it hard to relax and take my foot off the pedal, because I had been on adrenaline for the previous five days. I could not even doze off because my thoughts were racing and I actually had to shout out loud to myself, 'Barry, go to sleep!'

I was getting bored of myself too. People were paying hundreds of pounds for my presence at these events – an awful lot of money in those days – but I found I was telling the same stories four times in six days. I was not finding them funny any more, boringly repetitive in fact. On top of that I felt under the weather, had bags under my eyes and could hardly boast I was in a finely tuned sportsman's condition, where rest is vitally important.

Wherever I went I found myself being fêted and I felt it had simply gone too far. Men would come up and hug me. On one occasion, while I was on a business trip to a bank in Rhyl, north Wales, an eighteen-year-old girl actually curtsied to me. That had already happened to me once before during a visit to a hospital in Swansea. Once was bad enough; twice was simply too much.

That whole trip to north Wales had been surreal because when I arrived with Gwynne Walters, Cardiff area manager for Forward Trust, we found the road had been blocked off and we were escorted in like royalty. These days I can laugh about what happened next, but back then it was an eerie, frightening experience. As Gwynne and I entered the bank everyone was lined up to shake my hand and began clapping and cheering. I walked slowly down the line, reached the eighteen-year-old bank clerk and was horrified and embarrassed as she did it – she actually curtsied in front of me. Everyone applauded her actions, but that simply made matters worse as far as I was concerned. That moment made me realise I was alienated from ordinary people, that things had simply gone too far, that I was not like a normal human being any more. I was being treated with so much reverence it was alarming. These people thought I was out of their circle and I really did not want that.

Every day, it seemed, people would rush up to me to say, 'You're *the* Barry John, aren't you, can we have your autograph please?' I have no problems signing autographs – nearly thirty years on I still willingly oblige people, although when I'm going for an appointment and have to tell people my name, I make sure I say it quietly – but in those days youngsters would frequently knock on my front door asking for signatures. There was one time when, having gone to a garage to pick up a car, I was surrounded by so many people with little bits of paper that I had to get them to write down their names and addresses, put the lot into a big bag and, over a period of weeks, send out literally hundreds of signed photographs.

One of the more bizarre incidents came one Sunday, when four people from Bristol decided their idea of sightseeing for the day was going over to Wales to look at Barry John's house. They could have gone to the zoo, the park, the beach, anywhere, but no – they woke up and decided to seek out BJ's abode. They stopped off in Cardiff, asked where Barry John's house was and duly arrived in our street. I know this because my wife Jan invited them in for Sunday tea and they told us the story!

As this went on around me I had no one to turn to for guidance and advice, apart from George of course, and he had enough problems of his own without worrying about mine. So I began to warn people that this attention was getting too much and that if it didn't stop I might have to walk away from rugby. No one believed me, insisting I simply could not pack it in with so many great days still ahead of me. They just thought it was Barry John getting up to one of his pranks again.

But a hoax this definitely was not. Things were getting so bad I was thinking about my future virtually every minute of the day. It had got to the point where I was literally asking referees how many minutes were left in matches and making sure I positioned myself near the players' tunnel so I could avoid the flood of people rushing towards me at the end. Invariably that meant I was the first person down the tunnel and my state of thought was not exactly helped when I walked into the darkness to be met by glaring camera lights after Wales had beaten England 12–3 at Twickenham in 1972. (By the way, I never lost to England – it would have been rude, as a Welshman, to do so!)

I was like a rabbit caught in headlights, temporarily blinded by the sudden brightness. Then out popped Eamonn Andrews brandishing his famous red book. 'Barry John, tonight this is your . . .' I was used to television lights but this was different, a bit sudden and very disconcerting. I was whisked away by chauffeured car to the studios where Jan, my nearest and dearest and my Welsh team-mates and friends were present for what was a lovely show. Jan had been keeping the secret from me for almost two months and suddenly the silence around the dinner table two weeks earlier began to fall into place. George had had the red book shown to him and I asked our dinner guests if they had seen the show. Everyone went quiet, almost coughing and spluttering, and the hush was only broken by Jan asking, 'Barry, do you want some more peas?' I remember thinking at the time it was an odd question because my plate was already piled high with roast beef and vegetables and I wondered where on earth she expected me to put them!

While it was prestigious to be one of Eamonn Andrews' victims on the show, though, there remained almost a touch of horror about the way the television people had gone into my room while I was playing against England and taken everything away to their studios without me knowing. In truth I found it a bit frightening.

Quite clearly by this point I needed a break. So, even though Wales were playing Scotland in ten days' time, I did a George Best and disappeared from public gaze for a while, spending a week around the swimming pool with Jan in Majorca. The Welsh selectors had every reason to drop me, even sanction me. I remember telling Jan this as we sunned ourselves and then laughing, 'They'll have to answer to the nation, though!' That night, on Spanish television, the Welsh team was announced and the name of B. John was there at fly-half. When I returned the other players smiled: 'Only you could get away with it.'

However, the enjoyment of spending a week away from the suffocation of fame simply increased my desire to call it a day. After playing against the Scots and France and then in that special fund-raising match, I made my announcement to retire in the *Sunday Mirror*. I received £7,000 for giving them the exclusive, but the sports editor actually pleaded with me to think again. He told me the newspaper would honour their contract with me, but urged me to put my retirement on hold for another two years and make my announcement with them then!

Unfortunately I could not oblige. Once I have made a decision I stick to it. I duly gave the *Sunday Mirror* their big exclusive over lunch at the Ladbroke Club in London and went upstairs afterwards to play in the casino. There I saw a young Saudi gamble away £200,000 that afternoon. He had lost his fortune; I remember thinking I'd lost mine.

How was I going to handle the next Wales match and the fact that I would be inside the Arms Park, but not down on the pitch dictating play in my accustomed fly-half position? The game was a big one, against New Zealand, and I had a ticket for the press-box. I made a point of literally running up the stairs to my seat, hoping that by the time I got to the top I would actually be panting and hopelessly out of breath. Just to prove to myself, 'Barry, you're not fit enough to play out there anyway'. It was, I suppose, my way of trying to justify my decision to myself at the time – but I have to be honest and admit it took fully three years to come to terms with the fact that I could not be out on that pitch myself. Remember, most of the Welsh players wearing the red shirts had been my team-mates for many years and my natural instinct was to tell myself what I would have done with the ball in certain situations. Yes, it was hard.

Slowly but surely, I did eventually become accustomed to the fact that my playing days were over and so did the hundreds of people who kindly wrote to me pleading with me to return. One lovely story surrounded an old widow in her seventies who had an apartment overlooking Cardiff Rugby Club's Arms Park ground. Grey-haired and slight, she approached me one day to say that she had heard rumours I might be retiring and assumed it was because I had a big money-making scheme in the offing. She said she did not have a lot of cash herself, but would give me everything she had if I carried on playing – which amounted to the grand sum of £750. 'You see,' she told me, 'I watch you play from my balcony and you are one of the few happy things I have to look forward to on a Saturday afternoon.'

It was an incredibly touching gesture on her behalf, but again I could not oblige. I did make a point of seeking out this pensioner when I made my official announcement, to explain the reasoning behind my decision. I think she eventually understood why I was doing it, even if she felt I should have kept going.

Still, at least that particular stranger knew exactly who I was when I pulled on the number 10 jersey for either Cardiff, Wales or the Lions. Another dear old lady, Jan's elderly grandmother, whom we simply called Gran-Gran, got a bit confused one day as she watched me play on television – or, at least, thought she watched me.

We often had Sunday lunch at Jan's house in Swansea and, having seen me play well for Wales against England, Gran-Gran complimented me on my performance. A few weeks on, after I had played for Cardiff against Swansea at St Helen's, Gran-Gran said over Sunday lunch: 'Last time I said you were superb, Barry, and I thought you were. So, being totally honest again, I have to say I thought you were pretty poor yesterday.' Knowing our match had not been on television I wondered what she was on about, particularly as I had played well anyway. Then, as the conversation went on, the truth began to dawn. Gran-Gran insisted she had seen me. 'I only watched bits of the game, but you were wearing the number 10 shirt again . . . against Northern Ireland!' The penny dropped. While Cardiff were at St Helen's, the Welsh soccer team were just up the road playing Northern Ireland in the Home International Championships at Swansea City's Vetch Field ground.

I have no idea who the Welsh soccer player wearing the number 10 shirt was that day, but I can tell him this – he did not play very well! Without wishing to let Gran-Gran down, I just smiled and said, 'Well we can't have good games every week, you know.' Momentarily, however, she had put the fame thing into perspective.

Playing in the Northern Ireland side that day, of course, was a certain George Best. Hmmm – George and myself on the same pitch together? That, Gran-Gran, really would have been one for the fan clubs to savour.

TWO

BESTIE AND ME

The first time George Best and I met, there was instant rapport and respect. He looked at me, I looked back – and we each detected an immediate, invisible bond between us, a sense of mutual recognition. This was a case of two men acquiring each other's exceptional standards in their own sporting field. You are capable of this; I'm capable of that. You are going through this adulation thing; I'm going through it too. The whole world had been looking at George and, to be honest, I detected almost a touch of relief in him. It was as if George had suddenly seen himself in the mirror – here was someone, at last, who could understand what he was going through, even if, in my case, it was a more diluted form of stardom.

With hundreds of other stars, George and I were at the Savoy Hotel in London for a sporting dinner. We were each in company of our own, so I held up the palm of my hand to indicate 'five minutes'. George nodded, we duly finished the conversations we were having, and strode towards one another to talk for the very first time. It was the start of what I would call a 'special' friendship. We were each in a unique position. He was able to comprehend my problems better than anyone else; I was perhaps able to understand his, even if, I must stress again, George's fame level was five times greater than mine.

Maybe because of that special bond, I have always been able to sympathise with George over his drinking problem. Others have spent more hours, days and weeks in his company and know him better than me. But having talked to George many times in confidence, conversations arising from our recognition of one another's sporting ability and the subsequent difficulties that such ability brought, I understood why his problems developed and slowly went out of control.

George once told me in private that he would make the front pages of the newspapers for the wrong reasons. 'One day, Barry, they'll find me in the gutter,' he said. We laughed it off at the time. Well, we *were* young and at our sporting peaks, so how could something as preposterous as that possibly come true? However, with the passing of every year since and with George's name being more and more in the newspapers for anything (it seemed) except football, that little comment began to concern me. It was not something to have a little giggle over any more.

Therefore, when I heard in April 2000 that George had collapsed and had been taken to hospital, it saddened but didn't totally surprise me. In the past close colleagues like George's managers – Matt Busby and Tommy Docherty – and his playing colleague Denis Law had covered brilliantly for him. But at fifty-three years of age, time and drink had finally caught up with George and even he realises that if it happens again, it will be the last time.

Naturally I have been aware of George's problem for years and occasionally I wonder why it developed into this. While you obviously have to say it was his fault, you may yet ask if it was inevitable.

To answer that, you have to remember that George was a total one-off. I once went to Manchester United's training ground at The Cliff to do some filming with George for a television show and I saw Bobby Charlton ask him for his autograph for a friend. We are talking here about an England World Cup winner and a football legend in his own right – yet even amongst the company of giants like Charlton and Law, George was on a different plateau altogether. The demands upon him overshadowed any I have known in sport. The impact he made was greater than Charlton, David Beckham, Ryan Giggs, Alan Shearer, Eric Cantona, Kevin Keegan or anybody you wish to name. He was the original soccer superstar and there were many traps and pitfalls ahead for him to tumble into.

George reached his Everest in just about everything, although to someone of his ability the targets were probably more like small hills than the huge mountains they would have been to anybody else. Take it from me, once you have done that as a top sportsman, it becomes very tough going. How do you translate the energy, drive and buzz that went into achieving your ambitions into re-challenging yourself? At that level of stardom, it can be extremely difficult and maybe drink was an escape for George. He himself has gone on record as saying that if there were any excuse, he would turn to the bottle. It was his way of coping, I suppose.

Having retired early myself, I can certainly understand more than most just why George often went missing from training and packed in football prematurely himself. When the Paparazzi glitz hit me, I was in my twenties and had a college education behind me as a qualified schoolteacher. It was hard enough for me, so imagine what it must have been like for George coming over to Manchester as a fifteen-year-old working class lad from Belfast to be thrown into that sort of environment? When it came to being in the media glare I was very much in the First Division whereas George was in the Premiership – and I thought First Division was bad enough.

Football was waiting for a genius to emerge and suddenly this Irish youngster with phenomenal skill, locks of dark hair, blue eyes and Irish charm entered their world in the Swinging Sixties. The media were screaming out for a pin-up like George and soon he was dubbed the Fifth Beatle. It was not just talk either, because George was right up there on the same level as John, Paul, George and Ringo. Yes, he was that big. Skill, style, charm, good looks – the dream had been answered.

If you want an idea of just how big George was, how highly regarded and respected he was by his peers, let me go back to that time we first met at the Savoy. What is the test of a true sporting superstar? I found out the answer that day as I sat at the dinner table surrounded by eminent people, the room jam-packed with household sporting figures from around the world. Everyone was chattering away as you do on these occasions, the hubbub of noise getting greater and greater. Suddenly the master of ceremonies, in his red suit, banged his gong and announced in his most posh of voices: 'Ladies and Gentlemen, Mr George Best . . .'

Suddenly these Olympic gold medallists, Wimbledon champions, Open golf winners and world boxing title-holders stopped talking and began staring. To a person they wanted to see George Best, at his very peak then, in the flesh. I have only seen that happen on one other occasion. That time the MC announced, 'Ladies and gentlemen, Mr Muhammad Ali . . .' Again everyone stopped to stare. George and Ali were total showstoppers.

No wonder I feel honoured to have known George at his zenith, to have been a friend of his down the years and to have been likened and linked to him in my own sporting field.

It was an even bigger honour to discover that the great man himself used to get up in the early hours of the morning when I was in New Zealand with the Lions to tune into the radio and find out how I was doing. His driver, who generally looked after George as his 'gofer' in those days, told me the story of how he was warned his job would be on the line if he did not wake his boss. We are talking about three and four o'clock in the morning here, but regardless of what state he was in, George insisted he *had* to be woken from his slumbers. His driver was even ready to throw a bucket of water over George if necessary, although I do not think it actually came to that. By hook or by crook, each time George managed to get up and turn on the radio – and I'm just pleased we were able to oblige and make his early-morning rises worthwhile by beating New Zealand.

How can I describe what went on between us when we met up? Perhaps it is simplest to say that we laughed in each other's company, found one another fun and easy going, just enjoyed going for a pint together when the opportunity arose. George is one of the wittiest, funniest and sharpest characters I have met, a far more intelligent person than some people give him credit for. George's one-liners, when he delivers them on television, are invariably beautiful – not the sort of rubbish Chris Eubank comes out with. Said with a twinkle in his eye, George just has this wonderful knack of getting his clever message across. His delivery is brilliant.

We were comfortable together because I could respect the standard he had reached in football and he could respect the level I had attained in rugby. We could see the dangers in one another's sport too. I greatly admired the guts George displayed when the studs were flying from some true soccer hard-men in the 1960s and early 1970s. He would watch me play and frequently tell me, 'I would not fancy those big forwards thundering in to tackle me.' It was, I suppose, a two-man mutual admiration society.

Several times I visited George's lovely house in Manchester, worth £250,000 even back then, so I wonder what that particular property is valued at today? George told me the neighbours were frequently approached by tabloid newspapers offering money if they would monitor his movements and report back to them. That was the sort of goldfish bowl he found himself in.

George also had the dilemma to resolve of who his real friends were. People would try to get on board with me because of who I was, but since rugby union was still an amateur game they knew full well I did not have money. George did have money – and he told me he never knew definitely whether certain people wanted to be in his company simply because of who he was, or because of the vast sums he was earning.

It is strange to think that I could have actually opposed George on the soccer pitch. I very nearly became a professional footballer myself.

Funnily enough, it was the unwitting intervention of a certain Jimmy Hill which made me choose rugby instead – as I always tell him whenever we meet.

If you were to ask sportsmen which other sports they enjoy, most would plump for soccer and golf. Most of us played soccer when we were younger and many of us go on to enjoy golf – unfortunately a game I have had to give up for the past ten years because of a back problem – when we are older. In fact I would go so far as to say that, deep down, rugby players, especially the backs, harbour ambitions of being top soccer stars.

I used to play the game to quite a high standard, as well as rugby, when I was growing up in the west Wales village of Cefneithin. I scored lots of goals and was due to have trials with Coventry City after being recommended to the club. Everything had been arranged and I was just waiting for the formal letter stating the date and venue of the trial, but it never arrived. Why? I was in the dark for many years until the answer surfaced during a chance conversation with Jimmy Hill at a BBC function.

Jimmy took over as Coventry manager at much the same time and, on discovering various files of paper stacked up in the out tray on his desk – including my trial details – he decided to throw the lot into the dustbin. He decided that he was having a totally fresh start and did not even look at the sheets of paper. He simply deemed them part of the previous regime, nothing to do with him. Bang went my trial and my budding soccer career. Deep down I always knew I would turn to rugby, but if I had gone to Coventry for that trial, impressed, been looked after and coaxed to come back again, you never know. Jimmy does not see it that way, though. On the contrary, whenever we meet up he makes a point of saying that I owe him one: 'Barry, don't you think you should say thank you to me? I made you into a rugby player.' I suppose he did!

Still, I did once get the chance to play on the same pitch as George Best and finally show off those soccer skills that never did come to fruition. The occasion was a charity match, played in front of 16,000 people at Crystal Palace's Selhurst Park ground. The game was between a London XI (boasting names like Alan Hudson, Peter Osgood and Martin Peters) and a Stars XI. George invited me to be in his Stars team and, as we sat side by side in the dressing-room before kick-off, he asked me, 'What position do you want to play?' I replied, 'Just stick me out on the right wing.' That is where I lined up and, after a couple of comfortable early passes when it became clear I was reasonably proficient on the ball, they actually began to feed me possession quite a lot.

We won the game 8–3 and I even scored one of the goals. George bagged the other seven! It was almost as if he had his own ball at times. Eleven people are supposedly required to play in a team, but George took on that London side almost on his own. And they could not stop him . . . any more than the best defenders in Europe could.

The one thing that has eventually slowed George down, these many years on, is the drink, and his extended spell in hospital is the worst problem he has known. I'm sure he will make a recovery of sorts, although 100 per cent reparation is open to question. But knowing George as I do, I reckon this one will have come as such a jolt to him that even he may suddenly realise that it's nice just to wake up in the mornings and do everyday things. That is why I'm convinced George will adjust. I'm also sure we will not see a massive change in his personality. The wicked sense of humour will still be there, the one-liners will still be delivered with stunning effect and the genial smile will still win people over.

After what has happened, and the headlines George courted on that last occasion, people will inevitably have their own views of him. He will also have noticed how, with every passing year, the number of 'acquaintances' in his circle has gradually dwindled. At the same time, however, his true friendships will have become stronger.

I certainly will never abandon George Best or speak badly of him. On the contrary, understanding George – and the reasons behind what has happened to him – perhaps better than most, I will defend him to the hilt. As far as I'm concerned, there was only one person whom I wanted to write the foreword for this book, and I'm absolutely thrilled George readily agreed to do it. He is top man, as far as I'm concerned. And always will be.

THREE

POP STAR STATUS

The biggest sports stars, a soccer World Cup-winning manager, his captain who lifted the trophy, royalty, major figures from the world of showbiz . . . and even prime ministers. I know this sounds like a name-dropping exercise and if it is viewed that way I hold up my hands at once and plead guilty. But rugby gave me the opportunity to mingle in a celebrity world beyond the wildest dreams of most: the chance to rub shoulders and, in certain cases, become friends with, some of the biggest household names around.

It was not just George Best or my legendary rugby-playing partners like Gareth Edwards and Gerald Davies. How about this little lot as an alternative? Sir Alf Ramsey, Bobby Moore, Bill Shankly, Jackie Stewart, Tony Jacklin, Joe Bugner, Prince Charles, Sir Edward Heath (Conservative Prime Minister), James Callaghan (Labour Prime Minister), Robert Maxwell, Richard Burton, Richard Harris, Stanley Baker . . . to name but a few.

The most interesting thing I discovered about world-renowned actors like Burton, Harris and Baker is that while they were huge figures in their own right, phenomenally successful and interesting men I was eager to meet, they were actually just as excited at being introduced to me! Sport is an extraordinary thing. Just about every famous man, if asked what he would like to do had he not made it in his own field, would reply: play for Manchester United, or play for the British Lions at rugby, or be a Wimbledon champion, win the Open in golf, take the Olympic 100-metre title . . . and so on. When you are the sportsman who has actually achieved that status of reaching the very top, you find these major figures from the entertainment world hanging on to virtually every word you say, loving to hear the inside stories and gossip from the dressing-room. Burton was actually reported as saying once that he would have swapped every one of his films, acting gongs and money for just one appearance for Wales at the Arms Park.

More of the showbiz world in due course. Invariably most of the contacts I made were within sporting circles – not just rugby but soccer, golf, cricket, motor racing, boxing, tennis, athletics and others. One notable friendship that I was particularly proud to strike up was with Sir Alf Ramsey, the man who led England to their one-and-only World Cup triumph (beating West Germany at Wembley in 1966). We met up when, having finished playing early, I signed a five-year contract to help promote sports footwear for Gola; soon afterwards they got Sir Alf on board too, following his unbelievable dismissal as England manager.

Rumours were rife about Sir Alf not being a good communicator, about him being stern-faced, cold and prickly in dealing with others. Well you take as you find, as they say, and I can only maintain that this was most definitely not the Sir Alf I was privileged to know. On the contrary, he was polite, kind and good-humoured. After having a few drinks and meals together, we warmed to one another's company so much that he began to tell me the World Cup-winning secrets which, outside the England dressing-room, are probably not known to this day.

One involved the famous selection issue of whether Sir Alf picked the great Jimmy Greaves or the more inexperienced Geoff Hurst as his main striker in the final. Greaves, arguably the greatest goal-scorer England have produced, was Sir Alf's number-one striker going into the tournament, but lost his place to Hurst through injury. Greaves was fit again for the final and everyone assumed he would be straight back into the team against the Germans.

As you have probably gathered through my friendship with George Best, I'm a football nut myself. At the time that Sir Alf's short contract with Gola was about to finish, and he told me he was not planning to renew it, I plucked up the courage to ask the question that had been playing on my thoughts – and doubtless those of millions of others – for many years. 'Tell me Alf,' I started, 'How difficult was it picking Hurst ahead of Greaves for that final when the whole nation wanted and expected Jimmy to be in the side?'

Sir Alf admitted to me that he, too, was one of those who had initially reckoned Greaves would be in the team at Wembley: 'In the build-up to the final I used to sit in bed thinking about the match, my starting line-up and how to beat the Germans,' he told me. 'Every night Jimmy was in my side. Yet when I put my head on the pillow and closed my eyes, the person I kept seeing in that shirt was Geoff Hurst. He was the one making the forward runs that would hurt the

Germans, he was the one who could suit our system best and he was the one bang in form. So Geoff it was – poor Jimmy had to miss out.'

History, of course, proves Sir Alf's judgement, even if it was with his eyes shut, to have been absolutely spot-on. Hurst went on to score his famous hat-trick in England's 4–2 win. There I was, getting my answer straight from the horse's mouth. I sometimes wonder if even Jimmy Greaves knows the truth behind his omission from that World Cup final.

I was genuinely honoured that Sir Alf felt he could confide in me that way, but it was an example of how close we became during our time working together for Gola. When I heard that the company had signed Sir Alf, and that we would be colleagues, I was thrilled because 1966 will always be up there with me as one of the great moments of British sport. It did not matter that day if you were Welsh, Scottish or Irish: you wanted Sir Alf's men to win that World Cup. If England had been playing Brazil, maybe a few of us would have veered towards the South Americans. But there was definitely a bit of an anti-German feeling at the time, so everyone was very much rooting for England.

Sir Alf was pilloried by many for playing without wingers and for dropping Greaves. But quite obviously he was a master of management – how many other men have led England to the World Cup, either before or since? None, that is the answer. The players acknowledged him as a great man-manager, someone who knew each individual's idiosyncrasies and how to speak to them on a one-to-one basis to coax the best out of them. Very much in the mould, may I suggest, of Carwyn James, who led us British Lions to our victory in New Zealand in 1971.

However, because of the bad press Sir Alf attracted from certain quarters, I privately wondered just what he would be like as we met up for the first time at a giant store called Dingles down on the southwest coast in Plymouth. Would Sir Alf be cold and impolite, as some would have led you to believe? I soon received my answer. The entire store staff were lined up to meet us as we walked in and on this occasion I was very much the supporting cast. Everyone wanted to shake Sir Alf's hand, ask for his autograph or have photographs taken with him; and he was incredibly patient as, one by one, he dealt with the requests, spoke politely to everybody and answered all their questions.

We travelled back to London together by train, agreed to meet up again and soon discovered we were very comfortable in one another's company. Hey, Sir Alf even started to smile about things I said, so I could see he was really coming out of his shell.

One trip I will never forget was to a sports shop in Aberdeen. We went up on the Monday and were due to fly back to Heathrow the following Thursday. It was in the middle of the 1970s oil boom and the hotel we were booked into was virtually empty: the huge oil companies had block-booked rooms at an agreed tariff, but because of bad weather people could not get in from the rigs. As we were sitting alone in the bar one night, Sir Alf drinking his customary gin and tonic, I with a pint of lager, he confided his Geoff Hurst/Jimmy Greaves secret to me and spoke in more detail about that World Cup win. I was chuffed to have got this close to a man about whom many said there was a real stuffiness.

On the Thursday evening it was time to fly back from Aberdeen airport. With the weather having at last relented, we were told to wait thirty minutes while the Sikorsky helicopters brought the workers in off the oil platforms so they could go home for the weekend. Again Sir Alf and I were virtually on our own in the airport bar, when suddenly we heard the roar of the Sikorskys outside. There followed the most incredible scene. The number of women behind the bar immediately multiplied ten-fold as they lined up dozens of pints of lager on one side of the bar, dozens of pints of bitter on the other and dozens of whiskies in between. It was almost like a mini-military exercise, as if they could see the workers forty yards around the corner: better get the drinks ready, the lads'll be here in eight-and-a-half seconds flat!

The oil workers stampeded in like wildebeest and knew exactly where to go – lager men to the left of the bar, beer drinkers to the right, those wanting a Scotch in between. They had obviously done this many times before. From near silence there was this crescendo of noise. Then, after sinking a pint or two, a few of the men began to turn around. There was a nudging of elbows as they spotted Sir Alf and me and the decibel level began to lower again towards silence.

One of them strode over and said, 'Alf, shake my hand.' That started it. Next there was a huge queue as they lined up to meet him. I ended up having to swing my legs around every time to let them through. Among this group there were Scots, Welshmen, Geordies, Londoners – someone, it seemed, from just about every region in the United Kingdom. It was a beautiful sight as Sir Alf greeted them warmly one by one. What should have been a thirty-minute wait for take-off turned into a one-and-a-half-hour wait. Stuffy, stern-faced, cold? Not the Sir Alf I knew, no way.

Another legendary soccer manager of whom I would love to say I was an acquaintance was Bill Shankly, the little Scot who started

Liverpool's domination of British football during the 1970s and 1980s. Unfortunately I only got to meet Shanks for a couple of seconds when the grand total of just four words passed from his lips. But what words – and how he delivered them!

I had become quite friendly with John Toshack and Emlyn Hughes, two of the main men in that Liverpool side, and Emlyn asked me to attend one of his testimonial dinners in Southport. This was a real gala occasion, the room packed with everyone who was anyone in the world of sport. I had travelled up with Gareth Edwards and Emlyn could not wait to introduce us to the great man himself. Over came Shanks, only about five foot five inches tall, very much Billy Bremner style in stature. In fact, I could have imagined Bremner, another fiery little Scot, being similar in retirement to Shanks, perhaps carrying a little bit more weight. There are not many people who physically look up to you, but Shanks did as we shook hands. What he said next left me gobsmacked. Shanks looked me straight in the eye and, in his broad Scottish accent, simply stated, 'Hey, you had style.' With that he turned on his heels, walked away and disappeared into the throng.

I was left open-mouthed. I didn't even have time to say thank you. But the brevity of the sentence spoke volumes for me. I remember those few words a lot easier than I would have done a bigger speech from Shanks. Talk about being a master of getting your point across succinctly. Emlyn told me that was typical Shanks, though. When the Liverpool players went into his office, whether to ask for a pay rise, to be told off or to be given a new contract, Shanks was always brief and straight to the point. Good, bad or indifferent, he stated his case – then got on with something else.

I had not even known that he liked rugby, but to receive a compliment like that from an icon like Shanks was indeed something to treasure. Over the years I have heard so many memorable tales about Shanks that in many ways I wish I had played under him just once, whether in rugby or soccer. Like Jock Stein and Matt Busby, he had this knack of quietly walking into a room and everyone would look in awe. These people did not need to resort to sergeant-major-type antics to command respect; it came naturally to them.

Another who falls into that category, and whom I was privileged enough to meet on several occasions, was Mr Cool himself – Bobby Moore, Sir Alf's eyes and ears on the pitch as England's World Cup-winning captain. He was a real gentleman. You could see why he was a leader on the field. Sir Alf thought the world of him, knowing that Bobby would ensure the rest of the team did not go off the rails, misbehave and court newspaper headlines for the wrong reasons (as the England players have so often done since). Bobby did not even seem to get rattled when those trumped-up charges of stealing a bracelet were levelled at him by the Mexican authorities while England were competing in the 1970 World Cup. A lesser man would have capitulated under the pressure. Not Bobby. He refused to let his emotions show and during that tournament he went on to play some blinders. His tussle with Pelé and the other great Brazilians, in one group game, has gone down in football folklore.

That was Bobby, though. The calm manner in which he strutted around the pitch was replicated off it. He had the same look as he walked around a room, shoulders back, almost as if the coat hanger was still in his jacket. Bobby could not have slouched if he had been paid to. I would have loved, one day, to have seen him dance – just to see what movements he really could have produced. Unfortunately the opportunity never arose!

The time I got to know Bobby best was when we competed together during the first *Superstars* competition at the start of the of the 1970s, at Crystal Palace athletics stadium. For those who do not remember, *Superstars* was the television programme where a number of sporting celebrities competed against one another in different categories. There was football (in the form of penalty shoot-outs), athletics, swimming, golf, tennis and exercises such as press-ups, pull-ups and squat-thrusts. It made for great television in the early days, but I have to be honest and say I don't know why they called it *Superstars* after the first three or four programmes: I had never heard of some of the subsequent competitors!

In that first *Superstars*, though, we really did have the *crème de la crème* of British sport. Perhaps only George Best was missing, but Bobby Moore was not a bad representative for football, was he? I was chosen from rugby. Joining Bobby and me were: Jackie Stewart, the record-breaking Grand Prix driver; Tony Jacklin, who had recently won the Open; David Hemery, the Olympic champion and world record-holder at 400-metre hurdles; Joe Bugner, who challenged Muhammad Ali for the world heavyweight title; and Roger Taylor, who reached the semi-finals in the men's singles at Wimbledon.

We were the big names in British sport, thrown together for three days, and let's just say we shared quite a few drinks as we had a riotous time. It was probably the most marvellous three-day period I have known. Most of us got on famously. Top sportsmen find it so easy to do that, know they have nothing to prove to one another. It's those people who think they *ought* to be up at the top who are the self-opinionated and difficult ones. Away from the television cameras we had plenty of fun; in front of them, the action and footage we produced delighted the television people.

The format for the competition was simple. You had to nominate seven sports (out of ten) to compete in and were awarded points depending on where you finished in the various events. Why I chose swimming, I still do not know. I can swim, but not with any particular speed or style – and I have certainly never raced in an Olympic-sized swimming pool like the nearby one we were taken to. As we stepped up on to the boards, and the starter announced 'On your marks', we suddenly realised just how high up we were. Jacklin, crouching next to me, muttered, 'This isn't swimming, it's more like a diving contest.'

As the gun went off to start us, Tony and I dived in and were still underwater, splashing around and scrambling to reach the surface while Hemery – motor up his arse – was halfway towards the finishing line. Let me point out that as the athlete, Hemery was always favourite to win the overall competition, but we did not anticipate he would beat us by that much in the swimming.

Finally Tony and I managed to splash our way forward to touch the other end of the pool. We were last and second from last respectively and Ian Wooldridge came up with a classic line in the *Daily Mail* the next day to describe the event. 'While David Hemery won, some of the other competitors were not so convincing,' he wrote. 'Barry John struggled to fifth place and he was followed in last position by Tony Jacklin, who looked as if he was the last survivor from the *Titanic!*'

What Wooldridge did not realise, however, is that the problems for Tony and me were far from over when we finished the race. Out of breath, we soon realised that this was not like your ordinary swimming pool. The edges of the pool were a lot higher and we simply could not summon up enough strength to haul ourselves up. Discreetly and somewhat sheepishly, Jacklin and John, stars in their own sports, began diving under the lane-markers so we could reach the steps and walk out! Why did I compete in the swimming?

Anyway, at least we fared better than Joe Frazier – or so the tale goes – who competed in the American version of *Superstars*. Apparently he did not take to water too well, but for some reason, entered the swimming, dived in from that huge height . . . and was last seen splashing at the bottom! They had to send in the special squad to haul him out.

At least I managed to win the football and tennis, came out joint top in the golf and passed the finishing line first in the 100 metres. Eventually. Why I say eventually is because Bobby Moore and I thought we had sussed out this athletics lark and decided that the fastest way to run was by wearing spikes. Trouble was, ours were so big that our trainers got stuck in the starting blocks. With 4,000 people in the crowd looking on in amusement, Bobby and I discovered we were trapped until David Hemery politely pointed out that we should change our footwear. We did, I went on to win with a little dip at the end and was chuffed as the public-address man announced in his deep voice, 'First, Mr B. John, 11.6 seconds. Second . . .' After going through the results he then announced, 'Next week we have the Ladies' Three As Championships here at Crystal Palace. And the winner, Mr B. John, would not have qualified for the semi-finals!' Everyone was just rolling over in laughter, no one more so than Bobby himself . . . and I had beaten him!

Still, a win is a win; but I quickly discovered that the swimming had taken so much out of my body that I performed really badly in the press-ups, pull-ups and squat-jumps. In the end it came down to the last event, a straight shoot-out between David Hemery and myself in the 600-metre steeplechase for the title of first Superstar. David, for obvious reasons, had to run 800 metres as a handicap but he ate up the ground in no time. Having just returned from a holiday in Majorca, I had looked absolutely superb – fit, fast and tanned. But what the television pictures did not show was that I had nothing left in the tank. My respect for steeplechase jumpers increased ten-fold as I approached the water jump. With my limbs becoming wearier by the second, I felt as if I needed a pole vault to get over it. Somehow I scrambled across, but David caught me with 100 metres to go and came through to win.

I still finished second overall, which meant I was asked to return for another show, the 'Superstar of Superstars' competition, involving the competitors who had finished in the top two in the first few programmes. I think the television people began to realise they did not have the really big names any more and wanted to give their ratings a quick boost with a special show. However, when the organisers telephoned me I declined their invitation, becoming, I believe, the first person to say no.

The competition was about speed, strength and stamina, but the organisers had forgotten another important 'S' – skill. That is something defined in any event where you have a ball. Even in ice hockey they have a moving thing called a puck. As time went on, sports like tennis, golf and football were replaced with events such as canoeing. With respect, it does not take much deftness and cunning to row a canoe, unless you discreetly damage the other man's boat to make sure it sinks! Or show the sort of cunning Lester Piggott once did when, having lost his whip, he nicked one off the jockey next to him, gave his horse a few whacks and then handed it back, knowing he had done enough to keep his mount going to the finishing line!

I felt that the *Superstars* organisers had replaced skill levels with what amounted to a 'Who is the fittest?' competition which, in my view, went against the concept of the original show. My team-mates will tell you I was never the greatest trainer in the world, but I was a touch player who thrived on the skill factor. It came as no surprise to me when *Superstars* eventually petered out.

I did have the last say in the original event, however, although I suspect none of my fellow competitors know about it to this day. Certainly Joe Bugner does not, so he will probably be somewhat shocked to read this. Jackie Stewart and I had tied for first place in the golf, and we had to have a play-off because Jackie and Bugner finished level in the overall competition. Token prize money was at stake, depending on your final position. If Jackie beat me in the golf play-off, he would keep the maximum points from that event and finish ahead of Bugner. If I beat him, he would be below Bugner.

Well, I wasn't going to let Bugner get the satisfaction of third spot and the extra prize money, was I? Whether or not it was a case of him feeling macho I don't know, but he seemed to think he should walk events like press-ups and pull-ups. I was not a bad golfer, but on the decisive par-three hole Jackie took seven shots – and I made sure I took eight! So he won the golf.

Earlier Bugner had done a 'refusal' on the steeplechase water jump. His flabbergasted manager Andy Smyth exploded, 'And you're supposed to fight Ali!' In the football, where we took penalties against that great Tottenham goalkeeper Pat Jennings, Bugner and I were in the final. He could not kick the ball properly, but, with Pat scarcely able to stop his laughter, Bugner's toe-pokes kept going into the net. We told Pat, 'You have to try, you know.' It would have been embarrassing if I had lost to Bugner at kicking a ball. Luckily I scored my next penalty – and his went four yards wide!

While there was a humorous side to that golf play-off, it also gave me an insight into the unique problems faced by Formula One racing drivers. Anyone studying Grand Prix records will discover that Jackie Stewart finished on the odd number of 99 races. The reason he did not complete 100 was because François Cevert, his protégé at Tyrell, had a disastrous crash while practising for the US Grand Prix. Jackie understandably declined to drive in the race and, with our play-off scheduled forty-eight hours later, I contacted the International Management Group, organisers of the *Superstars* event, to say I accepted that the golf would be cancelled. However, they soon came back to me saying, 'Jackie will see you on the tee as agreed.'

Immediately after the Grand Prix Jackie went into hiding in France. He emerged by flying in from Paris especially to compete against me, but out of respect for Cevert told me he was never going to race again. It made me realise how easy my own sport was. If I made a mistake, it cost my team a try. If racing drivers make a mistake, as Cevert discovered, it costs an awful lot more.

Meeting these fellow sporting household names was a great honour in its own right. Being introduced to, and chatting to, royalty and prime ministers is something I will always cherish for different reasons. I found myself invited to functions at Buckingham Palace and indeed the Prince of Wales was the Welsh Rugby Union's guest of honour for our 1969 Five Nations match with Ireland. It was the year of his investiture and Prince Charles and I shared a few words. We met again thirty years on in the hospitality room at the brand new Millennium Stadium in Cardiff for the opening of the 1999 World Cup. 'Hello Sir,' I said humbly, 'My name is Barry John.' The Prince replied by saying, 'Oh yes, I know who you are.' We chatted together for a few seconds, discussing the new stadium, the state of Welsh rugby and what was in store during the World Cup.

Ted Heath and James Callaghan, the two prime ministers I met, were more interested in rugby than the Prince was. Mr Heath, of course, was in office when the Lions won in New Zealand and on our return we were invited by him to Downing Street for a lovely reception. He was also a keen sports participator in his own right, winning sailing races in his yacht *Morning Cloud* on the Tasman Sea at the same time we were winning our rugby matches nearby.

It was away from the sporting scene that I got to know Mr Heath best, though. At a dinner hosted by the Cardiff business community we were put together on the same table. Mr Heath did not want to talk politics – he just wanted to know the gossip in rugby circles. It was his way of escaping from the pressures of running the country, I suppose. All the same, as the evening wore on, official duties still had to be performed. That day Mr Heath had flown from the United States, where he was on government duty, to Zurich, then to London and on to Cardiff. He must have been exhausted from this taxing journey, yet he stood up and with no notes in front of him delivered the most wonderful speech. I could not help but think, however, that he had to slow down a little. No one could last many years with that sort of hectic schedule. Not even a British prime minister.

As a fellow Welshman I suppose Mr Callaghan's interest in rugby was somewhat more inevitable. But I still found it a great honour when, although I had finished playing by then, he invited me to Downing Street for a luncheon. Like Mr Heath, he wanted to escape from politics. Rugby, rugby and more rugby was what Mr Callaghan wanted to talk about and I was happy to oblige.

Powerful men in powerful positions, the pair of them. Publishing tycoon Robert Maxwell would never have made Prime Minister, but if anything he carried even more clout within his own circles than the men who held down the number-one job in the country. A huge man physically who possessed a deep booming voice, Maxwell was domineering, the sort of person who thought money could buy *everything*. It could not, of course, but that did not stop him trying.

The 1986 Commonwealth Games in Edinburgh were in danger of turning into a complete non-event because the black African nations had withdrawn for political reasons. Without the African world record-holders, the credibility of the Games was down the chute, leading to inevitable financial problems with sponsors and advertisers pulling out. The organisers suddenly found themselves cash-strapped until – typical Maxwell – the big man rode to the rescue by hosting a fundraising luncheon at a London hotel.

Even allowing for the influence of royalty and prime ministers, I have *never* seen anything done quite as quickly as it was that day. Maxwell only had to snap his fingers to get whatever he wanted in an instant – including, it seems, my presence at the function, for I was working as a rugby writer for the *Daily Express* at the time when my sports editor, John Morgan, ordered me to attend. 'Barry, whatever you are doing, drop it. We want you to go – you'll have to have a leg amputated not to make it,' he told me.

There were probably more prominent people gathered in that room than on any other occasion I have attended. The Duke of Kent represented the royals. The richest businessmen in Britain were present. I found myself sitting with Terry Wogan, while many more celebrities from the world of sport and entertainment were on other tables. Our presence was demanded by Maxwell for a particular reason: to give the businessmen a memorable afternoon to remember, so they could forget the money he was asking them to part with!

Huge favours were being called in. The man on my left was supplying printing ink to Fleet Street, including Maxwell's Mirror Group newspaper company, and he put £25,000 into an envelope. I have no idea how much was raised in total, but on our table of twelve alone I estimated the figure to be a quarter of a million. Multiply that by more than forty tables and you are talking about up to £10 million. In the end it was not the most memorable of Games, but Maxwell had certainly tried his best.

He didn't know the meaning of the phrase 'taking no for an answer'. Maxwell, of course, went on to fall from the heights over the pension scandal. Having met the man that day I could fully understand how his thousands of employees felt totally overpowered by him; how his big, booming voice would have dominated board meetings; how he would always have got his way. It did not surprise me that the moment Maxwell was off the scene, having supposedly fallen into the sea from his yacht, those same employees suddenly started coming out of the woodwork in their droves to tell the truth about him. They would not have dared do that before.

I have come across many characters from the acting world in my time and, as I explained at the start of this chapter, I find it fascinating that they seem to be more in awe of meeting sports celebrities than we are of meeting them. Recently, for example, I was introduced to Neil Morrisey, star of the hit comedy show *Men Behaving Badly*. Considering I had finished playing almost thirty years earlier, and he is part of the younger generation, I was pleasantly surprised to discover he was as delighted to meet me as I was him, saying: 'I don't believe this, you're *the* Barry John.'

I suppose it goes back to that desire of those in the entertainment world to be sports stars themselves, although I should point out that there's a big difference between the two professions. Showbiz celebrities work to a script. Rugby players, and in particular fly-halfs, have to make it up as the game is in progress.

Three actors who really loved their rugby were Stanley Baker, of *Zulu* fame (more of him in another chapter); that great wild Irishman Richard Harris, who has tamed down these days; and his big mate Richard Burton. Harris is an out-and-out rugby nut, a Munster man who follows the Five Nations tournament with a vengeance. He used to love hearing the stories about what was going on. At his age he was suddenly getting this unique dressing-room information from the matches he was so keenly following – and he was almost star-struck by it.

I actually only met Burton on one brief occasion (even though he was Welsh); but his wife Sally once told me, 'You've caused me more problems at home than anybody!' Apparently when rugby internationals were being played, Burton would invite his acting colleagues like Harris and Peter O'Toole to his luxurious home in Switzerland, where they'd have the games beamed in by satellite. Sally would look after the food, Richard would be in charge of the bar and Sally would then either book into a hotel for the night or go to a friend's house.

'I would return the following morning to total and utter chaos in the house – beer cans strewn on the floor, wine bottles everywhere . . . It was as if a bomb had hit the place,' Sally explained to me. 'Then, for the next few days, I would get, "Barry this, Gareth that. Barry did this in his heyday; Gareth did that in his heyday". I got fed up with you because Richard never stopped talking about you! We've only just met – but it is as if I have met you a million times already! So this is what the fuss is about.'

I would love to have had a day or two in Burton's company, but it would have to have been out of season, because we would have partied so much I probably could not have played for a fortnight afterwards.

At least, albeit fleetingly, I did manage to meet Burton. Muhammad Ali, I'm afraid, was the one who got away. On the many occasions I took the Cardiff–Paddington route, British Rail rarely let me down. On this particular trip I was going to a London hotel for an interview with the *Daily Telegraph*'s David Miller, but something went wrong in the Severn Tunnel and there was a sizeable hold-up.

I eventually arrived at the hotel forty-five minutes after I should have done to find David and a few others looking perplexed. 'Do you know who we've been desperately trying to keep here to meet you?' he asked. 'Who?' He replied, 'Only Muhammad Ali, that's who.'

The great man, undisputed world heavyweight champion, was in town on a promotional tour. He was The King, but then rugby fans called me 'The King', so David and the others were licking their lips in anticipation of an exclusive picture of us both together. Even Ali's people, apparently, made him hang around for an extra fifteen minutes, in an attempt to oblige. He was being held up for me – and I had just sauntered in there without a care in the world! As I conducted my interview with David over breakfast, a sense of devastation came over me.

Muhammad Ali, to me, was the most charismatic sporting figure of the lot. In fact, with icons like Nelson Mandela, Winston Churchill and JFK, he was one of the most extraordinary people the world has known, someone whose effect on the human race was so profound that everybody could identify with him.

Ali's courageous stance in refusing to fight in the Vietnam War was vindicated when, after he got out of jail, American public opinion was very much with him. Once he got his licence back, we had those three epic fights with Frazier. I hear stupid people asking if there was a fix. It must have been some fix when, after the Thriller in Manila, Frazier had big lumps coming out of his head and Ali, the winner, could not talk!

No, Ali was genuine and when I see him appear on the television these days, for example accepting his award as BBC Sports Personality of the Century, I deliberately make a point of going out of the room to make a cup of tea. The Ali I see these days disturbs me.

The Ali I missed by minutes in the mid-1970s, on the other hand, was at the height of his powers. What a man. Yes, I think you will agree I have bumped into a fair few famous people down the years, but that was the meeting I would have treasured above all others. A picture of The King meeting the man the rugby public called 'The King'. If only . . .

FOUR

A STAR IN THE MAKING

The first time I pulled on a representative shirt for Wales, believe it or not, was in making my senior début against Australia at Cardiff Arms Park in 1966. The selectors who picked the team at lower levels, including the Welsh schools representative side, decided I was not good enough to merit a place. You may find that hard to follow, but it is true. I have often wondered since what those men who decided to overlook me make of their decision.

I will let you into a little secret, too. At the time I was so upset and angry that I felt like packing in rugby altogether at the tender age of fifteen. Those record points for Wales and the Lions, the magnificent times I had, the pleasure people said I gave them when they watched me play, could so easily not have happened. I was playing soccer quite a bit in those days too, pretending I was Pelé and banging in the goals. Sometimes I was even made to go in goal so that the opposition could make more of a game of it.

If that was what the Welsh selectors thought of my rugby, maybe I should give it up and throw my lot into soccer instead, I felt. That I did not do that owes an awful lot to the enormous encouragement given to me by two people. The first was my old physics master at Gwendraeth Grammar School, Mr Edwards, who would ferry me to and from trials and keep my spirits going; the other was Carwyn James, who gave me a boost by stating that the selectors had made the wrong decision and urging me to stick at it.

Carwyn came from the same place as I, the west-Wales coalmining village of Cefneithin, around ten miles from the town of Carmarthen. He went on to coach the Lions to our memorable 1971 victory in New Zealand. I think it's fair to say he knew a bit more about whether someone was a good rugby player than those Welsh schools selectors who, in their wisdom, decided I was not up to it. Don't you?

I was actually a scrum-half in those days and I was bubbling after being selected to play in the Welsh under-15s trial at Carmarthen. It seemed the entire village of Cefneithin had travelled in force to support one of their own and I did not let them down – or so I thought. I played really well that day and thought it was a certainty I would be picked for the final trial and then for the Wales team. Imagine my devastation when two rivals, Pete Evans and Owen Freeman, were given the nod for that final trial at Llanelli's Stradey Park ground, while I was stuck as first reserve!

Bang went my hopes and dreams of pulling on the famous red jersey for the first time. When I heard the news I was nearly in tears. This was where Mr Edwards stepped in. To be honest he didn't know that much about rugby, but he did know enough to feel I deserved a chance. So, week after week he would turn up in his beaten-up old Ford banger – chug, chug, splutter, splutter, the car almost crying out to be left alone for a day – and ferry me off to trials and matches in places like Merthyr and Quakers Yard. They may have been towns in south Wales but, hey, for a young lad more accustomed to a twenty-mile radius around Cefneithin, those weird-sounding places might as well have been on Mars.

Inwardly Mr Edwards must have been hurting at my Welsh schools snub as much as I was, but he never once gave up, and kept on encouraging me. The same applied to Carwyn, although he went public with his views, telling the local newspaper: 'We simply MUST NOT allow talented people like young Barry to slip through the net.' Their positive attitude rubbed off on me and strengthened my resolve to prove the selectors wrong. Because of what everyone, bar those selectors, felt I was unjustly forced to go through, I decided to stick with rugby. A sort of 'I'll show them' attitude, I suppose. I think I did, too.

The following year, as a sixteen-year-old, I began to play regularly as a fly-half for the first time. The various journeys to trials and matches around Wales in Mr Edwards's beaten-out old banger paid off as I was chosen to represent Cefneithin at senior level. Then, as an eighteen-year-old, I received a letter from Llanelli asking me to play for them. Talk about going up in the world. I was still at school, yet here I was, about to play for one of the greatest clubs going. My rugby career was set to take off and the rest, as they say, is history.

In the end, rugby gave me that opportunity as an adult to mix with celebrities and to be invited as guest of honour to the grandest of functions and bashes. But one thing I have never forgotten is my council-house upbringing – nor will I. Perhaps that very humbleness, with absolute basics like saying 'please' and 'thank you' instilled into me at an early age, made it difficult for me to cope with the fame that came my way. As I have already made perfectly clear, beneath the 'fame' exterior I am just an ordinary human being.

I certainly would not change anything about my upbringing. I am fiercely proud of my working-class roots and always will be. I'm just as proud, too, of the Welshness in our household. Even in telephone conversations before she passed away – which was the saddest moment I have experienced – my mother, Vimy Madora, would always speak to me in Welsh.

Little did anyone know there was a so-called superstar in the making when I came into the world on 6 January 1945. Least of the lot Vimy (she was named after the great battle of the First World War); my father William John, who worked down the mines; my grandmother Mam-Low, the matriarch of the village; my brothers Del, Alan, and Clive, good rugby players the three of them; or sisters Madora and Diane.

Far from hitting the headlines by playing rugby for Wales and the British Lions, the natural role for me – and anyone growing up in our village, for that matter – was to follow our fathers down the mines. But let me tell you another little secret: I promised my father I would never go underground. To this day I have kept that vow and if he were still around today, he would have been as proud as I am of the fact I have maintained that pledge.

'Barry,' he would tell me after I came home from a day at Gwendraeth Grammar, 'if you don't do your homework, you know where you'll end up, don't you? Down the mines with me. And believe me, you don't want to be doing that.' I knew exactly what he was getting at. That is why I made sure I never skipped on my schoolwork!

Every morning, at 4.30 a.m. my father would rise and get ready to catch the bus to the Great Mountain colliery at Tumble, just a few miles from our home. How he would work once he got there, occasionally breaking for his sandwiches hundreds of yards underground (if the rats had not got at them first). Not only would he come home utterly exhausted and flop straight into his armchair, but there were times – if he was doing a double shift – when he'd not even see any daylight for ten days at a time. He would go to work in the dark, come home after 6 p.m. when it was dark, and in the meantime would be working down there in the pitch black.

No thanks! I had the utmost respect for the tens of thousands who, like my father, worked in such horrific conditions to earn their money.

But what for? You see some old miners today scarcely able to breathe after the horrific effects of working countless years underground, taking in the dust, and getting a paltry £50,000 in compensation money for their troubles. Oh, and they get little masks to put on their faces to help them cope with their breathing difficulties. What are the masks going to do – help them run the London Marathon, or something? I find the whole thing so extraordinarily sad.

To earn some money when I was eighteen, I actually had a seven-week spell working at the colliery during the summer holidays. Fortunately I only worked up at the top for a company called Thyssen, cleaning up a couple of huge pipes and giving those going underground a helping hand by supplying them with tools if they suddenly realised they had forgotten something.

Those seven weeks simply underlined to me why my father was absolutely right in urging me to do my homework. Suddenly I was up at the crack of dawn and on that same bus with him. I was young, fighting fit, playing a good standard of rugby and had just started a teaching course at Trinity College, Carmarthen. Every single morning I looked around the bus and saw men in their early twenties and thirties with their eyes shut, only to jerk suddenly out of their sleep by coughing, spluttering and wheezing – a legacy of breathing in coal-dust every day. Many had been at school with me and should have been at the peak of their fitness. Indeed, on Saturdays some were either team-mates or opponents of mine on the rugby field. I used to wonder how you could have a busful of people with so much vibrancy and spirit at the weekend, yet full of such utter exhaustion during the working week. I also wondered how they could contemplate running around a rugby pitch with me on Saturday afternoon, when in reality they should have been tucked up in bed catching up on their sleep.

By the end of my seven-week spell I began to understand how most of them felt because I too was utterly exhausted – and I had not even ventured underground! My main task involved sprucing up those pipes by chipping off the rust and giving them a coat of black paint. In my naïvety I started off going at them hammer and tongs until a colleague of mine called Bert took me to one side to politely spell out the working rules of the colliery: 'Barry, you can either go at this pace, get it done in 14 days and receive two weeks' wages; or you can take seven weeks and get seven weeks' wages.' I got the message and ended up taking my time, as he suggested. But seven weeks of those 4.30 a.m. starts still managed to take everything out of me and merely hardened my resolve to make sure my career path would go in another direction.

Not that I could complain about the money I earned working up top. I was paid well – more, in fact, than my father, which caused me no end of potential problems at home. I'm only talking about a £10 difference, but the actual amount didn't matter. It was the principle and there was the rather important matter of how my mother would react. Would she feel that I was devaluing the hard work put in by her husband day after day, week after week, when he was supplying the food for our dinner table?

When I received my first wage packet I was in a blind panic and did not know what to do. My first instinct was to take out the extra £10, give it to my father for a few drinks and pretend I had earned exactly the same money as him. But it was not quite as simple as that in our household. Every week, you see, my father brought his little brown wage packet home untouched and put it in a drawer where my mother dealt with the money. Never once, not a single time, did he open the packet himself and my mother expected the same of me. After mulling over various panic-stricken thoughts, I finally came up with a little ruse and told her the reason there was more money in my wage packet was because as a student I did not have to pay tax! It seemed to work.

The other point those seven weeks in the colliery rammed home to me were the dangers of working underground – which I used to see at first hand because I worked next to the trapdoor where the miners would get out after coming up the lift shaft. The lift automatically took them a few feet above the trapdoor and, once at the top, there would be a click, the trapdoor folded out and the shaft carrying the men would come back down to settle on it. Out they would then file, to go home at the end of their working shift. Sometimes, however, after going underground the men would discover they needed something – a screwdriver, hammer, bucket, whatever – to do some work below. If they were in a hurry they would come up and stop the lift manually themselves right by the trapdoor. Because the automation had not clicked in, the trapdoor had not fully covered the opening and there was a gap of about a foot either side. Such was the confidence and experience of the men, they would simply step out over the gap, grab the tool or whatever they needed off me, and back down they would go.

It meant less time was taken, but considering we were talking about a drop of a few hundred feet, I always felt it was a bit risky. Still, these men were seasoned miners who knew what they were doing. Or so I thought. One of them was a German called Heinrich, a wonderful fellow who used to receive a bit of banter but who gave as good as he got. Often Heinrich would say to me, 'Barry, come down and see what we're doing.' I would reply, 'No way, I've promised my father I won't go down there and I plan to stick to that promise.'

I went into work one day and after a while asked a colleague, 'Where is the German then, I've not seen him yet today?' I was told, 'There is no Heinrich,' and in my naïvety replied, 'What, he's gone home already, has he?' But it was much worse than that, I'm afraid. Heinrich had tried the trick of stopping the lift shaft manually once too often, lost his footing and fallen down. A truly horrible story.

Not that pit accidents were anything new to me. The school I attended was near the colliery and I will never forget the time when the wailing hooter, which signalled the shift changes within the pit, went off at the wrong time of day. When that happened you knew the result equalled disaster. On this occasion the siren sounded in the middle of the afternoon. Our school overlooked the pit and I looked down upon a scene of total devastation and utter panic and pandemonium. We were such a close-knit community that everyone in the school and in the village knew someone who worked down the mine. As the hooter wailed, the teachers ran out of the classrooms and into the playground to try to see what was going on. We were running up and down corridors and in the distance we could hear the wailing sirens of the emergency service vehicles.

We were like ants, rabbits, rats – just running into one another in blind panic, asking 'What is it? What's happened? Is everyone OK?' Sadly the answer was no. There had been a huge blast down the pit. My father was so shell-shocked by the incident I don't think he spoke for three days afterwards. He was never a great man for words anyway: just a proud, honest breadwinner who did his duty by bringing his pay packet home every Friday and who offered encouragement to us every so often. But on this occasion he said nothing, just tried to come to terms with what had happened.

One victim of the blast was a chap called David Pennington, an idol of mine from just down the road. I, and several of my mates, used to look up to him. Far from working down the mines, David should have been riding in the TT Isle of Man races, such was his love of motorbikes. He was the Evel Knievel of his day and used to have us in hysterics with some of the antics he got up to.

As you can imagine, our school was rugby orientated and David used to follow us to games to cheer us on. Follow us, did I say? How could anyone follow our old ramshackle of a bus? Chug, chug, chug it went at an average speed of about five miles per hour, somehow getting us to our destination eventually. One day we were going to play in the Gareth Edwards territory of Cwmgors and David provided the pre-match entertainment by doing wheelies in front of the bus. Then, bang, he was gone in one change of gear. As the bus spluttered on we said, 'Where is the git?' The answer came around the next corner because we saw David again – standing on the handlebars with his motorbike still going! An amazing character.

Another abiding memory I have of him was the day he dressed up as the Michelin man for the Cefneithin carnival. The entire village stopped for this annual event and I thought *I* looked a big enough prat dressed up as a Beefeater in big hat and the full works . . . until I spotted David. With his great big shoulder pads and shinpads he could barely move – and yet he decided to go in goal so youngsters could take penalties against him in a football competition. The first teenager to have a go could hardly kick the ball, but he made just enough contact with his toe to enable the ball to dribble slowly towards David. An easy stop – except David suddenly realised that because of his padding he could not reach down. He could only watch on as the ball crept past him and into the net. I think the lad won the coconut for that, too! But that was David for you. He would take the mickey out of the world, but he was happy to have others make fun of him as well. A tragic loss.

Apart from incidents like that, I have nothing but happy memories of my Cefneithin days when the name of the game was giving and sharing. I was taught that advice early on by my mother. The other great tip I received came from my grandmother, Mam-Low. She used to give me money for cutting coal for her. One day, as I was growing up and beginning to make a name for myself in rugby, she came out and said to me in her deep Welsh accent, 'Barry, whatever you do, and I know you're going to go far, always remember these little words – please and thank you.'

She pointed out that whatever mistakes I made, provided I started with please and finished with thank you, people would understand more. How right she was and what marvellous advice to take with me. It is frightening, though, to think back in hindsight of how I used to cut her coal. Hammer in one hand, no glove, slam it on to the coal in my other hand – and this was often on a Friday before a game for Llanelli!

My mother followed Mam-Low as the backbone of the village and she was a wonderful lady. Every night she made a point of checking my homework and never once did I hear the words 'no good' from her. She always offered encouragement and that made such an impact upon me that it was one of the main points I emphasised when I was asked to do the *Desert Island Discs* radio show a few years ago.

When my mother passed away it was as if I had had the guts ripped out of me. The saddest part is that I was not there to speak to her one last time. I was in Cardiff one morning when I received a call from my brother Del, who said, 'Barry, she's not well.' I knew by the tone of his voice what was about to happen. I didn't say anything to Jan other than that I was going to fill up with petrol and would be a little while, jumped into my car, then headed off to west Wales. It was an awful journey, eerie, quiet, just myself and my own thoughts. Even the huge Port Talbot steelworks you pass on the M4 motorway seemed to be different, as if the sulphur was keeping away so that my sniffling was not affected by the strong smell you normally have to put up with as you drive by.

I arrived just after 8 a.m. in our little street – the one they said I had made famous because so much had been written and broadcast about my rugby exploits – and there was total silence. I stopped the car, got out and walked into the house to see my father totally distraught. He looked at me, I looked at him and my two lungs pumped out at the same time. I was inconsolable and hugged my father, probably for the first time. We were not a tactile community: touch just was not involved when I grew up. Del, red-eyed and tearful, came down the stairs and said, 'Come and see her.' I went up, sobbed, hugged Del and felt awful that I had not been there with him.

I would certainly like to think some of my rugby exploits made my mother immensely proud of me. I'm just pleased I had the opportunity to do well on the sporting stage. That I did was despite, rather than because of, the efforts of a few Welsh schools selectors who patently did not know what they were talking about.

FIVE

LIKE PLAYING FOR MAN UTD
AND LIVERPOOL

Can you imagine being fortunate enough to play your entire club career for Liverpool and Manchester United? – two of the world's greatest soccer clubs with fantastic tradition and aura about them, not to mention trophy cabinets which have been filled with the complete set of major honours in the game.

Well, transfer that into the world of club rugby and you will get some idea of what it meant to me to spend my playing days with first Llanelli, then Cardiff. Not just the top two clubs in Wales, but amongst the most charismatic and glamorous anywhere. Speak to anyone in rugby circles, whether in Great Britain, New Zealand, Australia, South Africa, France, Japan or wherever, and there will come a point in the conversation where they will have a story to tell about the Scarlets or the Blue and Blacks. Someone will say, 'I was there when Barry John kicked that goal,' or 'Gareth Edwards scored that unforgettable try,' or 'Gerald Davies weaved that bit of magic.' It's just like Liverpool and Manchester United in football, with legendary tales about men like Kevin Keegan, Tommy Smith, George Best and Bobby Charlton!

In rugby terms Llanelli and Cardiff each drew huge crowds, home and away. The support we received from exiled Welshmen, when we travelled to play teams like Rosslyn Park in London, even vastly outnumbered the home support. Such was the pulling power of my two clubs.

What times, what characters, what memories. Including, perhaps, the cheekiest moment I have produced on a rugby pitch – one which, even by my standards of trying to do things out of the ordinary, still managed to amaze those watching at the Arms Park. Cardiff were playing Coventry, who were skippered by my great friend and Lions team-mate David Duckham. In those days Coventry were very much the big noises of the English game and boasted a star-studded line-up, although we had a pretty useful team ourselves.

I specifically remember this particular game for two reasons. The first is because Gareth Edwards, my regular scrum-half partner at club and international level, went off injured and Mervyn John, our open-side flanker and captain, took over the number 9 duties. That created the novel half-back pairing of John and John – one for the record books, no doubt. The second reason I recall the match so vividly is because of my moment of impudence. I can still picture it today, plus the look of sheer horror on the faces of Duckham and his team-mates as it happened.

Coventry had dominated possession, but were only narrowly in front when we were awarded a penalty twenty yards out, slightly on the right-hand side of the field. I stepped forward to kick the simple penalty goal that would put us right back in the game, or so everyone assumed. However, as I picked up the ball referee Ernie Lewis stopped me, saying, 'Hold on a minute Barry.' A Coventry player was down, injured. While this man was receiving treatment and there was a hold-up in play, Duckham had gathered his team-mates around him under the goalposts – the customary position as you wait for a penalty – to read them the riot act. My old mate was furious that his side were in danger of letting the game slip. It was at that moment, as I looked towards Duckham and his huddle of players with their backs to me, that I had my mischievous little thought.

'By the way Ernie,' I told the referee, 'I've not said what I'm going to do yet. I've not said I'm kicking for goal – so don't mess this up for me, will you?' Ernie nodded his head, blew his whistle to restart the game and with that I turned to the crowd on my right, put my finger to my lips and whispered 'Shsssshhh'. I took another look at Duckham, getting redder and redder as he ranted and raved at his team, tapped the ball to myself and ran the penalty, sprinting towards the empty try-line. Briefly the crowd respected my wish for them to remain silent and not alert Coventry to what was happening, but they could hold back no more. A huge 'Go on' roar went up around the ground and the bewildered Coventry players suddenly looked up and in desperation began rushing over to try to stop me. No chance. I had too much of a head start, crossed for the try and converted. Game, set and match: thank you very much, Mr Duckham.

David went absolutely ballistic afterwards. 'You cheat,' he yelled at me, although I quietly pointed out that I had *not* signalled what I was doing from the penalty. 'You were too busy reading the riot act to your team to notice,' I told him, before turning on my heels, smiling to myself and going back to the dressing-room to savour yet another Cardiff victory. Ironically David was to get the last laugh when we played Coventry again the following season. But more of that in due course.

Before I could even think of playing those sort of tricks as a Cardiff number 10, I was to have three-and-a-half wonderful years with Llanelli. The Scarlets are the nearest big club to my home village of Cefneithin, so it was a dream come true when, as a teenager, I received my invitation to play for them on a freezing January afternoon at Moseley. What an introduction to the big time, too. Llanelli lost 6–5, but I had the honour of scoring our entire points haul with a try (remember it was three points for a try in those days) and conversion. It gives me shudders to think about it today, though. There I was, fresh out of school classes, and suddenly finding myself on the same rugby pitch as Mike Gavins, the England full-back, no less.

So, as Gavins began bearing down on me, what was this complete rookie doing – feinting to go one way, side-stepping the other, running past my opponent's flailing arms and going over for the try? That is not how you are supposed to respect your elders, although in my defence I can look back upon it and say everything just happened instinctively. I did not have time to worry about the occasion or the fact I was being confronted by the England full-back – which was just as well, I suppose.

If this teenage unknown had given Gavins a bit of a shock, I then received one of my own when our skipper Marlston Morgan strode up, patted me on the back, said 'Well done' and followed that with, 'Put the kick over too'. Oh well, in for a penny, in for a pound. Over went the conversion, although I did miss a left-footed drop-goal attempt at the end which would have won the game for Llanelli.

Still, I had to be pretty pleased with the way things had gone for me personally. The Monday morning newspaper headlines declared, 'JOHN, THE NEW WELSH WONDER'. The good press continued as I played well in the next few matches, too. I even returned from one match against Rosslyn Park in London – where this starry-eyed youngster had seen the wide world of the Houses of Parliament, the West End and the Tower of London for the first time – to discover that my mother, father, brothers and sisters already knew I had produced another good performance, for the game had gone out on radio.

Hey, newspaper headlines, radio broadcasts – it was time to put my new-found fame to good use as I hatched a crafty little two-part plan to secure the place I wanted on a teacher-training course at Trinity College, Carmarthen. I'm sure one of the main reasons I went to college, on leaving Gwendraeth Grammar, was to give me another three years to think about what career path I should follow, for at the time I did not have a clue. I was certainly not a handyman, so I could hardly become an electrician or carpenter; I was not over-fussed on the financial world; I did not fancy joining the emergency services. How about teaching? Well, three more years to consider everything – that would do nicely.

However, wanting to do teacher training and actually being selected for a place in the college were two entirely different things, particularly as I was literally the very last student to enrol that summer. Hence part one of my little plan. A friend had advised me that if I wanted to get into Trinity College, first I had to check where the vacancies were. For a subject like English there were twenty-odd vacancies, and as it was such a popular subject every one of them had been snapped up months before.

Rural science and farming, on the other hand . . . Don't laugh – that's what I put down on my application form. Well, the college *did* have a farm, I *had* done zoology in the sixth form and I *was* the outdoor type!

I duly went before the Deputy Principal, Miss Jones, to explain just why I wanted to study rural science. Considering I did not know the answer myself, it was hardly going to be an easy interview. Miss Jones was flanked by two teachers on either side – it felt like facing the Big Five selectors who used to pick the Wales team – and she began asking about my farming interests. Let's see: I did haymaking in the summer holidays, I told her, and I was raised on a farm, although I declined to mention we moved to another house after just six months!

Eventually the subject of rugby came up and Miss Jones said she had heard I was a very good sportsman who had played for Llanelli. Aha, I thought, she knows who I am, so I've got a bit of a chance here. 'They tell me you're very good,' she went on, as I modestly replied, 'Do they?'

'So come on, are you optimistic or pessimistic about playing for Wales?' followed up Miss Jones. By this stage my thoughts had become so scrambled from keeping up the rural science pretence that I could not remember which was which. I just mumbled 'Yes' in reply to her question, received odd stares from my five interviewers, and left the room assuming I had blown it. Fortunately I had not because within eighteen hours I received a letter from the college stating I had been accepted for the course. I enrolled, picked up my grant forms, received my money – the huge sum of twenty pounds a term, in those days – and opened my first bank account, with NatWest.

On to part two of my little ploy. I soon decided I did not fancy getting up at 5 a.m. every day to milk cows as part of my training. No thank you very much. The important point was that I had my foot in the college door, so I went to ask the Head of Physical Education, Mr Griffiths, if there was a place for one more person on his course. This is where my early headline-grabbing exploits for Llanelli worked in my favour once more, because Mr Griffiths, I think, felt I could bring some honour and prestige to the college through my rugby.

So I had my dream ticket: PE as my main course, supplemented by two subsidiary programmes, science and horticulture. Horticulture? I hate gardening, but I can talk about double digging, single digging and the other technical jargon until the cows come home. Putting a fork in my hand and doing it, on the other hand, is something I'm not too fond of. I suppose it is a bit like the difference between talking a good game and going out there and playing a good one.

I have to be honest and own up to putting my rugby status to good use again shortly afterwards, this time to make sure I had the best food from the canteen. Well, Olive, the lady who ran the kitchen, was a Llanelli nut – so after eating typical student dietary fare in the refectory for a while, I decided it was time she and I had a little chat, as we shared a mutual interest. With Llanelli in those days everything was geared towards the matches with Cardiff and local rivals Swansea and Neath, huge games played before sell-out crowds. I approached the kitchen on the Friday before we played Neath and said, very matter-of-factly, 'Olive, you know we are playing Neath tomorrow and we have to win. Trouble is, I've got a bit of a tummy bug and have to be careful what I eat.'

Looking back into the canteen I could see the students on one side, piling into their typical junk food, and the lecturers on the other eating beef, ham, pork, chicken – the very best cuts, too. I told Olive I would love a bit of everything the lecturers had, but she looked at me as if to say, 'Barry, I can't do that.' 'But if I'm not well tomorrow and miss the Neath game . . .' I pointed out. That did the trick, although as a student I could hardly join the lecturers' queue for the best meat. We had to be a bit more subtle than that, so Olive piled the food on to my plate, covered it with huge leaves of lettuce and back I went to my table to share the tasty meal with my mates. Talk about being in their favour for the rest of the term!

I think it is fair to say, though, that while I pulled the odd stunt like that, the college did indeed enjoy the profile my rugby exploits brought to Trinity. Not least in my final year, in 1966, when I won my first Wales cap against Australia and the college switchboard was swamped with telephone calls of congratulations. I was taken to the bursar's office where there was a big bag of telegrams waiting for me. There were hundreds of them, yet – and this is uncanny – I dipped my hand in and the first telegram I opened read, 'Many congratulations. You've done it. David Watkins'. In this big lucky dip the first one I picked out came from the man whose red number 10 jersey I was taking over.

I was supposed to sit a mock exam before the game, but Wales were training and Mr Griffiths gave me permission to go with my country instead. 'Don't worry,' he told me, 'I'll give you another paper to sit in due course.' I still haven't received that exam result!

I owed my Wales call-up to my form with Llanelli, although not everyone seemed totally happy with my performances. One day Handel Rogers, a great man who was a former President of the Welsh Rugby Union and the secretary of Llanelli for years, sidled up to me to offer a bit of cautionary advice. In his booming Welsh accent he said, 'Barry, you are playing well, you are getting some rave reviews. Let's hope you are not like the others and forget it when you go past the Loughor Bridge.'

The Loughor Bridge was just a few miles down the road on the way to Swansea. Handel was saying that if I could produce match-winning performances away from our own fanatical support at Stradey Park, then I really had made it as a player. Over the years Handel had seen too many 'homers', players who simply were not the same when the going got tough on visiting grounds. I think I satisfied him that I could do it home *and* away.

I still had to win over some of Llanelli's own hard-to-please supporters, though, as I discovered one morning during an amusing lorry ride when I hitched a lift to college. Hitchhiking was fair game in those days (although today I wouldn't contemplate doing it). Up pulled a huge lorry and the driver, unshaven, gruff-looking and with spiky hair, told me to get in. When I mentioned I was going to college I could see him thinking, 'Oh aye, one of those student softies.' During the twenty-five-minute journey we began talking about rugby and he said he knew a few players from the local village. I did not let slip who I was and he clearly did not recognise me because he said, 'I'll tell you who is from Cefneithin and who goes to your college. That, what's-his-name, that kicker for Llanelli. That one who only kicks and does nothing else in the whole game?'

I decided to toy with him and said, 'Do you mean Barry John?' He replied, 'Yes, that's the one. If you see him tell him to take up football because my mates and I go to Stradey Park and we are fed up with him. Kick, kick, kick.' I told him that we did not particularly like Barry John at college either, and he said, 'I'm not surprised. He comes across like that, right arrogant if you ask me.'

He asked me my name and I replied, 'Charlie.' Then, as we reached my drop-off point, I asked which part of the ground he and his friends went to. When he said they always sat in the same seats I opened the door, jumped down and turned to say, 'Next time I'll give you a wave, then. My name is Barry John.' Oops, his jaw dropped. Whoosh, I have never seen a lorry move so fast. He must have broken every traffic law in the book as he raced off in embarrassment. Next time I played at Stradey I looked across, saw him and gave the thumbs-up. You could see his chest pounding out. He may have been embarrassed with me, but he told his mates the story and probably dined out on it for years.

Talking of Llanelli fans dining out on stories, what about the one involving a betting scam, with yours truly innocently at the centre of it? Inside knowledge, I think, is the technical phrase used for it. I travelled by car to home matches with my father, David the local ironmonger and a friend of ours called Harry Bach. I was known for dropping a few goals by this stage and as we got closer to the ground, the conversation would quietly go, 'Fancy yourself for a drop-goal today, Barry?'

I would reply, 'Well, if the conditions are right, I'll try a couple.' This happened over a period of a few weeks and I thought nothing of it, even when a spectator came up to me in the main bar after one match and put what looked like tiny little rolled-up sweets into my shirt pocket. When I unrolled them, I discovered they were not sweets but lots of one pound notes.

In the next game I dropped another couple of goals and the same thing happened again, this time the man saying, 'Have a few drinks on us, Barry.' Eventually it began to dawn on me what was happening. My father and our two great friends were seeking odds on how many drop-goals I would score in a game. The inside information I was unwittingly supplying was also being passed on to their mates, so there were schools of bets going on around the whole ground. When people had scooped a particularly tidy little sum, they would come up and give me some of the winnings as a thank you. I knew nothing of what was going on, but I suppose you could argue I had been 'professionalised' through being given that money!

At first, when I found out about it, we had a laugh – but I had the last one because I felt it was getting out of control. During the car journey to the next match the conversation duly started again. 'How many drop-goals do you reckon today, Barry?' I told them, 'It's a dry day, conditions are perfect, their back row are slow, I really fancy three. Yes, three. It should be a piece of cake.' Do you know what? – I didn't even attempt one, even though I reckon I could have put at least two efforts over with my back to goal, so easy were the opportunities! I think you can say my travelling companions were not best pleased when they got back into the car after that match.

Despite these highly enjoyable and amusing times, I began to get itchy feet. I decided that, as I was twenty-one, it was time to move on. This was nothing to do with Llanelli. I had been given a taste of pastures new during our away matches and I did not think I could remain in west Wales any more. When I first alerted Llanelli to my plans their attitude was one of 'Yes, yes, yes . . .' In other words, they did not believe me; nor did they take any notice when I suggested a few months afterwards that they should give some of the younger fly-halfs a run-out because they, not I, were the future for the club.

News that I wanted to broaden my horizons eventually filtered back to Johnny Millions. His real name was John Thomas and he was the president of the club, but we knew him by his other name because he was so rich. One Sunday Johnny Millions said he was coming to see me at home in Cefneithin to try to talk me out of leaving. Our little street always resembled Brand's Hatch on a Sunday, with everyone out working on their cars or lorries. Many of the vehicles had bricks under their wheels because they were being repaired.

If you imagine Concorde coming in to land at a small runway packed with beaten-up old aeroplanes, you will get an idea of what it was like that afternoon as Johnny Millions drew up in his Rolls-Royce. Two of the lorries with bricks under them could not be moved to let him through. Sitting high in his seat looking down on this mayhem, Johnny Millions had to wait for twenty minutes before enough space was created for him to squeeze past the parked vehicles, drive to the bottom of the street, turn his Roller around and pull up outside our house.

Still, at least the wait helped the John household overcome a dilemma, because we had suddenly discovered that the parlour door, which we never used, was stuck rigid. We had to free it for this 'special' occasion and the twenty-minute wait gave us time to do that.

In came Johnny Millions, out came the best china for cups of tea and down we got to talking. 'I'll give you a car, I'll sort out a house, I'll arrange a job,' said Johnny. When I kept politely declining, he felt I was driving a hard bargain and basically told me to name my price. He explained that people had seen me develop at Llanelli and they could not believe I wanted to walk away at just twenty-one. But call it wanderlust, or whatever, I had to try my hand further afield and Johnny Millions finally conceded defeat – probably for the first time.

At first I imagined going to England and joining Bristol or Northampton. But news filtered through to Cardiff that I was leaving Stradey and once they expressed an interest it was the perfect solution. I could remain in Wales; and as David Watkins had just gone to Rugby League, provided I picked up my blue-and-black number 10 jersey, I was a virtual certainty to be my country's fly-half too.

I had won two caps already. But caps or no caps, at Cardiff you have to prove you deserve your place in the team at the pre-season trial. This is where I first came face-to-face with a character called P.L. Jones. He was the most unlikely shaped rugby player I have seen, possessing the sparrow legs of a gymnast like Olga Korbut, but the torso of a prop forward. PL played on the wing and apparently the Cardiff crowd loved him, although I must admit I did not know much about him – not then, anyway, but I soon did! As PL ran towards me in this trial I thought he looked like a big bag of wind whom I could simply shadow into a cul-de-sac and push into touch. Bad decision, Barry. Next thing PL dropped his shoulder and barged me out of the way. I was dumped on to the ground; my fingers were numb; I could not move my shoulder and I was certain I had broken something.

My new Cardiff colleagues came to stand over this youngster from Llanelli with the big rugby future ahead of him and, smiles on their faces, said, 'Oh, hadn't anyone told you about PL?' No, they had not, but this was his way of saying 'Welcome to Cardiff, pal'.

I went on to play many matches with PL and found him a truly amazing player – a bit like the cartoon character the Road-Runner, darting here, there and everywhere in weaving patterns. One try he scored against Coventry from sixty yards was, in reality, more like a hundred yards because instead of going straight, he kept zigzagging sideways past Cardiff players as well as Coventry men. In the end the rest of us had to stand still like statues to help him! John Reason memorably described the score in the *Daily Telegraph*, saying PL was the only try-scorer who had gone past the same players three times on his way to the line!

PL was typical of the great characters in that Cardiff dressing-room. A lot of us were West Walians, including Gerald Davies and myself, and we teamed up with some fantastic people like our props Roger Beard, Gerry Wallace and John O'Shea, hooker Gary Davies, lock-forward Maurice Braithwaite and flanker John Hickey. Cardiff was also the place, of course, where my famous half-back partnership with Gareth Edwards blossomed. Not only was it a dressing-room studded with great players, it was one full of wit, camaraderie and a high degree of intelligence. Like a football team, we would have our share of tabloid newspapers and the *Racing Post* on the team bus. But, unlike a football team, there would also be a fair smattering of quality broadsheets like *The Times*, *Daily Telegraph* or *Guardian* as we caught up on the political and financial news.

What perhaps summed up the terrific team spirit best was the fact that myself, Gareth and Gerald, the supposed superstars of the side, were the butt of most of the jokes. 'Who do you think you are, you prima donnas?' Beard and the rest would rap at us. Everything was in good spirits, though, and we like to think we gave as good as we got. If any nasty situations started in a pub, with some idiot fancying his chances and trying to impress his mates by picking on myself or Gerald, we would suddenly notice Roger or Hickey straight by our side. 'Are you OK, BJ?' they would say, and the provocateur would soon skulk away – particularly when Hickey fixed his brilliant blue eyes on the man. When those stared at you, the message was soon driven home.

We loved playing for the most famous club in the world, a tag Cardiff still arguably have, in my opinion. Even when we played what I would term knockabout games, against Oxford University on a wet Wednesday night, almost 10,000 spectators would turn up. When the really big showdowns with Newport, Llanelli and Swansea took place, the atmosphere was electric. When we played away against the big English teams, their treasurers would even take out insurance against the game being called off. The Cardiff match would make their season financially, such was our pulling power.

Several times I would receive telephone calls at home from those treasurers who would enquire, 'Barry, are you and Gareth definitely playing?' I would reply, 'I can't vouch for Gareth, but yes, I'll be there.' When we did duly arrive, the local evening newspapers would have big banner back-page headlines declaring, 'THEY'RE HERE – EDWARDS AND JOHN ARE IN TOWN'.

There was one occasion, though, when I'm told the Coventry

treasurer was pacing up and down like a nervous kitten. That day, instead of travelling up on the team bus, I went in a car with some of the supporters. Well, they did give their hard-earned money to come and watch us play every week, so why not treat them to a little rugby gossip? What you sometimes do not realise as a top sportsman is that everything is done for you. You are shepherded from A to B, escorted here and there, there is always someone to pick you up. So when, an hour before kick-off, we arrived in Coventry and my car companions asked where the ground was, my reply was that I didn't have a clue. How should I know? – I had always been escorted there before!

After driving around for a while we saw some floodlights in the distance and headed in that direction. Only when we got there, we discovered it was Coventry City's Highfield Road ground . . . I had promised the Coventry treasurer I would definitely play and yet here I was, completely lost and with kick-off fast looming. Panic time. After asking a few people for directions, we did eventually arrive at the ground, with seconds to spare. I discovered the kick-off time had been put back fifteen minutes, so I rushed in to get changed. Apparently the public-address man had announced it was because of traffic congestion. The real reason was rather different – they were hoping I would make it in time!

That day we had travelled with just one spare player, Stan Thomas, who has gone on to become one of Wales's richest men. He's a multi-millionaire through his business expertise. Stan had never got beyond the Rags, the second side, but in my absence he had been told to change and was about to achieve his ambition of finally wearing a first-team Cardiff shirt – until I suddenly rushed in. To compound matters, we lost a player after just eight minutes, but because you were not allowed to use replacements in those days, Stan still could not come on. There are some things even money cannot buy!

Someone once told me that I scored twenty-four tries and dropped thirty goals for Cardiff in ninety-three matches over five seasons. A pretty good record by anyone's standards, I suppose. Drop-goals may be part of the modern game, but in general they were a rarity in the 1960s and early '70s. *Four* in the same match was unheard of – until I did it against Llanelli in the most riveting and memorable game of my Cardiff career. The script was pure theatre: two in-form clubs; a packed house at the Arms Park; Barry John against his old club; their coach, Carwyn James, Barry John's rugby mentor – and to cap everything the man marking me, as Llanelli's flanker, just happened to be my brother Clive. My other brother Alan, another flanker, was also due to play but had to pull out because of a foot injury.

The pair of them were fantastic players and there is a lovely little photograph on the wall of the Red Lion pub in Llannon, near Tumble, of the three of us together before another Llanelli v. Cardiff encounter. I'm in the middle like a chimpanzee, trying to push my shoulders out and look big next to their muscle. Anyway this particular Arms Park game, I decided, was going to be won by skill from the John household, not muscle; but what happened next surpassed my wildest dreams.

The two sides were littered with capped players, and I mean 'true' internationals (not like today where you see so many players called internationals, but only, in my opinion, because you have to have fifteen on the pitch). On that occasion, most of those thirty Cardiff and Llanelli players were the real bees-knees and it was the Llanelli ones who fared best early on as they went 9–0 up.

In truth they would have been out of sight had it not been for a mixture of dropped passes by them and superb tackling by ourselves. Just before half-time I dropped a goal to bring it back to 9–3, but we had been given such a run-around that even our most partisan of supporters felt Llanelli would simply blow us away in the second half.

Not so. Just after the restart I dropped another goal. Then Gareth Edwards gathered a badly sliced ball forty yards out, threw out a twenty-five-yard pass to me and – one-two-three – it was back through the uprights again. Our crowd started to go bananas. Next thing I remember is again receiving the ball, stepping like a matador inside my opponent and chipping over from twenty-five yards. From 0–9 down to 12–9 ahead. Four drop-goals out of four and each from a different range.

I know Jannie de Beer kicked five out of five for South Africa against England in the 1999 World Cup, but these days, if you do not have a drop-goal expert in your side you are foolish. Modern playing surfaces, the quality of the ball and everything else is in favour of kicking. The opposition stand back because of stricter offside laws, giving more time and space than we had. In those days, however, it was regarded as freakish and Llanelli could not believe what had happened to them. When the final whistle was blown Clive came up and sarcastically said, 'Oh, the only way you can win is by dropping goals.' I smiled and was running towards the darkness of the tunnel when suddenly an old man in his sixties wearing a Llanelli scarf appeared on my left and threw a punch at me. Luckily he just grazed my chin, but it was not what you expect after winning a rugby match.

A policeman saw the incident, grabbed the man and asked, 'Barry, do you want to press charges?' I looked at the old man and felt sorry for him. He was clearly thinking, 'I'm in big trouble here, what have I done?' But funnily enough I could understand his actions. He probably felt betrayed because he had just seen his side lose a dramatic match thanks to four drop-goals from a man who used to play in Llanelli colours, someone who he probably used to cheer at Stradey Park. To take the sting out of the situation I just put my arm around the old man, told the policeman, 'If I had been him I would have made sure I landed it,' and invited my aggressor into our dressing-room. He was a bit embarrassed, but his actions underlined the passion of the occasion.

I'm not sure if he'd have missed with his punch, though, had I succeeded with a *fifth* drop-goal attempt. Another opportunity arose towards the end of the match, but I spurned it and chose to run the ball instead – finishing an arm's stretch short of the try-line. In my confident mood, I really should have gone for the drop-goal. But as I began to pull back my right leg, the name Brigadier Glyn Hughes suddenly entered my thoughts. He was the man who ran the Barbarians and I remember one match against East Midlands when we were leading 17–3, only for them to haul it back to 17–17. I attempted a drop-goal to win the game, but the ball missed by a fraction and I was devastated.

Afterwards, Glyn marched into the dressing-room in his military manner, pointed his finger at me and said in his posh voice, 'Listen John, the Barbarians do *not* resort to dropping goals to win matches. Is that clear?' Well, Cardiff and the Baa-baas share the same rugby ideology. Suddenly recalling the Brigadier's words, I decided against the fifth drop-goal. That said, my Cardiff team-mates reacted somewhat differently to the great army man because they were jumping on me after the four I *had* scored, saying, 'Well done, Barry – you were brilliant.'

Members of the Llanelli committee, who used to love it when I won games for them, chose to see things differently. Speaking to the media afterwards, one of them said, 'Oh, we know Barry is a good kicker. It is part of his game, but if that is how he wants to play we think it would have been better if he had left us to go to Ninian Park, rather than Cardiff Arms Park.' Ninian Park is the home of Cardiff City Football Club. I just put the comments down to that particular committee man not counting to ten before opening his big mouth.

I didn't always have things my own way at Cardiff, though. Remember when I put my finger to my mouth, went 'Shsssshhh' to the crowd and confounded my old mate Duckham and his Coventry team by running in for that try? Well, David got his revenge the following year.

In those days Cardiff and Coventry each supplied one touch judge. During this game Duckham began racing away down the side where the Coventry touch judge was running the line. A few of us, including myself, were in hot pursuit when suddenly the touch judge stepped marginally onto the pitch. Dave weaved outside him, ran back inside and raced clear for the try. The rest of us had virtually stopped, assuming the touch judge's flag would go up – only it did not. The try stood.

And Duckham took great satisfaction in coming straight up to me and saying, 'There – that's to get you back for last year!'

Oh well, you can't win the lot, I suppose.

SIX

THE DREAM TEAM

They used to call the Welsh side of the 1970s the Dream Team. When you look at the personnel we had and study our winning record you can fully understand the tag. The talent around me in the back division reads like a Who's Who of rugby greats: Gareth Edwards, Gerald Davies, J.P.R. Williams, John Bevan, John Dawes (the greatest captain I have seen), supplemented earlier by men like Maurice Richards and Keith Jarrett.

To defend against that speed, slickness, athleticism and blockbusting ability must have been nigh on impossible. No, not must have been – it *was* impossible, as our opponents found to their cost. In the four-year spell before I finished, covering the Five Nations tournaments of 1969, 1970, 1971 and 1972, we won four Championships in a row, two Triple Crowns, one Grand Slam; and we would have had another had it not been for a daft decision by the Welsh Rugby Union to withdraw from a match against Ireland in Dublin because of political troubles.

That was a pretty impressive sequence of wins, which made us the undisputed kings of the Northern Hemisphere. No wonder it was called Welsh rugby's golden age, and after I retired the likes of Gareth, Gerald and JPR went on to win many more honours. However, what is forgotten in the passage of time is how everything could so easily have collapsed at the start, and how the Dream Team very nearly did not even get off the ground. Of my first seven matches for my country, we won only once (5–0 against Scotland in Cardiff, and that was with a try from a forward pass!) but luckily the selectors stuck by us. By the time I had finished in 1972, not only were we the undisputed top dogs, I was also fortunate enough to be the proud owner of the Welsh points-scoring record, my tally of ninety from twenty-five games surpassing the previous best landmark set by Jack Bancroft way back in 1914.

OK, I know modern-day goal-kickers like Neil Jenkins or Jonny Wilkinson get ninety points from about five games. But back in the 1970s rugby was a more fluid game, the onus very much on try-scoring and the opportunities to kick penalty goals arising less frequently. These days you can lose by sixty points and still score fifteen yourself, such is the proliferation of penalties. You have to carry a kicker in modern rugby – in fact, I would not be totally surprised if we soon follow the American Football lead and have a gridiron-style kicker who comes on especially to take the penalties and conversions!

Another thing that tends to be forgotten, as time passes by, is that I only actually did the goal-kicking duties for Wales in six matches. I never got a look-in before that. Clearly people thought I had better make up for lost time, because someone once worked out that in those super six games, every one won by Wales, my tally was sixty-six points. I went through the card too: tries, penalties, drop-goals and conversions. Fittingly, I suppose, it was in my very last international, our 20–6 win over France in Cardiff, that I eclipsed Bancroft's fifty-eight-year record with a thirty-five-yard penalty. The Arms Park crowd knew the significance of the three points as the ball sailed through the posts and they roared their approval, while my team-mates came across to offer their congratulations. But my joy at setting the new record was tempered by my own knowledge that this would be the last time I pulled on a Welsh jersey. Still, if there was a way to go out, what better than as a record-breaker.

There was a time, however, when being Wales's top points-scorer was the last thing anyone could have anticipated, because in the very early days we were anything but a Dream Team. Deep down the players sensed we could be on the verge of something special, that we could be an exciting side if we gelled, but the results suggested otherwise as we managed just that solitary win during my first seven games. Full credit to our coach Clive Rowlands for believing in us, giving us the opportunity to find our feet at international level and refusing to panic into making changes! Maybe Clive put our poor run of results down to the innocence of youth, with our back division having an average age of just twenty. Maybe he had butterflies in his stomach, wondering what was going to happen next. Whatever, he stuck by us and his confidence was justified when we suddenly clicked in beating Scotland 17–3 at Murrayfield. I scored one of the tries that day and from that point onwards we never looked back.

Once everybody fired there was simply no stopping us. I had complete freedom to run games instinctively as I saw fit, thanks to the encouragement given to me by our skipper Sid Dawes, still a great friend of mine. Sid never grabbed the headlines as much as the rest of us but he deserves a large chunk of the credit for what we achieved because he was so positive in everything he said, never once cautioning, 'Hold on a minute Barry, play conservatively.' On the contrary, he was more likely to tell me to go for it and for a running fly-half that was a bit like letting a greyhound off the leash. That said, many times I could have put on a duffle-coat out there and still no one would have noticed me. What I mean by that is that it would have been an insult not to give the ball to the hugely talented three-quarters around me and let them get on with it. You still have to choose the right moment to give it, though, and I like to think I did.

I hope this does not come across as arrogant, but there were times when we would run in tries, the crowd would go potty, yet we would look at one another on the pitch as if to say, 'OK, we will take the points, but that was not really a true Welsh try.' Subconsciously we were giving ourselves marks out of ten – and we would say that next time we would aim to run it from fifty yards and put together a ten-man handling movement. Those were the standards we had attained and if we fell below them, we were not satisfied.

How do I begin to describe the men around me in that Dream Team? Gareth Edwards, my half-back partner, acknowledged anywhere in the world – New Zealand, South Africa, Australia, France – as one of the greatest players rugby has produced. Our partnership was so special it deserves a chapter of its own. Read on.

Gerald Davies. They used to call Gareth and Gerald and myself the Three Musketeers because we hung around together for club and country. Gerald goes down as one of the greatest wings in the history of the game, but he actually started out as a centre with Wales. He was put out on the flank for the first time when we played New Zealand in Auckland and, while I will not say he was hurt, there was a feeling from Gerald towards the management of 'Oh, you don't think I'm good enough as a centre, then?' In fairness the Welsh management did Gerald a favour because the moment he went wide the tries started –and they kept coming and coming and coming.

Gerald was blindingly quick, possessing the most remarkable balance which enabled him to use that famous side-step which so often wrong-footed defenders. He was the Nureyev of the flank and we always knew that if Thomas Gerald Reames Davies was in the team, we were *never* out of a game. What was often overlooked, amid his sheer brilliance as a try-scorer, was Gerald's courage. Many a time he would dive head-first into the corner flag as big burly blokes were rampaging towards him to attempt last-ditch tackles. Sometimes the boots would come flying in, but Gerald never worried, he was only interested in scoring. Some of the tries he did get I'm convinced only Gerald could have scored. He was that good. Imagine Gerald on the right wing and the giant Jonah Lomu on the left? Little and Large . . . Hmm, that would have been a partnership to savour.

We were not exactly lacking in ability on the other flank either. Maurice Richards was a super player who never received the credit he deserved, possibly because of the headlines Gerald kept capturing. I did not exactly help Maurice's cause, either, when we thrashed England 30–9 at the Arms Park in 1969 – the first game where people began thinking, 'Yes, this is a team going places.' Maurice scored four tries that day, a fantastic feat and a record at a time when records really mattered. OK, four individual tries in a game, if not commonplace, does happen a few times these days. But, with respect, those achievements tend to come against the likes of Spain, Portugal and the USA. Those ones do not count, as far as I'm concerned. Maurice's feat, against proper opposition, most certainly did.

The trouble for Maurice was that the following day everyone was talking about our fifth try of the game – scored by none other than yours truly! If I say so myself, it was a beauty too. Actually when people ask me to go through my great tries, they assume I will spend ages talking about them. They tend to look rather surprised when I reply that I only scored about six great tries in my career. In reality that is not a bad number for a fly-half: normally the scores with which number 10s are associated tend to be classical support tries, or a race for the line after an attempted clearance has been charged down.

However, that day it was one of my better efforts as I went on a zigzag run, checking one way to go past one opponent, side-stepping the other way to get around another, dropping a shoulder next. Done at pace, soon I was over in the corner. As I got up I noticed four-try Maurice glancing towards me and I pointed to my chest as if to say, 'Hey, that one was mine.' His look of thunder said everything. He had scored four but he knew the headlines were coming my way. The next day that duly proved to be the case and one newspaper described my effort in this fashion: 'Barry John's try was one of the finest anyone will see. It was poetry in motion and should have been put to music.' I could not have put it better myself!

John Bevan eventually replaced Maurice on the left wing. Once he got his rag up, he could run through doors. Talk about sheer strength.

Someone once said to me that if Gareth and John were locked in a room and got into an argument, we'd never know who would walk through the door standing; but what we did know is that even the winner would have to be hospitalised. When we were with the Lions in New Zealand there was a training drill where our Irish prop, Ray McLoughlin, and John went head-to-head in a scrummaging duel. Our winger versus the hard-as-nails prop; should have been a no-contest really, but the backs were shouting, 'Come on John, show the pansies up front what real strength is.' It was almost like an amphitheatre and Bevan simply would not give ground. McLoughlin had packed down against the very best front-row forwards in the world, but he told me afterwards he had never known strength like that.

In one provincial match on that tour the Lions had been subjected to eighty minutes of constant dirty play. We were punched, kicked and gouged. Towards the end John had had enough and decided it was time for revenge. Receiving the ball in space he started on a typical rampaging run down the wing, full head of steam up, and began homing in on the try-line. That is what John should have done, anyway. Instead, at the last minute, he changed course and headed straight towards two Kiwi opponents who had been needling him during the match. A yard from the try-line, John just launched himself at them. Down they went like skittles, one falling backwards, the other sideways; John fell through the middle, grounded the ball and got up triumphantly to give that trademark left-hand fist of salute of his. 'Yes, have some of that.' The Kiwis certainly did, in more ways than one.

If that little lot did not get you, J.P.R. Williams most certainly did – as England, more than any other nation, found to their cost because he never seemed to stop scoring against them either at Twickenham or in Cardiff. JPR: what do you say about the man? A law unto himself, he will know this is tongue-in-cheek when I say that if no one told him for three days that he was a great player, he would probably have rung himself to say it. It was fantastic to have a man of such unbelievable self-confidence behind you, a full-back who knew that no one and nothing was better than him in that position. The crowd loved him. Socks rolled down, hair flowing in the wind, he would take on anyone – opposing full-back, hooker, prop, lock-forward, whoever, no matter how big. JPR took a great deal of pressure off me, allowing me a free rein to play my own game, because I knew I never had to worry about the full-back covering me. JPR was invariably there and on the few occasions he was caught out of position, he still managed somehow to get back in time to make last-ditch covering tackles. Actually, far from worrying about JPR's defensive positioning, I had to be on red alert, in the knowledge he might launch an assault from deep, and make sure I was up there in support.

These were the men who time and again captured the plaudits and the try-scoring headlines. It is somewhat ironic, then, that the Welsh back who rarely grabbed the spotlight just happened to be the one who held everything together. That man was John Dawes in the centre, perhaps best described as a player's player, a sentiment the rest of that Dream Team back line would echo. The best way I can describe the Dawes factor is this. If, before matches, the public-address man announced a sudden change to the selected Welsh line-up, and either JPR or myself was missing through injury, you could hear the moans and groans reverberate around the ground. In the dressing-room, however, it would not worry us in the slightest because these things happen in sport and we had good back-up players anyway. If, on the other hand, the public-address man announced John Dawes was missing through injury, the crowd would not bat an eyelid. In the dressing-room, however, there would be a mood of panic because we knew just how important his presence was to the way we played.

Sid, as we called John, was simply brilliant in the way he encouraged us. 'Don't worry about it,' he would say if a pass had gone astray. 'Keep trying things.' His attitude meant the rest of us had the confidence to play with panache and style, to attempt off-the-cuff moves. A truly great captain. What is more, to this day I believe Sid has never received enough credit for his own playing ability, for he was a master of passing superbly under pressure and had a big hand to play in many of our famous tries.

As for the forwards in that Dream Team, well I merely say a big thank you! No, I'm only joking. What those men did, the effort and commitment they put in, was sometimes beyond the call of duty. On occasions I saw one or two scarcely able to cough without wincing in pain because of injured ribs, yet they still went out to play eighty minutes of hard international rugby. They were big men who produced big performances when it mattered on the big occasions. Men like Denzil Williams and Jeff Young in the front row, Delme Thomas at lock, Mervyn Davies and Derek Quinnell in the back row. The respect I had for them, and continue to have today, is immense.

That admiration grew even bigger during one training session after I had taken the mickey out of Jeff, our hooker, almost sneeringly asking him: 'Tell me, what do you think about when your nose is down there half an inch off the ground in a scrum?' I should have kept my big mouth shut because at the next training session our coach Clive Rowlands suddenly stopped play, announced scrum down and told me I was going as prop! 'Me?' I queried. 'Yes you,' said Clive, to a chorus of approval and smiles from Jeff and the other forwards.

Clive came up and explained, 'Listen Barry, if you drop the ball or knock on, these eight ugly gits have to go through a scrum. You don't know what it is like, do you? So have a go and find out.' I have never done wrestling, but if I had I think it would be fair to say that the experience of a combination squeeze would probably be similar to that of being prop for one day. That is the only way I can begin to describe what happened next. Down I went, only to be pushed right up in the air, head popped out like an idiot, totally trapped. I was there for thirty seconds, which seemed like thirty minutes, unable to move; and to make matters worse people suddenly started clicking away with cameras to take photographs. My team-mates, I discovered, were in on the act and were laughing their heads off. I had been well and truly done.

I made sure I did not take the mickey out of Jeff after that and I also tried to ensure I never dropped a pass or knocked on. But I would still like to have seen Jeff and the other front-row men try their hand at kicking a goal or making a break from fly-half!

It was a truly amazing feeling to run out for matches knowing there was such strength – literally and metaphorically speaking – around me among forwards and backs. Together we formed an awesome and unstoppable combination, as England, more than any other side, discovered to their cost. In five games against them I never once lost (I repeat, it would have been rude for a Welshman to do so!). JPR's record was twelve unbeaten games.

The Five Nations matches against France, Scotland and Ireland were big encounters; but with England there was that extra edge, perhaps among the Welsh public even more than the players. Whenever we played England I used to be deluged with letters beforehand from Welsh people urging, 'Please don't lose' or 'Please don't miss a kick'. Never please *do* this or that, always please *don't* do something wrong. We used to get more letters for our visits to Twickenham than for our Cardiff games, principally from ex-pats who spent a year taking bets on the outcome of the game with their English neighbours or work colleagues.

One such letter duly arrived for me shortly before we went to Twickenham in 1972. It was from a chap in Oxford who explained that he worked at the local Ford factory and was one of only two Welshmen in his section. He wrote to say he had just totted up his bets and discovered that the total, if he lost, came to more than two weeks' wages. Needless to say, his wife knew nothing about this and he wrote, 'I'm going to be unbelievably nervous. Please tell Gareth, Gerald and the others not to do anything silly, and try not to miss any kicks.' Talk about having a burden to bear! I had this man's hard-earned wages, two weeks' worth of them, hanging on every one of my kicks.

Luckily, for him more than me, I had a 100 per cent record in the game, three successful kicks out of three, and we duly won 12–3. (Hey, it would have been even ruder as a Welshman to lose to England on that occasion with so much riding on the result!) The following week I answered this particular individual's letter: 'I'm glad we were able to do the job for you and that I scored eight points in our victory. But let's learn a lesson from this. Gambling this amount of money simply is not on.' I mean, what if I had missed my efforts at goal? I'd not have liked that one on my conscience.

The only time my proud record against England looked like being broken came when, after winning the Championship and Triple Crown in 1969, we tied for the title in 1970. The fact we managed to achieve that owed little to the men who normally made up our scintillating back line. No, Twickenham 1970, and our astonishing 17–13 win, owed everything to Ray 'Chico' Hopkins, the little man from Maesteg who replaced Gareth Edwards as my scrum-half.

We were 13–3 down, David Duckham was in supreme form, England were flying and there seemed no way back for us, particularly when Gareth went off with a hamstring injury with twenty minutes to go. On came Chico for his first cap and he totally turned the game on its head. It was as if he'd been waiting for this moment. I know that to this day, Chico feels let down and aggrieved with Gareth because he feels the great man did not properly congratulate him on his wonderful performance.

Gareth, like every great sportsman, I suppose, was prone to mood swings. He had set himself standards, challenges, mountains to climb, but on this occasion we were definitely down and out until Chico somehow pulled it out of the bag. I scored a quick try to bring it back to 13–6, then booted the ball down to the England corner. From there Chico set up JPR, who crashed through two tackles to score. Soon we were right back in it as I kicked the ball down to the corner again – I was too lazy to run that far. The line-out turned out to be a mess and Chico emerged from the confusion to grab a début try. When television clips of that great Wales comeback are shown, they always focus on a successful drop-goal by myself near the end. But the more pertinent kick was JPR's old-fashioned toe-poke to convert Chico's try, which put us into a previously unthinkable 14–13 lead.

The Welsh fans inside Twickenham could not believe what was happening; nor, for that matter, could the English followers. But having got this far, we were not going to let it slip. In those days you did not look at the clock to see how many minutes were left, you gauged it by the light. As darkness began to fall upon Twickenham, I decided we were going back down into that same right-hand corner once more. Boom, the ball went off my right boot into touch, Delme Thomas won the line-out, Chico fed a perfect pass out to me and over went the drop-goal. I reasoned that if I scored we would be 17–13 ahead, if I did not, England would have a 25-yard drop-out and would probably concede possession back to us anyway. Over the ball sweetly went, though, and shortly afterwards the Welsh fans began swarming on to the pitch, picking us up and tossing us around, to celebrate a most famous Chico-inspired victory.

I actually felt a little sorry for England because they blew it. And if they believe that, they will believe anything!

If we were on a high that evening, we soon came back down to earth as we lost the next game 14–0 to Ireland in Dublin – breaking a nine-match winning streak. I had a lower back problem that filtered down to the hamstring. It badly restricted my movement and sharpness and that is why I have been able to sympathise with top footballers like Michael Owen and Ryan Giggs who have been troubled by that sort of injury in recent times. To be honest, we could not have complained had we lost by a further ten points, for we had just one chance in the entire eighty minutes. If Gareth had scored from it, the Irish might have cracked. He did not and instead the Irish got stronger and stronger, as they do when they are on top in Dublin. Their number 8, Ken Goodall, still thanks me for helping to put them there, because I kicked one clearance right down his throat and he ran straight up the other end to score. Ken still pays me in pints of Guinness whenever we meet!

That Irish defeat proved to be just a blip, however, and the following year, 1971, we duly marched triumphantly to the Grand Slam. We easily beat England 22–6 in Cardiff and followed that with a comfortable 23–9 win over Ireland. But our two away games that year, in Scotland and France, were true epics.

At Murrayfield we were losing 18–14, going into the final moments.

I was virtually out of it, having been concussed when Billy Steele clattered into me as I scored a try a few minutes earlier. I can recall some periods of play in that game, but the rest are a total blank. I should not really have remained on the pitch. One thing I do remember is our one last big effort as we managed to peg the Scots back near their own 25-yard line. Of the thousands of line-outs Delme won in his great career, none was more important than this one. As the Llanelli captain palmed down the ball, I was shouting out loud to myself, 'Catch it and give it' as Gareth fed the pass to me. Only by concentrating hard like that could I overcome the concussion problem and focus on what I needed to do.

My little message to myself worked. I passed the ball down the line and it eventually reached Gerald Davies, who raced over in the corner. John Taylor converted from the touch-line. Phew, we had scraped through 19–18. When I watch videos of those final moments, I notice the sea of Welsh people on the bank behind the goalposts just erupt in joy and delight when, first, Gerald scores and then Taylor converts. I must admit I did not notice them at the time, such was the state I was in.

Then it was on to the game of my Welsh career: France in Paris, and a case of 'winner takes the lot', as the pair of us had each won our three other matches. It was the Five Nations game of Five Nations games, although I'm not sure I should even have been playing because I had felt terrible, really giddy and weak, after taking that bang against the Scots. Still, if I thought concussion at Murrayfield was bad, a lot worse was to follow in Paris. I rushed in to tackle the huge French forward Dauga as he was about to crash over for a try, and managed to swing him around; but as he toppled off balance, the Frenchman fell on top of me and his elbow smashed into my nose with a horrific thud. Needless to say my nose was broken. In fact it was so bent I could see most of the world on one side, but hardly anything on the other because my vision was totally obscured. I have still got a scar on the bridge of the nose today.

Just my luck after Murrayfield, I thought, and in my groggy state I immediately signalled to the bench to get a replacement on. By a strange quirk of fate, the French player Barrau had just been injured too, and after dealing with him the French doctor came to look at me. I do not speak French very well so I can plead privilege of ignorance about what happened next – but it didn't half hurt at the time.

The French doctor kept looking at me in a concerned manner as he felt around the nose, asking questions to which I gave nodded replies.

'Oui, oui, oui,' he said in a quizzical fashion, as I nodded my head again. On that, he looked me in the eye, put one hand on my forehead, the other on my nose and pulled it down and across to straighten it, letting the nose slip back into place like a wooden joint. It took just a couple seconds, but the pain was totally and utterly unbearable. The waterworks started in my eyes because the tear ducts had been broken, cotton wool was stuffed up my nose and I was in agony. Then it dawned upon me what the doctor had been saying. He was asking if I wanted to have my nose straightened there and then, instead of going to hospital.

Due to the fact that the last French I spoke was during lessons in school, I was totally oblivious to this, of course. If I had understood the doctor I would have run a mile and been halfway down the Champs-Elysées before he could even put his hand to my nose. Hey, yellow is my favourite colour. No wonder he had that quizzical look. 'Oui, oui, oui,' was his way of saying, 'Are you sure?'

Next thing I knew I was back in the thick of the action, with the little matter of a rather important rugby match to win. Gareth scored a brilliant try after we ran at the French from fully eighty-five yards and I kicked a second-half penalty to put us 6–5 ahead.

Then came perhaps my best try for Wales. Not bad timing, was it? Jeff Young took a scrum against the head and, as their defence stood back, I noticed my opposing fly-half, Bérot, slightly out of position. I stepped nine inches in the other direction and started a sweeping run, gliding down the blindside as a number of French players converged upon me. The nearest was Bertranne, but at the last moment I changed course again, wrong-footed him and swept over for the try. I must have been in a groggy state because normally, once over the line, I would put the ball down immediately. This time I kept going and my team-mates feared I was going to over-run the try area. Just as I was about to, I eased their worries by touching down.

We had done it, 9–5 to Wales. Our first win in France since 1957. There was a big party in Paris that night, although unfortunately I had to miss out on the fun because of the tablets I was on to ease the pain from my nose. I remember with pride the salute given to us at the after-match dinner by the French Rugby Union's President Farrass. Everyone who was anyone in France was at that function, including President Pompidou, and as we walked in the entire room got up to give us a standing ovation. In his address at the end, Farrass said in broken English, 'My team, Français, great season. But we salute the wonderful Wales. They, better.' It was a lovely moment.

That moment was surpassed, however, on our return to Cardiff airport, where thousands of back-slappers were waiting to greet us. Once you get that sort of reception you know you really do represent the entire nation. I was immediately whisked away by car to appear on a television chat show where the other guest was Eartha Kitt, the American soul singer. I said to the make-up woman, 'You'll have to earn your money tonight.' The nose still hurt, but this was one occasion when the sweet scent of victory conquered everything.

I'm convinced we would have had another Grand Slam the following year, having comfortably beaten England, Scotland and France once more. But our game against the Irish was called off following IRA bombings and mutterings about security problems. That proved a double setback to me: firstly because Lansdowne Road was the only Five Nations venue where I had not savoured victory; secondly because I knew this would be my last opportunity to do so, as I was retiring.

So for selfish reasons I was downcast. That said, I was genuinely against cancelling the match and to this day I still cannot fathom why the Welsh Rugby Union agreed to do so. The first I knew of a problem was when I heard on the HTV news that the game was off because of security reasons, due to pressure being put on by the Welsh players. A list of names was read out, including mine. I immediately telephoned the newsroom at the television studios to say I knew nothing about this and to stress that I personally would go to Dublin with *any* fourteen Welshmen to play the match.

To no avail, I'm afraid. The one blot on my curriculum vitae was not to be erased. The following year I did go back to Dublin, as a journalist with the *Daily Express*, to watch Ireland play England. I have never seen such a fantastic reception given to a visiting side – and remember, we are talking about England in Dublin. The game passed off without any trouble and it dawned upon me just how pathetic the Welsh Rugby Union, and the players who had complained, had been in not wanting to go there. We are supposed to be closer to our fellow Celts, yet it was England who managed not to let the Irish down.

Still, if that Irish no-go upset me, at least I had the satisfaction of bowing out as a record-breaker in my final international, against the French, which we won 20–6 in Cardiff. We did not play particularly brilliantly that day and, interestingly, the crowd left the Arms Park saying we had produced an 'earthy' and 'workmanlike' performance.

At least that proved we could grind and battle it out with the best of them. But I think it fair to say we served up plenty of romantic rugby on the way. To have played my part in that is an honour. To have become a record-breaker was the icing on the cake. Roll on the next Welsh golden age, whenever that may be.

SEVEN

GARETH AND I

You throw it . . . I'll catch it! With those few innocuous-sounding little words my half-back partnership and friendship with Gareth Edwards was formed. Our famous alliance, and what we went on to achieve together – including Five Nations Championships, Triple Crowns, the Grand Slam and victory for the British Lions in New Zealand – is still talked about today. Not only were we partners on the pitch, we were partners-in-crime off it, rooming together for many years with Cardiff, Wales and the Lions. Edwards and John: they say we are part of rugby history.

What isn't so well documented, however, is how the partnership started in the most unlikely of circumstances. Those few words were uttered by myself on a cold, wet, gloomy, windswept January day as Gareth and I practised together on a lonely playing-field in west Wales. No one else was around for a very good reason. While we were getting drenched and my hands were numb with cold, the more sensible members of the human race were probably tucked up snugly in front of a fire, watching television or reading a good book. Just what I wished I was doing. Having had enough of getting soaked, when Gareth asked how I wanted the ball thrown to me next I just replied, 'Oh, you throw it and I'll catch it . . . Let's go home.'

More of that in due course. What is also not so commonly known is how Gareth's career very nearly came off the rails in New Zealand, and indeed may well have done had it not been for a private chat I'd had with my scrum-half partner. We know about Gareth's brilliance, his stunning success, rave reviews, one magnificent try following another. But I often wonder whether Gareth would have gone on to achieve the greatness and stature he still holds in the sporting world today had it not been for our little conversation.

Let's just say Gareth had a crisis of confidence. Hard to believe that, isn't it, from someone who went on to become a world-class player, whatever era of rugby you are talking about? But there were plenty of self-doubts and question marks on the victorious 1971 Lions tour. The way Gareth overcame them, to stamp his mark as one of the true rugby legends, is an object lesson for any up-and-coming young sportsman or sportswoman today. Proof, if you like, that even the very best sometimes wonder privately whether they are up to it.

In Gareth's case it was not so much a crisis over his ability. He felt people were questioning his want, the desire to be out there and produce the goods on the big occasion. You know, every player must stand up to be counted and that sort of thing. Gareth had played well early in the tour and the New Zealand press were talking very favourably about the Edwards–John partnership. Come the first Test in Dunedin, which we won, he was complaining about hamstring trouble and was duly replaced early in the game by our reserve scrum-half Chico Hopkins, he of Twickenham fame.

With wave after wave of New Zealand forwards hitting him, poor Chico took such a battering in that match, and in subsequent provincial games, that come the third Test in Wellington he could barely walk. The other players noted the sheer courage of little Chico; there was not exactly friction in the camp, but people would say, 'Gareth, look at Chico. We need you.' We did, too, because our captain John Dawes was on standby to play number 9 – and he was a centre!

In the build-up to the Wellington shoot-out, perhaps the biggest game in the history of Lions rugby, we were still hearing about Gareth's hamstring problems. Knowing full well this was win-or-bust point, our coach Carwyn James and manager Doug Smith approached me a few days before to ask, 'Barry, what's the situation with Gareth and what can we do about it?' As I was Gareth's colleague on and off the pitch, the Lions management knew I was as close to him as anybody in the party. When I told them Gareth said he still did not feel 100 per cent right because of the injury, Carwyn and Doug numbed me by replying they had put the Scottish scrum-half Ian McCrae on alert to fly out – just in case. They made it clear they wanted me to pass on the message and that Gareth, because of our great friendship and mutual respect, might take notice of me.

I went back to our hotel room, sat down with Gareth and spoke bluntly to him. 'I'm not coming here on a proper mission from the management,' I stressed. 'But they are worried about Chico and unless you play, they are sending for Ian McCrae.' I don't know if it was down to that threat to his place, but Gareth shrugged off his hamstring trouble, played in the Wellington Test and in the first twenty minutes produced the best rugby I have seen from him as we soared into an unassailable 13–0 lead. I am convinced those twenty minutes against New Zealand were as important to Gareth's entire rugby career as they were to the outcome of the victorious Lions tour. Any self-doubts he had were suddenly cast aside as Gareth realised he was a player who could produce the goods when and where it mattered most.

From that moment on his career simply took off. It never came back down again until the moment he retired as the greatest scrum-half the game has seen. During those make-or-break twenty minutes Gareth set up two tries, including one for myself; and there was one fantastic picture in the New Zealand newspapers of him palming off their fly-half Bob Burgess just before offloading his pass to me. Burgess was a bit gypsy-looking, with flowing locks of blond hair. In this picture Gareth had his hand underneath his opponent's chin – and Burgess' hair was about two feet out to either side! Such was Gareth's immense power.

I hope when young players read this insight into Gareth's early self-doubts, whatever level they play at and whether their sport is rugby, soccer, cricket or even darts, they take the message on board and realise that even the greatest have those moments to themselves when they just wonder a little bit. It happened to me on the same tour to New Zealand when I missed two straightforward penalty kicks at goal early in the first Test in Dunedin. I finished with a Lions record of 188 points on that tour, but that afternoon I could hear the whispers going around the stadium. 'Aye, aye, this new British star on the block has an 80 per cent success rate in the provincial matches, but can he do it when the real pressure is on?' If I missed the next one, I was ready to hand over the kicking duties to our Irish centre, Mike Gibson, because the team is more important than any individual's pride. Fortunately my next kick sailed over and I came through my own private worries.

The important point is that, when you have those inner fears, there's someone you can confide in whom you can trust and respect. Someone who can make you feel invaluable again. If I needed to chat about something during my career, I could turn to the Welsh coach Clive Rowlands on the rugby side, or off the pitch to my business partner Gwynne Walters, a former international referee. If I moaned about a strain or a pull they would say, 'No, no Barry, the team needs you. Get out there and win the game for them.' Out I would go feeling ten feet tall again and capable of achieving anything.

I suppose in Gareth's case the Lions management felt I was their last throw of the dice simply because I knew him so well. I did not read the riot act to him and I most certainly did not sit down for our little chat wearing the hat of management. But if, as an old ally of Gareth's, I helped him and the Lions management at the same time, to overcome a potential problem, I did it quite willingly.

But that was the Edwards–John partnership for you. If either one of us was in trouble on or off the pitch, the other would be the first on the scene to ask, 'Are you OK, mate?' We were more than rugby colleagues. We were, and still are, friends, a bond that stretches back more than thirty years to that miserable January afternoon on the lonely playing-field when we first got to know one another.

Gareth and I had been selected as the half-back pairing for the Probables team in the upcoming Welsh trial at Swansea and, although I had already been capped once by my country, Gareth was hoping for his international début. So, being extra keen, he got in touch to suggest we had a training session together beforehand to get to know one another's play. I was playing for Llanelli at the time; Gareth was Cardiff's up-and-coming star, but he was prepared to travel down to west Wales.

To be honest, I had forgotten about this arrangement when Gareth and Maureen, then his girlfriend, these days his wife, turned up one Sunday at my student HQ – Room 3C in the tower block at our Trinity College campus in Carmarthen. I had been to a college party the night before and, student bashes being what they are, I was unshaven, in need of sleep and feeling very much under the weather when Gareth knocked on the door.

When he said, 'Let's go', my first response was, 'Do we have to?' He insisted we did, but, in my fragile state, the last thing I needed was to go out in the pelting rain to the college playing-fields one and a half miles down the road. To compound matters, I had left my boots at Llanelli the previous day and my clothes were in the wash. So in a hurry I had to put on a pair of white daps and borrow tracksuit tops and bottoms from my college mates, depending on what was clean and dry.

There we were, the future half-back partnership for Wales and the Lions: Gareth, splendidly attired in his designer tracksuit and spanking clean boots, darting, diving, sprinting with a bouncy stride; me, looking like a gypsy in multi-coloured gear, slipping and sliding on the mud and feeling like a drowned fish as we jogged a few warm-up laps of the pitch. The only other person watching was Maureen, although she had the comfort of being able to remain dry as she sensibly waited in the car.

After a few minutes of this so-called warm-up, when in truth I was getting colder and colder, we began practising rugby routines. Gareth would pretend to pick up the ball from a scrum, ruck or maul, and I would shout 'Right', 'Left' or 'Behind', depending on where I wanted the ball, to enable him to become familiar with my voice. When you are playing in a stadium full of 60,000 people, with the noise, buzz and bustle going on around you, that sort of know-how between scrum-half and fly-half is vital.

This was not the day to practise it, however. After about fifteen minutes of these routines, with the rain getting worse, the gloom drawing in, the mud thicker and me barely able to stand up in my daps by this stage, Gareth got ready for another move, saying, 'How do you want it this time?' I had had enough and just replied, 'Oh, you throw it and I'll catch it. Listen, Gareth, we'll be OK. Let's go home.' After a couple more manoeuvres we trotted back to the car and went home for a shower – a world-beating half-back partnership well and truly forged. On the journey Gareth said, 'Don't worry about my passes because they'll be fine. Just make sure you do catch them.' Then he grinned, 'You're as confident and big-headed as I am!'

Gareth and I went on to play for the Probables XV at the trial in Swansea, but, believe it or not, I was injured by one of his very first passes. So much for the 'throw it–catch it' plan! Not that Gareth was to blame, as someone caught me and took a huge chunk of flesh out of my knee. I had to go to hospital to have stitches inserted, which I removed myself and covered in bandages to make sure I played in the game against Scotland when Billy Hullin (not Gareth) was selected as my scrum-half.

We lost and Billy and I were dropped. David Watkins took my place at number 10, but shortly afterwards he went to rugby league. I always joke that I gave David a huge amount of money to persuade him to go north – and that I'm still paying him off! But with David out of the way, I was recalled to play against New Zealand in Cardiff when Gareth was named as my scrum-half partner for the first time.

After that there was no stopping us. We were partners for the remaining twenty-three of my twenty-five Wales caps, played together for the Lions and, of course, shared a fabulous partnership at club level with Cardiff. I can honestly say that, apart from that miserable January day on the college playing-fields, we never once specifically went out to practise together again. We were regular room-mates on away trips, but even in the privacy of our hotel we did not discuss definitive tactics. Sure, we would talk generally about the game ahead, but we would leave it at that. What happened between us on the pitch just happened. A tandem that worked, a natural gelling of two talents, I suppose.

We got on famously from day one because our backgrounds were similar. The pair of us were essentially from council-house stock, there were only two and a half years between us, and the other special bond we had in common was that we spoke Welsh. Let me tell you, we put that to great use, particularly against the English. In games I would deliberately tell Gareth where to pass the ball in Welsh – 'i'r olde', if I wanted to go right, 'i'r chwyth', which meant left, 'ty-ol', which meant behind if I wanted space for a drop-goal attempt. The poor opposition did not have a clue what was going on, giving us an enormous advantage. At certain set moves I would tell Gareth in more detail, again in Welsh, that I wanted the ball in a particular position on the count of two. I would move into that position, say 'Un, dau', he would give me the ball and we would be away for a try. Time and again we caught the opposition, and in particular England, napping with that little ploy.

I first heard about Gareth on the rugby grapevine where reports reached us down in Llanelli about this highly rated youngster playing for Cardiff, but I never imagined he would be quite as good as he turned out. Good? The man was phenomenal. When you look at truly great sportsmen there is often something different about their build. Mike Tyson is one case in point, smaller than most heavyweights, but with amazing leg strength which helped him launch into those ferocious knock-out punches. The squat little Diego Maradona, with his extraordinary low balance, is another. They can also possess a short fuse, perhaps a temperament thing which actually helps take them to the top.

Gareth was the same. He was only five foot eight inches tall and looked pigeon chested, but his torso was in actual fact huge. I would sometimes try on his blazer for size and on me it was like an overgrown coat. The blazer would not only come down to my knees, the shoulders were about a foot out on either side! What this build helped give Gareth was huge upper body strength and this was complemented by enormous power in his legs. Everything he did was explosive – just take that famous try he scored for the Barbarians against New Zealand as an example of that. Huge second-row and back-row forwards would come charging at us, only to be unceremoniously sent tumbling backwards through the air by Gareth.

He worked hard at his physique, doing loads of weight-training and often trying to rope me in. No thanks, I always told him. I was once sent through the post a Charles Atlas book which detailed how you could have a so-called body beautiful. It was so heavy I couldn't pick it up! No, each to his own. Gareth did things his way, I trained my way. Put together, what we did simply worked like a dream.

One of the biggest reasons for our success was that Gareth and I never competed against each other. Individually we scored brilliant tries, but we also knew the team was what mattered most. We were delighted for one another if either of us scored – but we loved it even more if a prop-forward like Denzil Williams went over for a try and we could take the mickey by asking how he managed to run in from fully three yards out!

There was no senior partner as such. Having said that, if Gareth had taken a couple of wrong options, I would put my hands behind my back and point to my number 10 as if to say, 'Hey, I'm the one who is facing play, I can see what is going on better. Give the ball to me and I'll make the decisions.' Gareth got the message, but in fairness he rarely did take those wrong options. Even when he did, his mistakes had a certain endearing quality to them because if Gareth went on a charge, he was so strong he would tie up two or three of the opposition back-row in trying to stop him anyway. Gareth also possessed this fantastic boomerang pass which gave me extra time and space to free the three-quarter line outside us. That was what made Gareth so special. He was a threat in two ways: when he passed the ball, or when he did not. The opposition simply could not afford to take their eyes off him until the ball had gone one way or the other. Throw in the fact that Gareth was a beautiful tactician, who kicked almost to perfection, and you have nigh on the perfect scrum-half.

It was not just at rugby that Gareth excelled, though. He went to Millfield school and to this day holds the English schools 400-metre low hurdles athletics record. The reason why is because they have dispensed with the race. So when people see the name G.O. Edwards in the school record-books, yes, it is the same Gareth Edwards, MBE. He was brilliant at tennis: he had no formal coaching, but his hand-to-eye co-ordination, ability to put his feet in the right place and sheer power of shot, meant very few could beat him.

The same was true with golf. I recall one charity game for the Welsh Conservation Society in Tenby when Gareth teamed up with the former Ryder Cup captain Brian Huggett in a foursome event against myself and another. In reality the pair of them should have been split because together they gave no one else any chance whatsoever that day. Brian was the professional and Gareth would ask him, 'What are you going to drive with?' Brian would take out a five iron and hit a perfect shot. Gareth would take a seven iron and get the ball to within two yards of the hole. When I did something like that it was a fluke. With Gareth it happened too often to be regarded as lucky and even a seasoned professional like Brian was impressed.

There *was* one sport Gareth did not seem to be any good at – cricket. At least, I thought that was the case until we played on opposing sides in a charity game at St Helen's, home of Glamorgan in Swansea. The match featured a mixture of professional cricketers, rugby players, soccer stars and showbiz celebrities and Gareth walked out to the middle to bat that day with a distinct 'what am I doing here?' look about him. I was on the fielding side and, knowing Gareth was useless at cricket, I sidled up to my team-mates and told them to keep the ball up as he would have a swing and be clean bowled.

I was proved right because Gareth was indeed clean bowled – the only trouble being, he had scored 72 by that stage and won the game for his side. Again, his hand-to-eye co-ordination was quite incredible as he hit some sizzlers, many of them across the line. As one shot came towards me at square-leg like an Exocet missile, I pushed the umpire to one side so I could duck out of the way. Even with that low trajectory the ball still only bounced once before thudding into the boundary, such was Gareth's power.

I'm not sure what my rugby partner made of it, though, when the former England swashbuckler Colin 'Ollie' Milburn ran in to bowl at him during that innings of 72, slammed his front foot down at the crease and pulled up without letting go of the ball. Ollie had had a false eye inserted following a car crash: here, it had come out and was rolling down the wicket towards Gareth. Undemonstratively Ollie walked towards Gareth, picked up the false eye, rubbed it on his whites like a cricket ball, put it back in – and got on with bowling the next ball. Gareth was out shortly after that! Even Gareth Edwards' concentration went sometimes.

No matter how naturally talented Gareth was, he would not have got anywhere in rugby without the right preparation. Take it from me, as someone who shared a room with him down the years, he was the consummate 'professional'. No nights on the tiles before games or anything like that. Gareth and I knew our responsibilities and made sure we respected the honour and prestige that went with pulling on that red shirt. The only time we did not room together was when Wales foolishly made Gareth captain at the age of just nineteen. He had enough responsibility on his plate as a newcomer and as a main decision-maker in the side, without having that burden put upon his shoulders too. The captain gets his own suite – hence our brief parting of the ways – but soon Gareth and I were back together again on the third floor of our Cardiff hotel where the Welsh team were based before matches (the pair of us driving the room-maids mad, as usual).

In the build-up to international matches, our rub-a-dub man Gerry Lewis would help Gareth and me to relax and go to sleep by draping us in steaming hot towels which had been covered with various oils, scents and potions. Neither of us wanted to get into a hot tub of water because that would simply have drained our strength, so Gerry's method of relaxing us was perfect. One day after two years of this regular routine, a chambermaid approached me as we were checking out of the Wales team hotel after another Five Nations victory. She said, 'Do you realise, Barry, that after you and Gareth have shared a room, we can't let it out again for days afterwards? . . . Because the smell is so strong!' Apparently they had to leave the windows open for a week.

Gareth and I roomed together for Cardiff as well and I recall one match away to Oxford University when we were very firmly put in our places – so-called rugby superstars or not. With Cardiff we always had the very best hotels, as the club really looked after you. On this occasion Gareth and I came down for dinner dressed in casual gear. As we stepped into the restaurant, Hubert Johnson, the senior official in the party and a Cardiff RFC man through and through, beckoned us over to him. I was wearing jeans and an open-neck shirt and hadn't shaved, Gareth was dressed similarly. Hubert pointed to other people dining in the restaurant and said to us, 'Look how happy they are eating away at their food. Notice the one thing they have in common – they are very well dressed. Then look at you two. Go upstairs, shave and change into your Cardiff blazers.'

So, like two little lambs, Edwards and John trotted up to their room, shaved, washed, put on their Cardiff blazers as requested and back down they went. 'Wonderful. Don't you feel much better?' asked Hubert. He never mentioned it again, but Hubert's message was clear – no matter how big a name you are, you are still representatives of the team and must look the part. Yes, even if you are Gareth Edwards and Barry John. Gareth and I knew Hubert was right, too, because while we may have formed a great partnership, we never lost sight of the fact that the team *always* came first.

I still see Gareth from time to time although, funnily enough, we do not tend to talk about rugby these days. I particularly enjoyed meeting up with him again when Wales played Argentina at the Millennium Stadium in the first match of the 1999 World Cup. Gareth and I, with a few other Welsh players of the past, were asked to walk around the pitch beforehand as part of the opening ceremony. It was a celebration of Welsh rugby's golden age for the 72,000 fans, with video footage of some of our tries being shown on giant television screens as we filed around.

The reception we received was fantastic and I remember writing about the experience in the newspaper column I pen for *Wales on Sunday*. I mentioned that at one corner of the pitch the file of ex-players was becoming stretched, saying: 'There was a gap, so I tucked inside Gareth. Just like the old days.' The newspaper made a great headline out of those words and doubtless the memories came rushing back to thousands of Welsh rugby fans.

Gareth, as I have mentioned before, was prone to mood swings like so many other top sportsmen and certainly did not seem to like it when we used to rib him about how well Chico might have been doing for us. Gareth wanted to be top dog, you see. But, then again, he was top dog and I doubt his like will be seen again in a number 9 jersey. Nice one, partner. It was a privilege to play with you for so many years and, like you, I'm just pleased we were able to give thousands of people so many moments of joy.

EIGHT

MANDELA'S BRAVE
NEW WORLD

Ask me to name my man of the twentieth century and one candidate stands out head and shoulders above everyone else: Nelson Mandela. Anyone who witnessed at first hand the two different faces of South Africa as I did – first as a British Lions player in 1968, then as a *BBC* Radio Five commentator during the 1995 World Cup – would agree quite readily with me in my choice. I have not the slightest doubt about that.

The transformation in the country, from the appalling apartheid regime I saw with the Lions to the remarkable free new world twenty-seven years on, was quite startling. I feel honoured to have been in the privileged position of actually describing the wonderful sea-change to hundreds of thousands of listeners back home as I held the BBC lip microphone to my mouth during the opening ceremony of the World Cup in Cape Town.

I never had any formal broadcasting training during my fifteen years as senior rugby analyser for the Beeb. In fact the only thing I had to teach myself was to slow down, because we Welsh are big yappers – when ten words will do, we prefer to use a hundred! So I had to make extra sure I did not get carried away with myself that afternoon as I looked down from my commentary position at the Newlands ground to witness perhaps the most remarkable scenes I have observed on or off a rugby pitch.

Ostensibly we were there to see the Springboks play Australia in the opening game of the tournament. That, however, was not the reason I made sure I arrived at the stadium a full two hours early. First-hand experience in 1968 of how the apartheid regime worked had left an unpleasant taste in my mouth and I wanted to be there in my seat to see the splendour of the new South Africa. I was not going to miss a single minute of it. Before the game I recall sitting outside with a bottle of beer, just taking everything in and sampling the atmosphere as whites and blacks had barbecues together, bands played music and everyone was having a wonderful time. The awful images of what I had seen twenty-seven years earlier flashed through my thoughts: in those days a scene like that would have had the riot police coming in with batons raised and dogs barking.

Once inside the ground I saw, thirty yards down there in front of me and receiving a rapturous ovation, Mr Mandela himself. (I feel I have no right to call him Nelson.) He was standing on a little orange-coloured box no more than six inches high – no big podium for this humble, wonderful man. I explained on air that it was more like Hyde Park Corner where someone comes out with a little stool to address the gathering crowd. As President of South Africa, Mr Mandela was guest of honour that day as he officially opened the third World Cup tournament. Yet I could not help thinking that to my left, as I spoke, was Robben Island, where South Africa's white regime had locked Mr Mandela away in 1962 – the start of his twenty-eight-year spell behind bars just because he stood up for the rights of black people.

Normally in those circumstances the main match commentator would put his own lip microphone to his mouth, a cue for me to stop talking, so he could go on to describe the opening ceremony himself. But on this occasion I was speaking so well that Bill McLaren, to my left, and my other co-commentator Ian Robertson, to my right, put their own mikes down. Without any notes in front of me I began broadcasting back home what was happening, ad-libbing about the spectacular dancing, the captivated audience, the beaming smile on the face of Mr Mandela as he looked on with huge pride. I told the listeners that if Andrew Lloyd Webber had been asked to orchestrate this, he could not have done a better job.

The organisers had performed a truly stunning task, for this was not like getting people from Manchester to London for dress rehearsals. No, we had Zulus from Durban who were a two-hour flight away; white Afrikaners; Cape Town coloureds . . . Different people, different cultures, different costumes, brought together under the umbrella of rugby. I said that those organisers who had brought these various factions together so well deserved a gold medal, particularly as the opening ceremony overran by a mere thirty-eight seconds. Then I thought that, more than anyone, Mr Mandela was the person who really deserved the medal, because without him none of it would have been possible.

Nor would have been possible the lovely moment I witnessed before the semi-final clash in Durban between the South Africans and France, when a flash rainstorm descended on the ground, throwing the match into jeopardy. As the weather finally began to relent, six black women went on to the pitch with huge brushes to begin pushing the water to one side of the pitch. Suddenly a little white ten-year-old emerged with his own brush to join in. In unison the crowd erupted with delight. This youngster was not interested in black and white. It was a game of rugby and he wanted to help make sure the semi-final went ahead – although I don't think he managed to move any of the water because it was too deep and his brush was too heavy!

This stunning turnaround in the country, from what I had witnessed in 1968, simply had to be seen to be believed.

When I was called into that Lions squad, it was undoubtedly the highlight of my career up to that point. There is no greater honour in the game than proudly pulling on that Lions blazer with its fantastic and unique badge. Unfortunately everything then went wrong and our trip to South Africa has become known as the forgotten tour of rugby. It turned into a personal nightmare for me because I broke my collar bone in the first Test in Pretoria and spent the next three months going from one cocktail party and drinks session to another to ease the dejection of having to sit out four Test matches that were ready made for me.

Rugby conditions out there were nigh on perfect: the playing surfaces were hard and true; I could kick a mile because we were 5,000 feet above sea level; and the South Africans were not used to anyone side-stepping, so I had the element of surprise on my side. I felt deprived at having to miss out on the ultimate test of pitching my fly-half skills against perhaps the best back-row trio rugby has produced in Jan Ellis, Tommy Bedford and Piet Greyling. Those three Springboks were quick and athletic and they knew the game inside out. Taking them on was a challenge. I had been licking my lips in anticipation of that.

It was not to be, I'm afraid. I had to look on as a frustrated spectator as, for the record, we lost three Tests and drew the other. No one remembers much about the rugby, hence the 'forgotten tour' tag. In fact, to close followers of Lions trips it became known as the 'kippers and wreckers' tour – named after those who slept in and who went out on cocktail-party patrol in the afternoon and early evening (like yours truly) after our hopes of playing any rugby had been wrecked by injury. In the end there were so many of us in that group, we even had our own minibus!

While the rugby is easily forgotten, though, I have to say the disturbing sight of apartheid at work is something I, and several others who were in that Lions party, could never totally erase from the memory. That's why the new world I witnessed in Cape Town twenty-seven years on had such a profound impact upon me.

As an educated twenty-three-year-old, I was obviously aware of the term apartheid. I knew that it meant one rule for whites, one rule for blacks – and that the set-up was basically no good, for the black people were regarded as second-class citizens. But when we flew out to Johannesburg, we quickly discovered the blacks were not so much second class as tenth class, as far as white South Africans were concerned. Things we took for granted, like going to a public toilet for example, were viewed differently out there. One toilet for whites, kept spanking clean; another for blacks, doubtless filthy. Signs up too, saying 'Whites only' and 'Blacks only', to make sure you didn't venture into the wrong one. There were even park benches with 'Whites only' signs, the same with bars, restaurants, hotels. In Durban we noticed the best beaches were reserved for the whites, with shark nets up so that you could enjoy the beautiful clear blue water and swim in freedom. Around the corner were the less salubrious parts where the blacks were allowed to go. No luxury of shark nets for them.

As we drove to training grounds we noticed that the further out we went towards the townships, the more startling the change in housing, roads and general conditions became. It was, literally and metaphorically, black and white.

We had a black chauffeur on our minibus called Josh and, as I did not play again after my collar bone injury, I became quite friendly with him. I kept asking Josh to pop into bars with me for a drink, but he insisted, 'I can't, Barry. If I do, you'll get into trouble, as well as me.'

At the rugby matches there was no escape, either, as there were black and white sections within the stadiums for spectators. The blacks were crammed into a tiny little part of the terracing. It had obscured views and a huge tennis-style fence in front to keep them in. That was their pen – once in, they could not get out. Guess what the whites had, on the other hand? The very best seats, overhanging the pitch, giving them a brilliant view of the action. Of course, we had complimentary tickets for some of those seats and often wanted to give them to people like Josh and our black waiters who were so attentive to us during the trip. But we might as well have put a match to the tickets, because the blacks would not have been allowed to use them anyway.

Most Afrikaners had this in-built anti-black feeling and could not understand why the Lions players were being so polite to black people, saying 'please' and 'thank you' and so on. As I explained earlier, those basic manners were instilled into me at a young age when I was growing up in Cefneithin. The blacks loved us simply because we treated them like human beings.

I found the whole thing oppressive and disturbing. I did smile, though, when reading in *The Times* recently that a black man had become co-owner of one of the big gold mines in Johannesburg. The Lions party visited a gold mine once and saw the black employees being ferried to and from work in a vehicle that resembled a cattle-truck. They were herded together in the back of it, like cows. They would then go underground in horrific-looking old crates and boxes. Remember, I had had experience of coalmining myself and I dread to think what the accident levels in those gold mines might have been.

It was during that particular excursion that we missed out on the opportunity to ensure none of us would ever have to work again. The mine owners put a huge slab of gold in front of us and decreed that if anyone could pick it up one-handed, that individual could keep it. No such luck for yours truly or any of my colleagues, I'm afraid: we quickly discovered that not only was the gold incredibly heavy, it was also slippery and you simply could not get a grip. None of us returned home with our bank balances heavily boosted – although legend has it that on a previous trip the great New Zealand second-row forward and captain Colin Meads, he of the huge shovel hands, once actually managed to budge the thing!

We had been given a foretaste of what was to come on that tour when, before flying, the Lions party was taken to the South African Embassy in London to receive a list of 'dos' and 'don'ts'.

We had earlier assembled for training in Eastbourne – a shrewd move I guess, on the management's part, because it was a town full of retired people so they knew we could hardly get into any mischief. I remember spending one evening playing bowls and listening to a brass band in the background! Not that any of us exactly felt 'with it' at that particular moment, since we had been 'encouraged' to go to the barbers. Dave Brooks, our English manager, said: 'It's going to be hot and sweaty out there, Barry, so you'll be much better off with short hair.' A number of us duly went down to the local barber's – and we came out looking like Marines! That may be the vogue today, but we're talking about the '60s then: flowing locks, different shades of hair, that sort of thing.

Once we travelled up to London just before our departure from

Heathrow, news began to filter out about our movements. We emerged from that visit to South Africa House – having been instructed quite forcibly by their diplomats not to sleep with a black woman (because it could lead to an international incident), not to go into coloured bars, not to do this, that and the other – and found ourselves facing demonstrators, many holding up banners bearing the words 'LIONS, DON'T GO'. Seeing people of my own age among them making their feelings on apartheid known did affect me; but I honestly did not know how bad things actually were in South Africa until I got out there.

Anyway, I could hardly not go after the most fantastic collection had been made for me in my home village of Cefneithin. News of my Lions selection was announced on the radio one Tuesday morning. The following weekend, after playing on the Saturday for Cardiff, I went home. What happened next overwhelmed me as I was presented with £900 – the staggering sum of money raised by the villagers. In those days this was a pretty large sum of money. It was quite unbelievable, but they felt that I was representing the village. The local youngster come good: 'We can't have Barry going over there and begging for food or going short of clothes!' Lovely little old ladies, with barely half a crown to rub together, contributed. Collection boxes were put in the butcher's, the baker's, the post office – everywhere. There was even a fundraising concert in the local school.

Then there was Millie, the landlady who, with her husband Mansel, used to run the little pub just outside Cefneithin. It was called the Dynevor Lodge. She stuck one of those huge Bells whisky bottles up on the bar with a 'Buy Barry a drink in South Africa' label on it. Millie knew who the high-rollers were and she made sure they put their hand in their pocket for that bottle. If they said they had no change, Millie would insist, 'Right, you're not getting a drink then.' They soon found their money from somewhere.

I have cracked open a fair few of these Bells whisky bottles at charity events down the years. Mostly people put in pennies, but the bottles are so large you can still raise as much as £200. In this particular one for me there was more than £500, because Millie had insisted on those high-rollers putting £5 notes in.

By and large I did not need the money because, as a British Lion, you get a tour allowance and everything is done for you anyway. But I was a newcomer and knew little about the protocol of what happened on tour. It was an incredible feeling as I sat at home and counted out that £900. Three years later the Cefneithin villagers raised a further

£300 when I was selected for the 1971 tour to New Zealand – and by that stage I was married and fully settled in Cardiff!

I felt I could not possibly let down those wonderful fellow villagers. I travelled determined to make an impact in the Test matches, which is why my collar bone injury proved to be so distressing for me. We had quite a good build-up to the first Test, beating Western Province, South-West Districts and Natal. Though the local South African journalists did not rate our forwards too highly, they felt that we could do well if our backs got the ball. I was getting a good press, so too was Gareth: we had speed on the wings and the brilliant Mike Gibson in the centre.

Within our own dressing-room there was a genuine feeling of optimism as we prepared for that first Test encounter at the Loftus Versfeld ground in Pretoria. But it soon went pear-shaped when, early in the game, we were given a penalty and our full-back and skipper Tom Kiernan told me, 'Just put it into touch.' I wish I had listened to him, but then hindsight is a wonderful thing, isn't it? I noticed a huge gap in the South African defence and decided to go for it, reasoning that if I could side-step their new and inexperienced full-back Rodney Gould, who was the last line of defence, I would be in under the posts for a try.

My ambitious move very nearly came off; but just as I looked like scoring, I noticed a shadow on my inside which turned out to be their outstanding flanker Jan Ellis. As this was the first Test I was wearing a new Lions jersey to mark the occasion and the collar was still stiff. As I was streaking away, Ellis managed to get just a finger under my collar and heaved with every ounce of his strength to yank me over. As I fell to the ground the pain was so excruciating that I knew straight away the collar bone was broken. The ambulance people rushed on and one kept trying to get me to move the shoulder. Gareth nearly hit him, because he could see the agony I was in.

I trudged dejectedly off the pitch, my tour over as a player. But what hurt me even more than the broken bone itself was the reaction, or rather lack of it, from the Lions management. Disgracefully, not one single member of that management team came to see me in the dressing-room to ask how I was, or to offer some words of comfort which might have cheered me up a little from my depressed mood. When a knock finally came at the door it was from Haydn Morgan, who had played with me when I made my Wales début against Australia two years earlier. Haydn, from Monmouthshire, had left Wales to emigrate to South Africa and sensed how I would be feeling.

So he left his seat in the stands to check on me and it was Haydn who actually ended up taking me to hospital, where the X-rays duly confirmed my worst fears about a break.

After having my shoulder put in a sling, Haydn drove me back to the official after-match function, where one of the first people I saw was Jan Ellis. His finger was wrapped up, too, because it had been pulled back so far he had ruptured the tendons.

Believe it or not, the Lions management remained hopeful I could play again before we flew home. Therefore I remained on the tour. Was that a problem? Well, we were being invited to cocktail parties every single day . . . And as the tour progressed there were plenty of injured Lions who only too willingly took up the offers of hospitality. Actually it became a bit of a routine. The fit players would be up early and off to training. The rest of us would get up afterwards, have some treatment, rendezvous in the hotel foyer and off we would go. Even our minibus became known as the 'Cocktail Bar'.

I ate and drank so much that I put on an inch around my neck. It was when we asked if we could have a bigger minibus that it dawned upon the South African Rugby Football Union, who were footing the bill for the tour, that while some of us might be fit to play again, others had no hope. Those in the former category were given a licence to carry on cocktailing. The rest had to catch the next flight home.

I was one of those expected to play again, even though my shoulder was still in a sling and I could not even do up my own shirt buttons. The Lions management sent me for another X-ray which somehow did not show up any mark on my collar bone whatsoever. I couldn't fathom that one out because I knew the agony I was still in, but the management were insisting I would soon be fit enough to go back out to play international rugby.

I suppose I did not exactly help myself by breaking my own record for press-ups – managing the grand total of eighteen! I must point out I have never been good at that particular exercise and my previous best tally was a mere ten. What the Lions management did not realise, as I 'soared' to a new personal best, was that I only managed eighteen because I was still under the influence from a particularly heavy session with a couple of the other players the night before. Because the injured players felt so low at missing out on the rugby, we would occasionally say, 'We need a massive.' This basically meant, 'Meet up in the foyer for a bender.' It was the only way to keep our spirits high and it was after one of these 'massives' that I managed those eighteen press-ups . . . Because the whisky was numbing the pain! Our beaming manager Dave Brooks said, 'Brilliant Barry, you'll be back in the side soon.' Some chance. As soon as the effects of the whisky wore off I was back in the sling – in complete agony.

To me, towards the end, the tour became more like a holiday than a traditional Lions trip. Parts of South Africa are very beautiful and as Lions, and thus guests of the country, our hotels were invariably in the best locations. This was enjoyable. But when I returned to Wales, I could not get rid of those horrible images I had seen of the unsavoury side of South Africa.

Not much had changed when I first went back, this time as a journalist for the *Daily Express*, to cover the 1980 Lions tour when Bill Beaumont's side lost to the Springboks. One day I was in my hotel having a drink when I noticed a familiar-looking face. I stared hard and realised it was one of the black waiters who had helped look after us so well twelve years earlier. We said hello. It turned out he was working in that particular hotel, so I ordered two bottles of champagne and invited him up to my room when he was off-duty for a good old chin-wag about the 1968 trip and what he had done since. He replied he could not do that because it would get us into trouble. I wanted to give him money for a tip, but he said the hotel owners would assume he had stolen it. When I said I would explain, he politely pointed out the whites would still refuse to believe the story. It was quite disturbing.

Roll on another fifteen years, to the opening of the World Cup in Cape Town, and perhaps you can begin to understand why seeing Mr Mandela down there on the pitch amid that sea of wonderment made such a startling impression upon me. Although I never like to think that as a top sportsman you are given the red-carpet treatment, fame definitely does help. To have the opportunity of witnessing something like that was a privilege: almost a case of those bad memories of yesteryear being wiped out in one go. Actually to be involved in describing the moment on national and world radio is one of the greatest things to have happened to me.

History, of course, has gone on to tell its own story about Mr Mandela. I never did get to meet the man, much as I would have loved to. But the effect he had on me, with what he achieved in standing up so forcefully against apartheid and losing his freedom for twenty-eight years as a result, came across loud and clear in the message I broadcast that day.

Man of the Twentieth Century? It is no contest.

NINE

THE LION KING

It is strange to think that I very nearly refused to go on the tour that made my name worldwide and led to people giving me that so-called pop star status – the British Lions' brilliant triumph in New Zealand in 1971. I had taken those two hefty bangs against Scotland and France during Wales's Grand Slam march a few weeks earlier and three gruelling months of high-pressure games in the most intense rugby hotbed of the lot was the last thing I needed. Instead, I planned to spend my summer in rather more genteel fashion, listening to the sound of leather upon willow by donning my whites and playing village cricket for Cowbridge, a delightful little club in the Vale of Glamorgan.

Let's just say I'm glad I was talked into travelling by Jan because for those present – players, management, spectators and even hard-bitten, seasoned journalists – it was the most absorbing, exhilarating and sheer stupendous experience imaginable. No British side had beaten New Zealand on their own patch before; no British side has repeated our feat since, and, three decades on, that pretty much puts our efforts into perspective.

To have scored 188 points on the tour, a Lions record that still stands today, is something I'm particularly proud of when you consider they were earned against the toughest opposition possible. At the time, though, I just took it with a pinch of salt, for while the vast majority of those 188 points came from my right boot, I cannot honestly say many of them were as a result of practice. On the few occasions I did go out on to the training pitch for kicking drills with Bob Hiller – the England full-back and our midweek goal-kicker who himself scored more than 100 points on tour – our routine would consist of him taking the pots at goal and me standing behind the posts giving the balls back! Two days before one of the Test matches, with my goal-kicking regarded as crucial to the Lions' chances of success, Bob suddenly stopped to say, 'I think there's something wrong here, Barry.'

Although records are made to be broken, as the old cliché goes, I'm not sure my 188 points tally will ever be overhauled – simply because modern-day Lions tour formats, which mean shorter, more intensive trips, do not allow for it. Sadly I also have my doubts whether a Lions side can go to New Zealand and win again, because the irony of our '71 triumph is that it led to the Southern Hemisphere nations emerging as rugby's superpowers in the modern game. Our thrilling brand of rugby – based upon style, space, speed, skill and use of hands – made New Zealanders change their entire philosophy. Previously their game was about big forwards grinding the opposition down and churning them out; then the New Zealanders saw that our method was the way forward and moved accordingly in that direction, with South Africa and Australia following suit.

They picked up the baton. Unfortunately in Britain, and in Wales in particular, we dropped it – to such an extent that in the 1990s we were losing games by 60, 70 and even 90 points to Southern Hemisphere sides. The majority of the victorious Lions team was made up of the Welsh Grand Slam XV – people like myself, Gareth Edwards, J.P.R. Williams, Gerald Davies, John 'Sid' Dawes, Mervyn Davies, John Taylor and Delme Thomas. We warned that a lot of effort needed to be put into the grass roots of the Welsh game, to ensure that those golden days didn't just come to an end. In the Southern Hemisphere they took note of that sort of concern. Around the corner in Wales, our words fell on deaf ears. While you never say 'never', you do have to question whether our exploits of 1971 can be matched, certainly in the foreseeable future.

The most astonishing aspect of our 2–1 triumph, with the fourth Test being drawn, was that we took rugby to totally new dimensions in terms of public and media appeal. Early on, the New Zealand Rugby Football Union was able to announce that the entire tour – not just certain games – was a sell-out! The demand for tickets reached previously unknown proportions. By the time of the third Test in Wellington, news also began to filter over to us about the headlines and unprecedented levels of exposure we were getting back home. Friends who had flown out warned me that I was being given this pop star image by the British media.

I must admit I tended to scoff at the suggestion at first. Then I came to realise it was true. We were not just capturing headlines on the sports pages, but on the news pages, in non-sporting magazines and, it seemed, just about every mainstream television and radio programme. Other sports took a back seat, including soccer, and I reckon it would have taken a Briton winning Wimbledon to steal the limelight away from us. Journalists were ringing Jan and knocking on the door to ask how she was coping with the adulation coming my way. Every aeroplane that arrived in New Zealand carried extra newspaper and television reporters as our feats attracted more and more interest. Everyone wanted an interview.

Letters would arrive for me addressed, simply, 'To Barry John, New Zealand' and invariably reach their destination at our team hotel. When my shirts, bearing my name, went with the laundry they invariably failed to come back. I assumed this was happening to the other players too; but after a while it was pointed out that I was the only one who had to keep asking for new shirts. Some people in New Zealand have still got Barry John mementoes from that tour.

When we flew home, *News at Ten* bosses extended their programme and beamed it direct from Heathrow airport to capture our victorious return from the other side of the world. There were so many people waiting on the tarmac to greet us that the Lions management called us to one side, just before landing, to order us to spruce up and have a shave.

I thought it was a trifle over the top, to be honest, but I'd already had a foretaste of what we were coming home to during a refuelling stop in New York. Clutching a sandwich and a cup of coffee, I wanted something to read, so I put my dollar into one of those newspaper slot machines they have in the United States. I unfolded the front page and peered down at what looked like a picture of me. I looked again and noticed it was indeed me. I was on the front page of the highly respected *New York Times*, clutching a can of Coca-Cola after our overall victory had been sealed in the fourth Test. I think, to be honest, it was more a promotion of Coca-Cola than anything else, but it was still staggering that a rugby player should be the main image on the front of an American newspaper.

To think I was within a whisker of missing this by turning down my invitation to play for the Lions! Those concussion and broken-nose bangs I had taken against the Scots and the French had taken an awful lot out of me. Two weeks after the France game I keeled over at a garage and had to be revived with water. I was still giddy, felt low and in need of rest, so when my Lions invitation arrived I did not reply to it. Our coach Carwyn James telephoned to ask what was happening. I told him exactly how I felt and I could sense Carwyn's concern as he said that provided I flew out with the team, the management would not ask me to train or play until I said I was 100 per cent ready. I was worried this would create a 'prima donna' attitude towards me from the other players, but Carwyn insisted that was his problem to deal with, not mine. He did gently point out, though, that there was a time limit to this and we agreed I would phone him at 11 a.m. the following day with a final decision.

That night I spoke to Jan in depth about my dilemma, telling her I would not care if I spent a lovely summer turning out for Cowbridge in the local cricket league. A lot of people accused her of putting me under pressure to quit rugby at twenty-seven, so let me put the record straight here and tell them it was *Jan* who insisted I went to New Zealand. She told me, 'Barry, you might as well go – otherwise we'll have three months of misery here with you wondering what might have been.'

The following morning I rang Carwyn as planned. I told him, 'Don't worry, put me on the plane' and asked if he wanted my measurements for the Lions blazer and the rest of my kit. Carwyn craftily said they already had my gear ready. He knew deep down I would go, although I can honestly say that for a while the answer looked like being 'no'. I'm told that on hearing my decision, the Lions manager Doug Smith poured himself a large Scotch. I genuinely had no idea I was such a big ace in their pack of cards.

The big pull to go, from a personal point of view I suppose, was the very fact that I needed to put 'Victory over New Zealand' down on my rugby curriculum vitae. Let me put into perspective what winning out there meant. There was, and to a degree remains, this aura of total invincibility about New Zealand. They were harder people physically, their players had the mental toughness to take pressure on the chin, to come out and dominate the opposition. When New Zealand put you under the cosh, there was only one way back to the halfway line – for the restart after they had scored, because invariably they did (as I had already discovered when Wales twice lost heavily to them).

I have learned that, while people will say complimentary things about you, you must still set your own personal standards and expectations. Top of my rugby ambitions had to be walking off the pitch at least once on the winning side against New Zealand. When the final whistle went, I wanted to meet my opposite number, look him in the eye and shake hands on different terms – as a winner. I wanted to say, 'Well played, hard luck', instead of the other way around. Until I uttered that tiny little phrase, something would be missing from my career.

When that happened in Dunedin, as we won the first Test 9–3, I felt as if I had climbed Mount Everest. It was a wonderful feeling; but I soon realised just how much the achievement had taken out of me mentally when we spent the following few days relaxing in Queenstown, a fantastic winter resort with white-water rafting, free-fall diving and bungee jumps. I did not participate in any of those activities because I spent most of my time asleep! People were asking me to go for a pint, but I would come down from my room, have one drink and virtually nod off on the bar. My preparation for the match, and the concentration level that went into the eighty minutes themselves, had left me totally and utterly exhausted. Then it dawned upon me I would have to do the ultimate not just once, but four times. There was a rather hurried re-thinking of my personal schedule.

Those were the demands placed upon our Lions party. We were up against truly great players such as Colin Meads, Ian Kirkpatrick, Sid Going, and Bryan Williams, and we quickly discovered that if playing the New Zealand Test side was not exactly tough enough anyway, no one else was going to make it easy for us either. Some of the provincial teams tried to claim the Lions' scalp by playing the dirtiest rugby I have encountered anywhere. Punches were thrown, the boot came in – dare I say it, in an attempt to try to knock one or two of our key players out of the Test matches.

If that little lot wasn't hard enough, in Australia, where we played two warm-up games before going down to New Zealand, we faced a character called Craig Ferguson. He was the referee in charge of our match against New South Wales at the Sydney Cricket Ground. I had spent my time before kick-off looking around our dressing-room with a sense of enthralment, wondering where Hutton and Compton would have been sitting before going out to score a century against the Aussies, or where Trueman would have warmed up for one of his big wicket hauls. But it definitely was not cricket weather that day, for it was raining cats and dogs and parts of the pitch were just total mud.

No one complained about Mr Ferguson's penalty count: nineteen to New South Wales, just five to the Lions. But what even those statistics do not tell you is that our so-called kickable penalties always seemed to be awarded in the same place – in the middle of the mud – while those for New South Wales were invariably on the grassy bits. I had had enough. From one of ours, deep in the mud, I went back to a two-foot square patch of grass I noticed behind me. The ball remained in the muddy bit, but at least I could give my non-kicking foot stability by standing on the bit of grass. You beauty! Over went the kick – and

I'm convinced that after that Ferguson took us back another five yards on the rare occasions he gave us a penalty.

We duly won the game 14–12, despite a lot of injury-time, and I got my tour off to a good start with eight points. But we did not win many admirers among the New Zealand press. They would not condemn us, as such, but they did write that we were coming to be slammed in their own country just like every other touring side. In fact, they maintained we'd have to improve just to beat their best provincial teams.

I could not understand that attitude because I knew there were mitigating circumstances. We were pulled up for anything and everything in that New South Wales match and I recall writing home to Jan to tell her this was a good Lions team, the spirit was great and our highly intelligent management trio of Doug, Carwyn and Sid Dawes was excellent. Doug – a Lion himself in the 1950s – was a brilliant manager, Carwyn, as coach, got on famously with him and had a great vision for the game, while Sid was unflappable as captain. Each knew his exact role; there was no trespassing on one another's territory.

We needed their know-how and expertise early on as the provincial teams tried to rattle us before the first Test – including the New Zealand Maoris, who were traditionally supposed to represent the fun side of rugby. Every Lion was adopted by a school, mine being Auckland Grammar. As I was not due to play against the Maoris, I took the opportunity to go to the school that morning to give a speech and hand out the highly sought-after and beautiful little Lions badges. I talked of the remarkable similarities between Wales and New Zealand, the lovely green countryside, music, culture, and above everything else, rugby. We each played the game in a hard but sporting manner, I was explaining . . . when I was cut short by a tap on my shoulder, to be told that Mike Gibson had pulled out and I was playing. There were huge cheers: the school's adopted one was in the starting line-up and they would be at the ground to see me.

Hard but sporting? This was more like brutal intimidation as the Maoris went wild with punch after punch. I looked up at one point to where the Auckland Grammar pupils were sitting and thought to myself, 'What was it you were telling them this morning?' We still won 23–12 and I contributed twenty of those points, setting John Bevan up for a try too. The game proved that this Class of '71 Lions were going to stand up to be counted, no matter what was thrown their way, which I suspect was music to Carwyn's ears.

However even that game was made to look like a teddy bear's

picnic, compared to the encounter against Canterbury at Lancaster Park. I sat that one out, the consensus being I was so important that I needed to be wrapped in cotton wool (in reality, though, I played in seventeen of our twenty-six tour games and only Sid and our Scottish prop-forward Ian McLauchlan featured in more). That afternoon I had bruises just watching from the grandstand. In the first scrum the two teams did not even bind, the New Zealanders came through with fists flying. Our two first-choice props, Scot Sandy Carmichael and the great Irishman Ray McLoughlin, took a fearful pummelling. Sandy was one of those characters who would not hit anyone and in the dressing-room afterwards he had four fractures down one side of his face and could hardly see out of one eye. It was blatant thuggery. Ray finished with a fractured hand after hitting one of their guys on the chin in revenge.

Carwyn had lost two-thirds of his front row for the first Test, but even amid this mayhem he could still see with clarity, beckoning me over to say in Welsh, 'Barry, diddorol.' 'Interesting.' What Carwyn had noticed was the poor positioning of their Kiwi full-back Fergie McCormick and he said, 'I don't want to see him after the Test next week.' He was asking me to make McCormick look silly with my tactical kicking.

It was the worst game of rugby I have seen. We won 14–3 and although the two sides were due to be entertained together afterwards, the liaison people suggested it was not such a good idea. Not so much to keep the teams apart for fear of possible violence, but to ensure the evening was not spoilt for the Lions. How could I, for example, shake hands with people I had seen slam my mates that afternoon? It is the only time I have known two rugby teams not to mix afterwards.

New Zealand suddenly realised we could not be intimidated by their brutal tactics. But what really shook them to the core, registerable on the Richter scale in its effect, was the stylish and sometimes scintillating rugby we played in destroying their domestic champions, Wellington, 47–9. You know how cricketers say they would love to roll up a certain wicket and take it home with them? Well, in my case, give me Wellington's Athletic Park pitch any time. In three matches there I scored 50 points, including 19 in this trouncing of the best provincial team in the country.

The city is known as Windy Wellington for obvious reasons. At its worst they even tie ropes to the lampposts so people can walk down the street without being blown over. The goalposts at the ground are the shortest in world rugby, because any higher and they too would topple over. Yet – and this is uncanny – every time I played there conditions were perfect. The moment I loved most in this particular game came just before half-time when we had the put-in at a defensive scrum near our own line. Everyone assumed I would clear to touch, but I noticed their defence was a bit flat and I told Irish centre Mike Gibson I was going to kick over the top for him to chase. The Irish tend to win one game and lose the next two, so Mike did not share my rugby confidence and said conservatively, 'Just put it into touch, Barry.' I insisted I was going ahead with my plan: if Mike wanted to be a part of it, well and good, if not, so be it. I duly kicked into space. Mike chased, gathered the bouncing ball and fed John Bevan outside him, who raced fifty yards for the try – one of four he scored in the game.

Even the great Mike Gibson was running around joyfully afterwards, punching the air and shouting, 'We did it, we did it.' That one moment of magic on our part gave him supreme confidence and for the rest of the tour he played some unbelievable rugby.

The crowd were left stunned by what they had seen. Suddenly the headlines were 'NEW ZEALAND BEWARE' and Wellington's captain Graham Williams was the first to go public in declaring that the Kiwis had to forget their own style of play and accept that the Lions had shown the way forward. Pace, space and creative thinking had to be the future for New Zealand rugby, he said. Even veteran British journalists were buzzing at our performance. J.B.G. 'Bryn' Thomas, who wrote for the *Western Mail* and had covered endless Wales and Lions tours, could not think of a more complete display. He eventually equated our performance to the 1955 Lions and their destruction of Orange Free State, but gave us the slight edge.

So the moment of truth was upon us, the first Test in Dunedin, the missing link on my curriculum vitae. Everyone in the country wanted to see the match and one quick-thinking train driver hit on the novel idea of treating his passengers to the action by stopping his locomotive on the stretch of track overhanging the ground. I'm sure the signal was not on red – not for the whole game anyway!

I kicked six of our points and Ian McLauchlan scored a try, but I still do not know quite how we managed to win 9–3. New Zealand battered us, wave after wave of black shirts rampaging towards our try-line, so much so that at one point I thought they had their own ball out there. But there was always someone to put in a last-ditch tackle or hack the ball away. Mike Gibson was thinner than the arms of some of the New Zealand forwards, but he did his bit. After one tackle on Colin Meads you did not have to ask Mike which part of his body hurt because you could see the lump come up straight away. Somehow we managed to hold on. One writer's description concluded: 'The thin red line bent, meandered, but refused to break.'

Then came my moment. The final whistle went, I shook hands with my opposite number Bob Burgess, uttered the words, 'Well played, hard luck' and trooped off a winner. I could look in the mirror that night knowing I was a true international because I had at last beaten New Zealand. For a while I had been worried because, after an exemplary goal-kicking record in the warm-up matches, I had missed my first two shots at goal and could sense people saying, 'Aye aye, Golden Boots, you can do it in the provincial games, but when the going gets tough . . .' I noted the relief throughout our entire side when my next kick went over. Yes, Mr John *could* do it when the pressure was on.

One person who seemed to enjoy the moment even more than me was Chico Hopkins, our bouncy little Welsh scrum-half terrier who had come on early in the game for the injured Gareth Edwards. Chico stood at just five foot three inches and, coming from Maesteg, spoke with a broad valleys accent. His room-mate and big sparring partner was the awfully well-spoken Bob Hiller, six foot two inches, of Harlequins and England, who taught English at a private school. Poor Bob was getting some fearful stick for his posh voice from Chico, who then turned his attentions to anybody and everybody. 'Hey, you big Irish lump,' he would challenge Willie-John McBride, 'Don't give me rubbish line-out ball like that to deal with again. OK?'

Chico's exuberance apart, the other buzz at the official dinner that night was, 'Has McCormick played his last game?' I *had* indeed carried out Carwyn's request to the letter and his plan for McCormick not to be picked again was duly answered in the affirmative. At the dinner, though, I made sure that I was never more than a yard from the side of our other big beefy second-row forward Delme Thomas! I could sense the vibes coming from McCormick were not great.

Then they started coming. Telegrams, telephone calls, messages and letters of congratulations from not only from the United but also from former Lions based in South Africa, Singapore, India – throughout the world, really. Most of the letters to me were addressed simply, 'Barry John, New Zealand', including one with an up-country Palmerston postmark from a dear old lady in her sixties who penned a lovely little note but would not give her name. 'You were wonderful,' she wrote. 'If you can keep winning and shake up the whole system here, it will turn out to be the best thing that could happen to New Zealand rugby.'

With the note was $12, which I thought was a strange sum, although in due course I realised it was double my six-point tally from the game. After the second Test, when I scored a further six points, she sent me another $12. In the third Test I scored ten points and $20 arrived, in the fourth Test I scored eight points and she sent a further $16. A total of $60. I appealed, via the New Zealand media, for this anonymous lady to get in touch so I could hand back the money. She did not. To this day I still have no idea who she was, although I suppose you could argue that by giving me the money, she was 'professionalising' me!

Having achieved my ultimate goal of beating New Zealand, there was a strange feeling inside me which top golfers or soccer players probably get when they win the Open or the FA Cup final. For a while there is an empty feeling, almost as if a bubble of emotion has burst inside you. What do you do next? I had to refocus sharply on the remaining internationals and I warmed up for the second Test by scoring one of my best tries in our 27–6 victory over New Zealand Universities. Do not be fooled by the fact we were playing students. In New Zealand that means past and present, with the emphasis very much on *past* – which meant a number of Test players in their line-up.

I scored twenty-one of our points that day and my try took me past the hundred-points mark for the tour, beating a record set in New Zealand by a South African called Gerry Brand back in the 1930s. John Reason wrote in the *Daily Telegraph*, 'John decided on a suitable and brilliant way to break Brand's record.' The ball came back to me from a scrum twenty-five yards out and as I began to move forward I dummied to drop a goal and then to pass outside me to Sid. My body seemed to move rhythmically as I did this and suddenly I ghosted past two of their men and over for the try. As I touched the ball down I thought to myself, 'Yes! I really fancy that try, it's one of your better ones, Barry.' For a split second there was total silence and I began to wonder if Chico had fed the ball in crooked. Then, in a millionth of a second, the decibel level went from zero to plus-whatever-you-can-count-up-to. Everyone erupted, even my own team-mates, acknowledging they had seen something special. When asked by the media afterwards to describe the try, I could not. It was almost as if I had created gaps without running.

One of those journalists, Bryn Thomas, said to me, 'Well King, that wasn't a bad one,' and went on to describe an extraordinary meeting he had with the New Zealand coach Ivan Vodanovitch the night before. Vodanovitch had asked Bryn to go for a drink and said, 'You've watched Barry down the years. How can we stop him? We've never seen anything like him.' Bryn, even if he knew the answer, would not have betrayed a fellow Welshman. But he admitted to me, 'To be honest King, it was the first time I've not had to tell a fib – because I truthfully don't know!'

On seeing my try our Irish prop, Ray McLoughlin, who had a huge IQ and was full of probability and possibility mathematical theories, asked Carwyn if he could room with me to find out what made me tick. 'So you want to spend a night with The King, do you?' said Carwyn with a wry smile. Ray and I duly got together and the following morning Carwyn could not wait to hear a report of what happened. Ray, in that lovely Irish brogue of his, explained how he had spent twenty minutes telling me what goes on in the front row, how the back row had to do this and that to beat New Zealand again. After a while he apparently asked what I thought and turned to hear silent snoring coming from the next bed. So much for finding out my views and what made me tick. He had sent me to sleep!

Poor Ray was flummoxed again that evening when a group of us was playing poker dice in the hotel foyer. Ray had thrown four aces and a king but I gazumped him with five aces. He reckoned the chances of that happening were about two million to one – but was lost for words when I then did it a second time. Ray did not say anything, just got up from the table and went to bed. His brilliant mathematical genius had been blown to bits. If he could not work me out before, he sure could not after that.

We lost the second Test 22–12, our only setback in New Zealand, but funnily enough we played better in defeat than we did in victory in Dunedin. It would have made more sense had the results been reversed, so despite losing we were far from despondent. The game turned on a refereeing decision by John Pring, who awarded a penalty try when he felt Gerald had tackled their left wing Bryan Williams deliberately early. Personally I felt Gerald had timed his tackle to perfection, but when Mr Pring said to me afterwards, 'I suppose I won't be refereeing you again after that decision,' I told him: 'On the contrary, you're the best and we want you in charge.' It was a tight decision and he called it as he saw it. There were no moans or recriminations from us.

One apiece, the third Test in Wellington was going to be arguably the biggest shoot-out in the history of rugby. We simply *had* to win. There was a bizarre moment *en route* when we beat Wairarapa-Bush 27–6 in a sea of mud at Masterton. Three players – Arthur Lewis, Chris

Rea and myself – chased a kick through as the bouncing ball went over the try-line. Arthur dived first but appeared to miss the ball. Then it was Rea's turn and he did not seem to ground it properly. The ball came backwards to me and I touched down. There was total confusion about who actually scored and even today statisticians argue about it, debating whether my Lions record is for 188 points or 191 points. The only thing I know for certain is that the Lions scored, so I think I'll claim one point for the try, with Arthur and Chris sharing the others. That gives me the record at 189 points. OK!

If that one was offbeat, Hawkes Bay was just another of those downright dirty encounters. The violence, punches and bad tackles got horribly out of hand, yet in between we played some sensational rugby and Gerald Davies scored four beautiful tries as we won 25–6. There were moments when Hawkes Bay could not care less if they kicked the ball or the man on the floor.

When you don't care, you are playing a dangerous game. The crowd were on our backs with the old 'Oh, you can't take it' rubbish. Towards the end I had had enough. From deep inside his own half, their full-back kicked the ball down into our 25-yard area where I was waiting. I trapped the ball with my arse and sat on it – although I made sure I was just inside my 25! The crowd were baying. The Hawkes Bay players could not believe what they were seeing and started charging towards me. As they got to within a few yards, I stood up, picked up the ball and slammed it right back down to where it had originally come from. It was hilarious because the Hawkes Bay team stopped, turned and ran back again, just like in a cartoon sketch. I stood there smiling with arms on my chest and then disdainfully walked off. The game was won, but if that was the way people wanted to play rugby I did not want any part of it.

In the dressing-room I threw my boots at the wall and asked Carwyn, 'What is this tour coming to? If this is rugby, let's go home.' I could sense the management wondering whether I had 'lost it' at this crucial stage and they even suggested giving me a little holiday in the build-up to the third Test, an offer which I politely declined. At least I could smile at the comments of the Hawkes Bay coach Kel Tremain, who was asked about Gerald's four cracking tries and whether he would love to have him in his own side. Tremain pondered for a moment and replied, 'I'm not sure I would want him in my team – I don't think he knows what he is doing!' He was referring to Gerald's jinking runs, movement and blinding acceleration. As crass statements go, that one took the biscuit.

Just before the third Test Doug and Carwyn took us to the Bay of Islands for a couple of days' relaxation. If anyone threw me out of Wales, these islands would be top of my list of places to go, with their beautiful scenery and tranquillity. Relax we did; rest we most certainly did not, as we had a riotous time, partying so much that we had to go on a four-mile run the following day to sweat it off. I never did like road running and to compound matters that day my ankles were hurting. I made sure I was at the back and, 200 yards into the run, I tucked into the hedges and woods to hide. When my team-mates were in the far distance I ventured back out, stopped a lorry coming up the road and asked for a lift to the top. There was the Lions' finest, preparing for the Wellington encounter crammed into a lorry surrounded by crates of oranges!

As I jumped out I noticed Doug and Carwyn giving a press conference just a few yards away – and everyone stopped to look at me. The New Zealand press, realising what had happened, asked the Lions management what action they were going to take against me as I had refused to go on a training run. Carwyn, aware of my ankle trouble, put a fag to his mouth and came up with a classic answer. Puffing hard on his cigarette he said, 'Well, I call it initiative,' turned on his heels and walked away. The press were left open-mouthed. I ended up cutting oranges for refreshments, so I did my bit anyway.

On to Wellington. This was it, the moment everyone had been waiting for. Neither side dared lose and it was at this point of the tour, as friends of mine arrived from Wales, that I began to realise I was carrying the expectancy of the British nation on my shoulders. One of those friends was the great Clem Thomas, a former Lion himself, whom I arranged to meet for coffee in the restaurant of our George Hotel base the night before the game. As I ventured down the stairs I spotted Clem and it took me fully fifteen minutes to reach his table, such was the deluge of autograph hunters, well-wishers and back-slappers. 'So this is what the fuss is about,' smiled Clem. 'You wait until you get home. You're like a pop star there. I guarantee they will want you on every TV programme and in every newspaper and magazine if you win this game.' He went on and on and in the end I had to tell him to shut up.

The importance of the occasion had already been made crystal clear to me when I visited the Athletic Park ground earlier that evening to study conditions and see how the wind might affect my kicking. There were queues of people stretching around the corner, waiting for any last-minute tickets that might become available. This was the night *before*, yet they were camped out with umbrellas, sandwiches and flasks of coffee. When Clem rammed the pop star stuff down my throat, I almost felt as if I needed an extra large pair of shoulders. It certainly affected my normal match-day routine, which was to wake up at 8 a.m., order breakfast for Gareth and myself (toast, marmalade and coffee for me, toast, honey and tea for him), have a quick shave, sprinkle my face with cold water and get ready for the game. On this occasion, because of that pop star stuff I had heard the night before, I actually felt nerves for the first time. At 8.30 a.m. I went downstairs, bumped into Terry O'Connor of the *Daily Mail* and we went for a little walk. It was the exclusive of exclusives for Terry as I opened up to him about the pressures I was feeling, but he knew it was mostly off-the-record.

The butterflies were still there as I boarded the team bus to the game. I reflected that if this match were in Paris, I would not have had time to worry about nerves because you spend most of the trip fearing you are going to crash. The French gendarmes just go through bollards and I'm sure at times they aim at people. Our New Zealand escorts were a bit more subdued in steering us through the throng of people going to the game. As we drew up by the players' entrance the entire team began singing in unison the folk song that Olivia Newton-John went on to turn into a hit single, 'Take Me Home, Country Roads'. It's a lovely, melodic song and it gave us a real buzz of togetherness.

Next thing we knew we were alone in the dressing-room, just the fifteen players, Doug and Carwyn. The time for talking and planning had passed; it was the moment for action, to put up or shut up, if you like. Do you know, I would have made a great world heavyweight boxing champion? . . . Right up until that moment alone in the dressing-room . . . I would have hyped the fight, ridiculed my opponent, sold tickets, but when crunch-time arrived, and I knew I would have to walk out to that ring, I would have lost my nerve! But that day in that dressing-room as a Lions rugby player was something else. Any self-doubts I had during the morning disappeared as I looked around and saw Willie-John, Merv 'the Swerve' Davies, John Taylor, John Pullin, Derek Quinnell. I looked at Gareth and Gerald, J.P.R. Williams, Mike Gibson, David Duckham, I thought 'I'm here too and I'm bang in form.' Yes, I knew I was in the right dressing-room.

We ran out full of confidence and I had a little smile to myself as the national anthems were played. Up in the stands I saw a cloud of smoke in front of two people sitting in the director's box. I knew it was Doug and Carwyn, puffing on cigarettes, as usual. How many fags they went through during a game, particularly that one, I will never know. But I would like to think we put them at ease almost straight away, because history will tell you that the Lions produced twenty minutes of the most thrilling, authoritative and spot-on rugby the game has known. *Everything* just clicked.

This is the question we were asking beforehand: 'Is Gareth up to it?' Remember the fears about him missing the game through hamstring trouble? Well, Gareth responded brilliantly. He was simply awesome and the New Zealanders could do nothing to stop him. I dropped a goal, converted a try by Gerald and then converted my own try after Gareth had set me up. This little lot had happened in just eighteen minutes and there was no way back for New Zealand as we ran out 13–3 winners. As the game wore on I gave myself a private pat on the back. I knew, after my doubts and fears that morning, I had passed not so much a rugby test, as a personality test.

There was one frightening moment in the second half when Bob Burgess collapsed spark out after John Taylor's elbow accidentally caught him right on the point of the chin. Luckily JPR, who is a doctor, raced over, prised open Bob's mouth and took out his gum-shield. Those horrible few minutes stressed to me that rugby is such a hard game, you simply cannot afford to have preconceived thoughts of dirty play (as some provincial teams did against us). We want to win: but win, lose or draw, we also want to go home at the end of the day. So how can you deliberately plan to kick someone in the head? – a fate Gareth had to put up with in the Hawkes Bay match. Bob duly recovered and I was thrilled when he was my last guest on the Eamonn Andrews programme the following year.

Pop star status! Back home in Cefneithin they had not known anything like it. Reporters were queuing up to knock on the door of the home where I grew up, for a reaction to our win and my performance. Chris Lander, of the *Mirror*, eventually drew this wonderful line out of Vimy after he asked her about my try: 'Well, if Barry had run through a field of daffodils, no one would have noticed.' In other words, you wouldn't even have seen a ripple. What a quote! With due respect to Chris I think that line deserved a more quality newspaper!

That night, beaming at our victory, Clem Thomas told anyone who would listen that he was the first one to spot me, that he took some of the credit for my rugby development . . . and that he would have marked me out of every game. As the party wound down in the early hours, it began to dawn upon the players that if we could keep our heads and avoid defeat in the final encounter in Auckland, we would go down as one of the best rugby teams in history of game. The financial rewards would not be monumental; but we would be up there with the true greats of sport.

I met my match in the build-up to that fourth Test: Mrs Angry, a pensioner who dropped me a telegram when it was announced I was missing the midweek encounter with Manawatu. I think the entire town was out in force to see our aeroplane fly over – our arrival was the biggest thing to happen there for years. The telegram read, 'I'm a pensioner and money is tight, but I have put a certain sum away for weeks to watch the Lions, and in particular you, as I'm a great fan of yours. Suddenly I read in the newspaper that you are not playing – you horrible Welshman.' I looked up her address and paid her a visit. She could not believe it as I knocked on the door and said, 'I'm Barry John – and by the way, I agree with you!' The neighbours got to hear of it and we had a little street party. She was like a queen that afternoon.

Those expecting me to be wrapped in cotton wool before the final Auckland showdown were perhaps surprised when I was selected in the matches against North Auckland and Bay of Plenty. That is why I smile when I hear modern-day players moan about pressure and too much rugby. Oh dear, how awful. New Zealand was the most gruelling, most intensive tour imaginable and yet I played in the last three games in the space of a week.

My team-mates were particularly delighted I had been selected against North Auckland because I threw a punch for the only time in my career – and it gave them the opportunity to spend the next few days laughing their heads off at my expense. It was another of those needle encounters and I'm convinced the provincial side thought that if they could take out key Lions players, we would not have enough time to recover for the Test. I had had enough of one particular guy having a go and when he whacked me again, giving us a kickable penalty, I snapped and retaliated by chinning him. The referee saw it, reversed his penalty decision and told me, 'Any more of that and you're off.' When I got to the dressing-room at the end of the game I was welcomed by a chorus of, 'Here's the big bully coming. What a brute. Watch your backs everyone!' They couldn't believe what they had seen. I think Sid Dawes dropped his gumshield and was still in shock!

At least it gave us something to smile about before the real business in hand. Were the newspaper journalists and television people, who were still flying in daily, going to go home with the most wonderful rugby story of modern times to tell – or were we to be nearly-men? We had climbed the mountain in Dunedin and proved we were not one-Test wonders by winning in Wellington; one more huge effort was needed in Auckland if we were to rewrite the record books and become the first Lions side to triumph on New Zealand soil.

Carwyn's pre-match instructions centred around not contesting the early line-outs because he knew there were going to be fireworks up front. Gordon Brown, our young Scottish second-row rookie, did not heed the words. He lost it in the adrenaline of the occasion and ended up with eight stitches in his face. And while we were down to fourteen men New Zealand went 5–0 ahead. After four months of effort and determination, not to mention some truly brilliant rugby, surely we were not going to let it slip at the final hurdle? *No way*. We had come too far as a bunch of men for that. Peter Dixon scored a try; I converted, and kicked two penalties; JPR dropped a goal; and we eventually drew 14–14. We had done it.

In the second half I played the percentage game by kicking deep into the corners when, aesthetically, with Sid and Mike Gibson outside me, I could have run the ball on two or three occasions and gone for the tries. It was the only time in my career I ignored such scoring opportunities, but the prize at stake was so great that these were not normal circumstances. If I could play the game again I would go for the tries because, believe it or not, there was a strange feeling of anti-climax at the final whistle. We had achieved so much, yet there was a certain let-down because we had not gone out in style. One try and I reckon we would really have cut loose. No one was complaining, though, least of all Doug Smith. He had forecast beforehand that we would win 2–1 with one Test drawn. I reckon he was delighted we did not triumph by twenty points because he could say 'I told you so'.

We had one big party on the flight home and as we closed in on Heathrow, Doug and Carwyn told us to spruce ourselves up because of the reception waiting for us on the ground. When we touched down and disembarked, the sight in front of us was phenomenal. There were thousands waiting to greet us including, it seemed, most of Wales. If you had been a burglar in the valleys that night you would have had a field day. They might as well have given you the key. Chico, JPR, Gareth, Gerald, I and the other Welsh members of the party were mobbed. We were the local ones who had done good.

Then, as the players eventually began to file away after more than three months together, the big six-foot-two-inch frame of Bob Hiller approached me. Putting on his best Cockney accent, Bob said, 'You see, John and Hopkins, you have to go home to fame. I have to go to Upper Tooting . . . And at the bus stop, if I've got more than two bags, the driver will say, "Sorry mate, one bag only please." And there will be no point in me flashing my Lions blazer to him and saying "Do you know who I am?" because it won't make the blind bit of difference. That's what I'm going home to.' Chico and I laughed our heads off.

I did indeed go home to fame and the pop-star-type talk and newspaper headlines. Gareth was given a massive, carnival-style procession – complete with pony and trap – in his home village, while the people of Cefneithin, when I went back six weeks afterwards, gave me a lovely party.

But that night, what I wanted to do most was quietly go home to No. 14 Graig Lwyd in Radyr, on the outskirts of Cardiff, offload my luggage and enter my own house with Jan, away from the spotlight I had been under for the past few months. I was disappointed, then, when local television broadcaster Martyn Williams, reporting on the pony and trap procession for Gareth, asked on air, 'And what did the people of Radyr do for Barry John?' I told Martyn he should apologise for the remark because I will tell you what the people of Radyr did – they kept my garden tidy, cut the lawn, mended a burst pipe, brought a pint of milk if it was needed and helped Jan when she asked for something. That meant more to me than any procession.

I had had enough of the headlines and the thought of the many, many, more to come. The quiet welcome was what I needed at that precise moment in time. Maybe Bob Hiller didn't know how lucky he was that the London bus driver failed to recognise him.

TEN

THE KING STEPS OFF
THE THRONE

I quickly came to realise over the next few months that everything had
changed quite dramatically for me – just as Clem Thomas had warned
– and in the end the hype and idol business proved so unbearable that
I made my reluctant decision to pack in rugby. So, what next for a
twenty-seven-year-old qualified schoolteacher, who had broken Wales
and Lions rugby records and who had spent the last four years working
off the field as a financial representative? A large part of that job
involved what amounted to debt collecting. Yes, the Wales and Lions
number 10 going up the Welsh valleys to check on people who had
not kept up to date with their car hire-purchase instalments! One
disgruntled pensioner looked me in the eye and barked, 'Hey, I know
who you are . . . I hope you break your leg on Saturday!' I thought it
was perhaps time to call that one a day too.

The one thing I was not short of was job offers. After what I'd been
through during the previous year, nothing should have surprised me;
but one approach did take me aback and make me really sit up and
take notice. It came from the big-money men of American sport who
got in touch shortly after my retirement had been announced, to ask
me to go over to California to play American Football. For pretty big
bucks, too. I do not know if they had seen that front page of the *New
York Times*, but clearly they were aware of my exploits with the Lions
because they wanted me to go out there simply to kick goals. On
they'd wheel me, once a touchdown had been scored, and boom! –
over the ball would go from my trusty right boot. That was the plan.

The approach was made via Stanley Baker, the legendary actor of
Zulu fame, who had been a big friend of the former Welsh rugby
international Bleddyn Williams since the days when they were
stationed together in the RAF. I knew that Stanley was a huge rugby fan

himself and when Bleddyn told me the actor wanted me to go to London to meet him about something, the inquisitive part of me wanted to know why. Bleddyn refused to tell me. I went to Stanley's amazing penthouse opposite the Houses of Parliament, overlooking the River Thames. I pressed the buzzer, went up in the lift and stepped out to see this huge open-ended room. The best way to describe it is to imagine putting a cricket pitch in there: bowl off a three-yard run and you could still have wicket-keeper and slips standing back. Stanley was at the far end and waved me over.

After brief introductions, Stanley told me we were off to the Carlton Towers hotel, in another part of London, to meet a friend of his called Mark McCormack – boss of the International Management (sports) Group – and Arnold Palmer, who was in Britain for the World Matchplay golf championship. I was introduced to Mark, then taken to meet a group of rich Americans, one of whom just happened to be the legendary grid-iron quarterback Namath. He was the Dan Marino of his era, every bit as big in his heyday as Marino was when he starred for the Miami Dolphins. Namath could hardly walk because his knees were so painful, a legacy of the countless big tackles he used to take. Even getting into a car was a difficult exercise; Namath had to sit down with his back to the door and have his legs swung around.

Anyway, it turned out that this American consortium wanted me to go and play for a team called South California in a new league they were setting up, a deal which would also involve games against the traditional NFL and AFL sides if we were successful. They were taken by my Welsh accent, believing it would be loved on the west coast of the United States, and they liked the fact that I was very much my own person. The offer they put in front of me was mouth-watering: £120,000 for just one season. Believe me, in 1973 that was an awful lot of money and the only thing I had to do to earn it was go on to the pitch and kick goals!

It seemed a dream deal, but there were stumbling blocks – and they came from me. Since retiring I had already signed various contracts, including one to write as a rugby journalist with the *Daily Express* and one with the sportswear firm Gola to promote their products. I felt honour-bound to the pair of them and told my American hosts that while their offer was very tempting, it would be unfair on the *Daily Express* and Gola if I just moved lock, stock and barrel to the United States.

Stanley turned to Messrs McCormack and Palmer and said, 'Well, that's a Welshman for you', deep down admiring the loyalty I was showing to the two companies who had come in for me first. Not to be put off, though, Stanley suggested I compromise by moving to the Home Counties where I would be within touching distance of Heathrow Airport and could fly out to California on a regular basis. When I pointed out that I already had a property in Cardiff, which was only a couple of hours down the Paddington line, Stanley insisted I had to be on-call at any time, virtually saying the Americans would own me.

Well, for that sort of money I suppose they were entitled to make some demands. But at that point I brought the negotiations to a halt by saying very slowly, 'I think we can cut it there. Thank you for the offer, but no deal gentlemen, I'm afraid.' The reason I gave, staggering though the Americans found it, was Glamorgan County Cricket Club! I explained to the Americans that cricket was a complex game, but one that I loved and couldn't be far away from. Of course, it was possible to look at the scorecards in something like the *Daily Telegraph* and read, 'Tony Lewis, lbw, 50.' But that was not enough. I needed to know details of how Tony got his runs and details of how he was dismissed. The only way of doing that was to buy the Welsh newspaper *The Western Mail*. Stanley just looked straight at me, turned to the Americans and said, 'Well gentlemen, the Welsh are entirely different from the English!' I was quite proud of that one.

I found Stanley to be one of the warmest, kindest people I have met, on top of his efforts to land me that lucrative American Football deal. If I mentioned in conversation that my stereo was not working, or that I needed a holiday, he would scribble it down on a small card, stuff it in his pocket, give it to his secretary afterwards – and next thing I knew the problem would be sorted for me. It never ceased to amaze me with world-renowned actors like Stanley, Richard Burton and Richard Harris that, no matter how famous they were, they always wanted to talk to me and get those little dressing-room anecdotes that fascinated them so much.

The South California offer was actually the fourth time I had turned down the opportunity to play sport professionally, the previous three approaches having come from the big guns of rugby league. The first two each involved Wigan while I was still at college and playing for Llanelli, although on the initial occasion they very nearly ended up signing my best friend and best man at my wedding, Pete Davies, instead!

I had been alerted that rugby league clubs were sniffing around and one Sunday morning the Wigan representatives did indeed turn up at our student halls of residence. I had been out on the tiles the night before and felt distinctly under the weather and in need of sleep when, at 10.30 a.m., these two huge men stepped out of the lift and knocked on the door. Pete, who is a big bloke, answered and the Wigan officials, assuming he was me, introduced themselves and started negotiations. Pete toyed with them for a while, mainly to stall them and give me a chance to raise myself from my bed – something I did with a start when he came in, threw a bucket of cold water over me and said, 'Go out there and try to look like a rugby player.'

As I sauntered out with my ten-and-a-half-stone frame, looking grey-faced and with bags under my eyes, I could see in the faces of these men that they were thinking, 'So why the big fuss about him, then?' Remember, they were accustomed to dealing with the big, strapping men who played the hard game of rugby league week-in, week-out. I probably sounded a lot better on the telephone when I had first been approached than I looked that morning.

Anyway, I politely explained I wanted to carry on with my studies – only for Wigan to come in again a few months afterwards, once more in hilarious circumstances. At college the Physical Education students were seen as the muscle-men, so when the school just down the road was vandalised (hooligans having thrown broken bottles and stones into the swimming pool), Red Adair and his team answered the call to clean it up. 'Leave it to me,' I said, and in I dived. Trouble was, some of the stones had gone into the filter nine feet down at the bottom of the pool, and as I was trying to get them out my finger became stuck. I had to yank really hard to free it, pulling off the skin, and I swam back to the top gasping for air. As I grabbed the side of the pool, the first things I noticed were the clean, shiny shoes of two men and I looked up to see them dressed smartly in blazer and tie.

'Are you Barry John?' one asked in a northern accent. After my escapade underwater I just wanted to be pulled out of the pool. These men had come to ask me to play rugby league – and they probably thought I was too weak to even swim!

Again I politely declined the invitation. But when I was next approached, this time as a Cardiff player who had just returned from that broken-collar-bone British Lions tour of South Africa, I was indeed on the verge of signing for St Helens. I even had the fountain pen in my hand ready to put my signature to paper; only a sixth sense pulled me back from the brink, enabling me to carry on with my rugby union career instead. I do not know if St Helens knew of my personal circumstances, but they timed their move to perfection because I was out of work at the time and in many ways felt abandoned. I was the British Lion without a job, having given up my teaching post at the Monkton House private school in Cardiff after just two terms to tour South Africa.

The St Helens officials arrived at our Cefneithin house in a limousine and put in front of me a very tempting package centred around an £8,500 tax-free signing-on fee, guaranteed match fees and bonuses and, as an extra sweetener, a part-time teaching job. I travelled to a second meeting at a Hereford hotel, had the contract put in front of me and was handed the expensive fountain pen. I considered my unemployed situation and thought, 'If this is what people think of me, I might as well go north.' My hand holding the fountain pen hovered over the contract and just as I was about to sign, I pulled it away and asked for another week to think about the offer. When I got home I realised, 'BJ, you're being a coward by taking the easy way out.' There is nothing wrong with going to rugby league, providing it is for the right reasons. But I was going for the wrong reasons and in the next few days I told St Helens, 'Thanks, but no thanks.'

To give you an idea of how low I was feeling at the time, I had not only given up my teaching job at Monkton House, I also questioned whether there was a future in the profession for me. It was not so much that I was disillusioned with the actual teaching. In fact I loved doing the job and, if truth be known, I would like to have carried on teaching right up until today. I honestly think I was made for the profession and I had the extra advantage, because of my rugby travels, of being able to let pupils know more about places like South Africa and New Zealand in geography lessons than you would find in the textbooks. There is no greater experience than experience itself.

What I did not find so impressive, however, were the salary levels: in my case the grand sum of £52 a month. I was broke at the end of every month and this was compounded by the fact that, because I was teaching at a private school, the pupils invariably had money. Lots of it, too. We used to take a school bus back and forth to Wenvoe, a few miles outside Cardiff, with the pupils paying a shilling for the ride. I was driving the bus one Friday before Cardiff were due to play a match at Northampton. Pay day was looming and, as usual, I hadn't two pennies left to rub together; so when one pupil handed me a £5 note I told him I had no change and that he would have to wait until Monday for it.

'Let this be a lesson to you to bring the correct money,' I said. We were only talking about a shilling so I should have simply put an IOU from him into the pot. No way! I needed spending money for the Northampton trip. In fairness, Cardiff looked after you so well you didn't even want for a packet of crisps, but you still liked to have your own money in your pocket. I gleefully went home that night and told Gareth and Gerald, 'We're OK for the weekend, I've got a fiver!' I repaid the money, of course, but it was an example of how stretched teachers were. This was not a case of survival, it was even worse, and I simply could not afford to carry on.

Because I was a famous rugby player who was also a qualified teacher, I was asked to contribute an article to a book Prince Philip brought out on the role of sport in education. As part of my article, I wrote about the Burnham scale for teachers and explained why so many people left the profession. The student teachers around me at college were a terrific gang of people who had bright futures ahead of them, but they found the finances just did not work. One left to sell dolly mixture sweets because the financial package he was offered, which included a car, was so much better. The point I tried to get across was that not only did you lose teachers, in my opinion you also lost many of the best ones – to far less stressful jobs, too, because teaching, with the preparatory work needed for lessons, is one of the most demanding occupations imaginable. I only did it for two terms and realised I had to be concentrating flat out for every second. Yes, I know teachers are paid a lot better these days, but in reality it is still not good enough.

It was under these circumstances, having just returned from South Africa, that I found the St Helens offer so tempting. People could not believe I was unemployed and time and again came up to pat me on the back, saying, 'Don't worry Barry, you'll get a job soon.' While I appreciated their sentiments, they were not the ones who had to go down to the local dole office to sign on. Not that I did that either, for I just couldn't bring myself to do it. I even asked my cousin Margaret, who worked there, to send me the forms to sign. 'Barry, I can't, you have to come in here,' she replied. But I could not, I felt too embarrassed. To this day the social security people owe me six weeks' worth of money which I never claimed from the summer of 1968.

Everyone assumed there would be a queue of people ready to employ me, but the only ones to come in at that particular point were those St Helens officials. No wonder I found the move north tempting. Then, quite out of the blue, I had the most extraordinary job advertisement broadcast for me on nationwide television by David Coleman, who was presenter of the BBC's hugely popular *Sportsnight* programme. There was only one telephone in our little street, owned by our neighbour Mrs Delyth Nicholas, and she mentioned to me that David had rung the previous day asking to speak to me. I told her to knock three times on the wall if he phoned again – they were so thin you could hear everything – so I would know the call was for me. The three knocks came and I jumped over the fence to take the call.

Sportsnight's main director was the one and only Cliff Morgan. David asked if what Cliff had told him about me being out of work was true. When I said it was, David replied, 'Watch Wednesday's programme.' I did and the very last item was about me. David spoke about the young Welshman who had given up his teaching job to represent the Lions, who broke his collar bone and who had been unemployed since returning six weeks ago. As job advertisements go, they do not come any better.

Gwynne Walters, a former international referee, was on the telephone the next day. He explained that he was the area manager for the Forward Trust finance house, which needed representatives in the Cardiff branch. Shortly afterwards, a big, gregarious man called Mr Williams got in touch to say Bulmers Cider might also be interested. I decided I would join whoever made the first formal offer and that was Gwynne, who telephoned again to say I would start on 1 October. Bulmers were back on the following day, but the Forward Trust move suited me down to the ground because I was playing for Cardiff anyway.

I rang Gerald and told him he had a guest coming to his flat in Cathedral Road, just off the city centre. Gerald explained they were only paying for four lodgers, but I said I would only be there for a week . . . It was a fair bit beyond that, by the time I left – the result of an ultimatum from the property owner who noticed an extra person was occupying his flat. 'He either pays or goes,' he told Gerald. I went. There are some things even fame cannot do for you.

So there I was in the big world of business. The next question I had to ask was, just what did a finance rep do? Forward Trust was the financial arm for garages, providing the money to enable customers to buy cars. One of my tasks was visiting people who fell behind with their hire purchase instalments. We had business targets to hit every month and if clients were not paying the money they owed, we had to find out why.

I was going up the Rhondda valley in the dark of winter, the weather cold, miserable and wet, knocking on doors and saying: 'I'm sorry, but you are behind with your payments'. The householders just looked at me in dread and every time they answered the door I could almost see a mirror of myself. I wouldn't have wanted 'debt-collectors' knocking on *my* door back in Cefneithin either. I could tell I was only one of many asking for their money, including the milkman, the coalman, the local corner shop owner and others.

There was that time when an old man shuffled to the door with the aid of a walking stick and told me, 'Hey, I know who you are, from television. You're that rugby player. I hope you break your leg on Saturday.' On another occasion, in Treorchy, a woman answered the door looking so haunted and ghost-like that the image of her face remains with me today. On her file her age was shown as 26, but when she came to the door she looked more like 46 – haggard, big bags under her eyes, you could see there was nothing left in her body. She invited me to come in and wait for a while and I noticed a smell that, if not foul, was still a bit unpleasant. Sitting at a table were a six-year-old, a four-year-old and a two-year-old waiting for their food. The woman brought in three plates, each with two tiny little sardines in batter on them and a very few baked beans which, at a push, you could actually count.

I thought to myself, 'What am I doing collecting money from her?' I asked where her husband was and, after a few shrugs of the shoulders, she eventually told me he had upped and left the moment the bills started coming. She had been paying for his car every month, a vehicle that was in such a state it was parked outside with no wheels and had grass growing through the bottom of it! You would actually have paid to take the eyesore away. I asked, 'Why didn't you tell us?' and felt disgusted with myself. I had a nice little car outside. I thought of my upbringing when, though we did not have loads of money, there was always a good table of food put in front of us – meat and two veg. I told the woman I would be back in ten minutes and I drove to the corner shop, bought milk, bread, ham and corned beef, paid £3 for it and took it back to her. I had gone to the house to collect money from her, yet I ended up out of pocket myself! Enough was enough as far as I was concerned. I had these big computer printouts on our clients and I ended up throwing them in the bin.

The following day I went to see Gwynne Walters and explained that I did not want to go out any more and that we should close this woman's account: put it down to a bad debt. That particular unsavoury experience was every bit as profound for me as scoring a try for Wales was, but in a different way.

There were plenty of lighter moments, though, including the day I went to see the owner of a little shop in Trebanos. He studied my business card, looked up to verify that it was indeed *the* Barry John, asked if I had enjoyed Saturday's match so he knew for certain it was me, then asked if I could return at 11.15 a.m. the following Tuesday when he would definitely have my money.

This shop was right opposite the primary school and the pupils used it during their break as their little tuck shop. I turned up as requested that Tuesday – only to discover queues of people outside. It turned out the owner had been to see the headmaster to say, 'Do you know Barry John is coming here? We are in business together.' In fairness he was not telling a fib, but he was not exactly telling the truth, either. He had set out a stool and table where I had to sit and sign autographs while the youngsters spent money on sweets, chocolate bars, crisps and drinks. I was signing pieces of paper so he could pay his debt to me. He soon raised his target and turned to say, 'We've done it, Barry.'

There was another client who was trying to strike a bargain with a bottom-interest-rate charge and I had to give him his way, not having the time to hang around and haggle. The reason? Wales were training, and I had to be there. He said, 'I'll tell my friends to do business with you, Barry, particularly when Wales have a match coming up!'

The Forward Trust management, in particular Gwynne and the Cardiff office boss Wynne Jones, were always fantastic to me – never more so than when I returned from New Zealand as part of that victorious Lions side. I reckon that through my rugby commitments I had used up about three years' worth of advance holiday. In fact, I probably still owe them. Yet Gwynne called me into his office and uttered the words, 'You've not got a job any more . . . But you've got a rise and you've got a new car.' He knew times had changed for me and said that I was to work, from that moment on, as his assistant. I was arguably the most talked-about sportsman in Britain at the time – ahead even of football players – and the mail started arriving for me at the Forward Trust offices by the sack-load. Gwynne even let me borrow his secretary Barbara to do the administration work for six months. She loved the new dimension this job gave her, sorting out my various invitations, replying to them and making sure autograph-hunters were not left disappointed. Every so often she would say, 'There is a pile over there Barry. Sign them, will you please?'

However, much as I was enjoying my time with Forward Trust, I fancied having a go at writing. The opportunity arose when the *Daily Express* sports editor John Morgan contacted me just after I had retired to ask if I would become their rugby columnist. As I had taken the *Express* since I was a teenager – still do in fact – this was an offer I was happy to accept, particularly as it gave me the perfect opportunity to remain in close touch with the game. I had to become a member of the National Union of Journalists, an organisation which insisted that to show loyalty and intent to the profession, 75 per cent of my earnings had to come under the umbrella of journalism. As I also had a lucrative contract with Gola, this meant the end of my marvellous association with Forward Trust.

My first assignment was to cover the New Zealand trials, where I first set eyes upon Grant Batty, who was to spring to prominence as a world-class wing. I filed my first report by telephone, having gone over and over it like an essay until I was 100 per cent satisfied, but then received a message from the *Express* telling me: 'Just enjoy the rest of your trip Barry. Your work commitments have ceased for the time being.' The Cardiff chapel of the NUJ had turned down my application to join them. Being on the other side of the world, and having given up my secure job with Forward Trust, it was an uncomfortable period for me because I didn't really understand what was happening and why. Fortunately Jim Hill, the *Express*'s Welsh-based journalist, sorted everything out for me on my return. I suspect it was more a case of a slap on the wrist from the Cardiff branch than anything else, the union officials trying to say that just because I was a big name I could not automatically expect to walk into their profession.

Membership was eventually given, then. I wrote for the *Express* for twenty-six years, from 1972 to 1998, covering matches on a Saturday and writing a column on a Thursday. I also worked for the BBC as their senior rugby radio analyser for fifteen years, covering the 1987, 1991 and 1995 World Cups. I love writing and I have been given the opportunity to keep my hand in as a columnist for the national Welsh newspaper, *Wales on Sunday*, in recent times. I'm glad to note that my zip and interest for the job has not waned down the years.

I was given no formal training in either broadcasting or writing, just told, 'Be yourself and say things as you see them'. But John Morgan did give me some excellent early tips, the best one concerning how to approach my Monday morning reports. He pointed out that the Saturday matches had been given hundreds of column inches in the Sunday papers and had received huge coverage on television and radio. The *Express*, forty-eight hours later, did not want yet another match report as such, but rather comment pieces from me. So the test I set myself was simple. If Fred Bloggs was sitting in a pub having a pint and thinking about the game, what question would come to his lips? What would he want to ask me and why? I could still have been out there playing, remember, so I was in a good position to give those answers.

The bulk of my work was in Wales, although fortunately I did not have to criticise too much in the early days, because the players I was reporting on – many of whom just happened to be my 1971 Lions team-mates – were among the very best. Pick a World XV of the time and at least six Welshmen would have walked into it. When the need arose, however, I had no qualms about having a go at people and I expected players, management and committees to take it as it was meant: that I always told the truth as I saw it.

One famous occasion concerned my old Wales and Lions full-back colleague J.P.R. Williams. He had a poor Five Nations match in Scotland in 1981, Wales lost 15–6 and, as we were travelling on the same flight back to Cardiff, I approached JPR at Edinburgh airport. I told him, 'Listen, you know I've got to write a piece about this defeat. I think you've lost it and I'm going to say so. By any other standards you had an acceptable game, but the JPR of old has gone, in my opinion.' I know that was brutally frank, but at least I was being honest. I told JPR that the best way out was for him to give me quotes about him retiring from international rugby. That way I would get a great scoop for the *Express* and JPR would have a lovely article written about him, based around his fantastic fifty-five-cap career. 'But, for this, I need you to give me the nod before we get off at Cardiff,' I said.

JPR did not give me that nod. So the following day in the *Express* I had to explain why it was the end of the road for him and how the next game against Ireland would present the Welsh management with a lovely opportunity to give a new full-back a game. Well, this was seen as BJ having a pop at his mate JPR, so it made big headline news in the other newspapers. I was on business in Southampton that particular day; when I arrived home, Jan said the telephone calls had not stopped.

Two weeks afterwards I walked into the lion's den to report on a game involving JPR's club side, Bridgend, at their Brewery Field ground. I received a mixed reaction that day, although I would argue that more were supportive of what I had said than against. One who most definitely fell into the 'against' category was JPR's father, Dr Peter Williams, a very fiery character. He proceeded to give me the biggest rocket I have known and if he did not go as far as to say I was a traitor, he did very forcibly point out how JPR had helped my own career to flourish. What a scene! It was a bigger talking-point than the match itself, although I have to say that JPR himself was fine with me. Anyway, I was proved right, because he did not play for Wales again. Gwyn Evans, of Maesteg, was the young full-back who got picked against Ireland.

Another hard-hitting report that landed me in a bit of hot water concerned the Varsity match between Oxford and Cambridge at Twickenham. The game was played on the first Tuesday in December and on this particular afternoon it was bitterly cold, with a pretty poor standard of rugby on display. Twickenham was three-quarters full and any game that draws in a near-capacity crowd should provide a certain level of performance. I wrote that this game resembled a sixth-form match and said it was like hiring the London Palladium and booking the Band of Hope to perform. If this was what the Varsity match was about, I felt they could keep it.

Twelve months on I was back at Twickenham again. Just as I was taking my seat in the press-box this old guy beckoned me to join him. He introduced himself as Charles, but then concentrated on the match – something like his fiftieth Varsity game! Half-time arrived and he pulled out a satchel that looked even older than him and probably should have been in the Victoria and Albert Museum. It had been battered and kicked, but he flipped it open, pulled out two silver goblets and some mulled claret, poured the wine, closed the bottle and put it back in his satchel. Charles handed me a goblet and said, 'You see Barry, this is also what the Varsity match is about.' Basically he was saying that it was not the players' fault they were not up to my standard and that the whole occasion was about more than just eighty minutes of rugby. He was right and I realised I had been unfair in slating them all the previous year. Equally, why shouldn't these players have the Palladium once a year? Charles's simple actions and words taught me a lot and the following day I made sure I wrote a complimentary article. Since that moment, I have always looked at the Varsity game in a different light.

There was only one assignment I refused to cover and that was the 1974 Lions tour to South Africa. Not just because I had no wish to see apartheid again, but because I was too close to it. I could still have been out there wearing the number 10 shirt next to the players who had triumphed with me in New Zealand three years earlier. The *Express* asked me to cover the last two Test matches, but the Lions were doing well by that stage (they won the rubber 3–0 with one drawn). I felt my presence would have meant I was encroaching on their victory party.

It's just as well I did not go, too, because I would have had to castigate the team for the dirty play I witnessed on my television screen back home in Wales. This was the tour where the Lions used the infamous '99' call. If any Lion felt he was being kicked or punched, he would shout '99' and his team-mates would rush to join in, hitting the nearest Springbok – whether that particular South African was involved in the incident or not. Sadly I saw great players run thirty or forty yards to throw punches. If their actions had taken place off a rugby pitch and on the street-corner instead, I have no doubt they would have been hauled up in court on charges of actual bodily harm. The saddest thing of the lot is that Willie-John McBride's Lions were such a fabulous rugby team there was simply no need for this '99' business.

The players shunned the *Daily Telegraph*'s John Reason, because he criticised their actions. Reason, whom I knew well, dropped me a note from the tour, starting it as usual by writing simply, 'Dear King . . .' He went on to say he did not think I would have put up with this attitude on the pitch and I agreed with him. As I knew so many of the players very well, I was genuinely shocked by what I was watching. Reason was made *persona non grata* and was ostracised by the players, but I admired him for having the guts to write what he did.

What made things even worse, in my eyes, was that I subsequently went to sporting dinners with some of the senior players and, instead of regretting the incidents, they tended to embellish them further. I actually heard fellow guests say, 'We don't want to hear this. It's a bad example to set our younger players.'

While I'm glad I missed that tour, funnily enough my most rewarding journalistic moment actually came in South Africa when I was working as BBC Radio Five's summariser during the 1995 World Cup. The Welsh accent was not as readily accepted as Scottish and Irish brogues in my early broadcasting days, but my voice was deemed to be OK and the South African jamboree was the third World Cup I covered as the BBC's senior rugby analyser. Again I had no training for the job. The producers simply told me to be myself. As I commentated on the opening ceremony in Cape Town I had such a feeling of immense pleasure and joy, doing my best to describe the new world that was unfolding in front of me. It was a marvellous moment, the start of a marvellous tournament.

After a couple of years of making personal appearances and promoting Gola sportswear – very much a full-time job for that period – I discovered I had some time on my hands again and could mix my journalistic work with another occupation. Therefore, when a man called Len Hughes got in touch to ask if I would join an insurance brokers, I said yes.

Len ran his own company in Birmingham and wanted to branch out in Wales. The best way to get into an area is to find a similar, but slightly smaller company, and buy them out. Not Len. He planned to start from scratch in Cardiff and wanted to use my name as a figurehead. A couple of others joined us, the financial projections were done for the next three years and within twenty-four months we were already in the plus column. The firm began to mushroom and next thing we knew C.T. Bowring, the Rolls-Royce of the industry, bought out Len and we moved to bigger and better premises.

I was with Bowring for seventeen years and brought in lots of new business, always doing my best to sell the professionalism of the company. I struck business with lots of clients at rugby matches, sporting dinners, even out on the golf course, and many of them became great friends of mine. One such account was struck with a man called Hwyel Meyberry, an abattoir owner from west Wales who was a typical butcher – a big, amiable, jovial character. I was participating in a golf tournament where various holes had been sponsored, so guess who won the par-3, 180-yard sixteenth hole? It was a complete fluke because I totally mis-hit my shot which was heading a good hundred yards out of bounds when it hit the top of a bunker, sprang around fifty feet in the air and came down to nestle within three inches of the flag.

My prize was a pig that I went to collect at the abattoir. There I got talking to Hwyel and struck an account with him at the same time. It was a pretty useful account for Bowring, too, because Hwyel is a big player at Smithfield meat market in London and has supplied fillets of beef to Buckingham Palace. On one occasion Hwyel asked me if I could get someone to come and say a few words at a function he was holding. I got a comedian friend to do the honours, but I warned him, 'Put something warm on – you'll be talking in a freezer!' He did a great ten-minute show, taking the mickey out of butchers and meat. Somehow he managed to keep it going, even if by the end his teeth were chattering!

Significantly, however, I was never a formally registered insurance broker. The idea was that I would bring in business on the back of my name, and that simple little fact was to cost me my job when American giants Marsh MacLelland bought out Bowring and announced there would be redundancies.

My boss and great friend, Brian Speed, was given the unfortunate task of telling me the bad news and he was nearly in tears as he explained what was going to happen. 'This is so unfair because you're responsible for 42 per cent of our total business yourself,' said Brian. Ironically, I had mentioned to him twelve months earlier that I felt a little precarious. What had made me uncomfortable was a television documentary I'd seen that centred on the fact that we are mere numbers in the high-pressure world of business, every one of us. I was particularly alarmed about one case featuring the next young high-flier, someone with the keys to his own future, who had had to take three months off work through stress. He returned to find someone else sitting at his desk, with boxes of his own possessions packed in the corner of the room.

There is always someone, somewhere to take your place. I have to say that what we achieved in building our little company up from scratch into one that flourished gave me as much satisfaction as anything I had done on a rugby pitch. But, like that young high-flier, I had begun to realise that Barry John was simply a mere number in the business world too. I was proved right, as well.

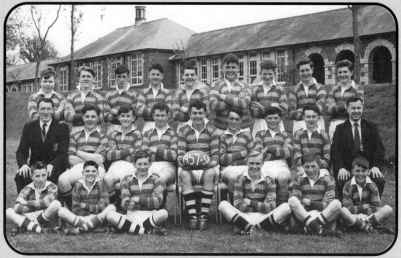

TOP: The young Barry, keeping up with his schoolwork to make sure he didn't have to go down the mines.

ABOVE: Barry John at school (front row, far right). I was only 12, but here I'm pictured in the Gwendraeth Grammar Under-15s.

Over I go. Try-scoring action for Cardiff.

Read all about it! I catch up with the news in this special souvenir edition of the Lions' victory in New Zealand published by Western Mail and Echo Ltd.

ABOVE AND RIGHT: You throw it . . . I'll catch it. But I meant with a rugby ball, mostly! Gareth and I take a break from our normal training.

BELOW: In you go. Tottenham and Arsenal legend Pat Jennings is beaten during the soccer competition in the *Superstars* tournament. Tony Jacklin looks on.

Wedding day. This is one occasion when I didn't worry about being at the centre of attention. [Courtesy of *Western Mail and Echo*]

The John clan. From the left: Kate, myself, David, Anna, Jan and Lucy.

With Bestie at Manchester United's Cliff training ground during our heyday. I think he's giving me some soccer tips!

Signing autographs was part of the everyday routine. [Courtesy of *Western Mail and Echo*]

Final match. The Barry John XV which played against a Carwyn James XV in the Welsh League of Youth fundraising game. It was my last time in a rugby shirt. I am in the front row, sandwiched by Gareth Edwards and Gerald Davies.

The opposition. Carwyn's selected XV.

GÊM Y DATHLU
The Jubilee Game

I nodi hanner canmlwyddiant Yr Urdd
To note the half centenary of the
Welsh League of Youth

XV CARWYN JAMES
v
XV BARRY JOHN

Y Maes Cenedlaethol Ebrill 26 1972/The National Stadium April 26 1972
K.O. 6.15 p.m. PRIS Y RHAGLEN 10c. PROGRAMME PRICE 10p.

LEFT: The programme cover for my final match.

BELOW: Over the line. Scoring a try in the Barry John XV–Carwyn James XV game. As rugby to me was primarily about scoring tries, I refused to take the conversion as my last act on the pitch.

"There, there darling. Grampy understands just how you feel – I was just the same when Barry John decided to quit the game!"

A cross-generational reference to the legend of Barry John. [Courtesy of Gren]

I'd love to become a winning racehorse owner one day. The horse would be called Caring and Sharing – one of my mottoes.

ELEVEN

BEHIND CLOSED DOORS

If everyone were like Jan, my wife for nearly thirty years, most of the world's problems would be resolved almost overnight. It is a measure of the respect and esteem in which I hold her that even though we separated a few years ago, I will never have a bad word said about Jan. Not that anyone would say hurtful things about her anyway, for Jan is one of those people who is universally liked.

We married in Swansea in 1969 and things cannot exactly have been easy for Jan after the way everything exploded for me in the following years when I returned from New Zealand. Because I was in such demand to attend dinners, sports functions and awards ceremonies, there was a period when I was lucky if I averaged one meal a week at home. But Jan remained fully supportive and she was the first person I took into confidence over my decision to quit rugby. Then, as she invariably did, Jan said to me, 'Barry, I'll back whatever decision you make.'

We had many years of wonderful times together and we remain great friends, despite the separation. We are not officially divorced, I must stress, but a few years ago the pair of us had the feeling within the house that things were not quite what they used to be. As with millions of other couples, we just grew apart. We do not really know why; I suppose it is just the next chapter for you, if you like. When this sort of marriage breakdown happened to friends of mine I never argued with them about it. I certainly never thought, 'That could not happen to Jan and me' – that would have been a dangerous thing to believe, even though we were extremely happy together.

The difference, of course, is that my friends could go through the process of separation in anonymity. With Jan and me, our marriage breakdown was inevitably splashed across the newspapers. As I am writing this book, there has been publicity surrounding the marriage of the television actor Robson Greene. The moment your name gets into the newspapers, be it through rugby exploits, showbiz or whatever, you have to accept you will always be in the headlines, particularly when it comes to something like this.

However, to show there was no nastiness involved, Jan and I actually used the same solicitor. We could hardly be at each other's throats in those circumstances, could we? I just said, 'Let's have half of everything each' and we got on with it – no fighting or squabbling. I would suggest to every other couple who land up in our situation after so many years of being happily married that, if it is emotionally possible, to do it the way Jan and I did. Make sure there are no verbal punches, let alone any other sort. I'm not exactly glad things worked out this way; no one would wish that upon themselves. But to continue sharing a house together under a false umbrella with holes in it would certainly not have been the right way forward. Jan and I realised it was time to call it a day and we made the decision to do so amicably.

We sold our lovely house in Radyr, on the northwest outskirts of Cardiff, and I moved into an apartment in the Cardiff Bay waterfront area of the Welsh capital. For the first six months I found it very strange being on my own. From the days when I grew up in Cefneithin I had been used to having everything done for me, particularly my laundry. In fact, in the four years I have been in my current apartment, I have not used the washing machine once. I should own shares in the public laundrette in the Llandaff area of Cardiff because once a week I take my shirts there to be washed, dried and ironed. Basically I had gone straight from home in west Wales to marriage with Jan. My second and third years at Trinity College, Carmarthen, were the only time I had to fend for myself. Even then I hardly did that, though: first I lodged with a lovely couple called Mrs and Mrs Brian Davies, who were extremely helpful when it came to doing the chores. Then, when I moved into Room C at the student tower block, I used to leave a bag of laundry outside my door. For a few complimentary tickets the cleaner would take away the washing and do it for me.

It was at college that I first set eyes on Janet Talfan Davies and we got to know one another at a Hallowe'en party in the Black Horse pub in Carmarthen. Her father is Sir Alun Talfan Davies, one of the country's leading QCs, a well-known figure in the publishing world, big in the banking and literary worlds, recognised as a great Welshman . . . and, most important of the lot, a very great friend of mine. The fact that Sir Alun had a high profile himself must have been of great help to Jan when our own world was suddenly turned on its head with the fame that enveloped me. I'm not saying that, because she was used to the way publicity worked, Jan could just take it in her stride. It was most certainly not as simple as that. But she had seen television cameras and microphones in her home before and at least she had some idea of how to deal with everything.

We hit it off fantastically well from day one and, to be honest, I'm not sure Jan was impressed by the fact that I was a rugby player. I was a regular in the Llanelli side by then and I would walk into the student common room after lectures to be met with a chorus of 'Well played last night, BJ' from my fellow students. But I don't think Jan even liked rugby in those days, although she did begin coming down with friends to the midweek games at Stradey Park, where we would draw in crowds of 12,000. I'm sure she enjoyed the occasion and the atmosphere more than the match.

Jan had spent six years at Cheltenham Ladies' College and had returned to Wales to study to become an English teacher. As we got chatting I quickly discovered she could certainly beat me when it came to little digs. Age-wise, Jan is six months younger – but in terms of having the last word or the last laugh she was a good year ahead of me. Despite getting on famously, though, we went our separate ways after a few months as I focused on my rugby career. Then, quite coincidentally, we bumped into each other again on a train a year afterwards. I was a Cardiff player by then and, having travelled up from Cefneithin to training one evening, I jumped on the train back to Swansea and Jan just happened to be travelling in the same direction. We struck up a conversation about old times and immediately we hit it off again.

As I could see we were so obviously made for one another I felt I did indeed have room for rugby and romance, that the two could mix. So, during one of our evenings out together, as we were discussing whether I should go north to rugby league or not, I stopped the car and popped the question. The romantic location? Outside the gates of the Smiths crisps factory in Fforestfach, on the outskirts of Swansea! Jan and I can smile about that one today, but the important thing was that she said 'yes'. I remember saying to Jan on our wedding day, 'I suppose you're going to be known as Mrs Barry John from here on in.' But I told her straight away I did not want that – Jan had to remain her own person. She could not simply become an accessory on my arm anyway, because she is highly intelligent, can draw cartoons brilliantly and could have written books if she wanted.

Jan has been teaching full-time for the last few years and I think she honestly enjoys the fact that the school where she is based is in the Ely area of Cardiff. Ely is well known for, shall we say, not the right reasons. It is a hardened, tough part of Cardiff where crimes from murder downwards are committed. Jan, remember, comes from a privileged background with Sir Alun as her father, Cheltenham Ladies' College and so on. Yet knowing her, I should imagine she genuinely loves working in that rough neck of the woods where normal rules do not apply, where every morning there are new problems, new questions, to be answered. They think the world of Jan down there. She has a marvellous ability to create the right atmosphere in the classroom and she is so dedicated that she went in during the school holidays to convert the room herself, to make sure it wasn't dreary and was full of bright colours instead. Jan, like lots of teachers, also spends her own money, making sure every pupil gets a present at Christmas time.

Once we were at a charity dinner in the old Dragon Hotel in Swansea when Jan, who was involved with the fund-raising, was asked to stand and say a few words. Normally I had to do that sort of thing, but on this particular occasion I just sat back to watch and listen – and I have never felt so proud of anyone before. Jan has a lovely voice and spoke with confidence and authority, everyone taking note of what she was saying. On another occasion she was asked by a television crew what it was like to share a house with me, for a programme they were making. Jan was open and honest, saying I was a bit of a gypsy. What she meant was that because of my fame I was not conventional, that normal rules went out of the window. She went on to say how useless I was at DIY, that I was slightly accident-prone and that she'd certainly not ask me to change a plug. When the interview finished the television producers approached me to ask if I wanted certain comments to be edited out. 'No way,' I told them. I respected Jan's views and insisted they should be aired.

When I was in New Zealand with the Lions, Jan would telephone to say the lawn looked great, the leaking tap was working and that the broken window had been fixed. She was virtually saying, 'If you remain away for another three months we will get it right in this house!' Our neighbours, Leighton and Glaswyn, had been brilliant in helping Jan while I was away. That is why, after Gareth Edwards and his wife Maureen had a horse-drawn carriage procession through their village on his return, I became infuriated with that television comment of 'And what did Radyr do for Barry John?' The villagers did the best thing possible in ignoring me, letting me settle quietly back home with Jan and Kate, who was one year old then.

Not that the quietness lasted, of course, and while I would not say that my sudden elevation to celebrity status put a strain on our marriage, Jan certainly had to become accustomed to the dramatic change just as much as I did. She had first realised I would spend my career in the spotlight when, after I had played just a few games for my country, HTV produced a thirty-minute programme entirely devoted to me and my background – with little mention of rugby. Suddenly everything was on a new plateau. We realised things would be totally different, but it happened so fast – within a matter of weeks – that Jan did not even have the luxury of a year to acclimatise to the change. I think what really made her realise things had gone over the top was when we were sitting in our lounge watching a Ronnie Barker comedy programme and I received a mention in one of the sketches!

It is to Jan's credit that she coped so admirably with everything and helped Kate, and afterwards Lucy, Anna and David, come to terms with having a famous father. I am immensely proud of the way those four have made their way in the world. Each is a talented sportsperson, with the four of them winning Radyr tennis titles, but the important point is that none of them achieved their success simply because Barry John was a top rugby player and they were carrying a famous name. No, they all did it through their own ability, never once pressing the button of having the John name.

Kate, our eldest, could turn her hand to most things and represented Cardiff in the sports equivalent of *It's a Knockout*. As well as being a super tennis player and representing South Glamorgan at hockey, she is a terrific swimmer. That, however, is the only time I have suppressed anyone's ambition. When Kate was younger I pointed out that successful swimmers had to train for two hours in the mornings and that unless you reached Olympic standard, it simply was not worth it. Anyway, she liked her bed in the mornings so I'm not sure she could have got up for training!

Kate went to the Ysgol Glantaf school and the only time I had concerns about her was as a fourteen-year-old when another pupil was almost 'stalking' her. This other pupil was known, shall we say, for her violence and when Jan rang me one day to say there had been an incident at the school, I was immediately worried. With no provocation whatsoever, this other person had smashed Kate in the face, cutting her lip. It was a frightening experience for Jan and myself, but that isolated incident apart, I never had any trouble involving the four of them. Apart from the times they would forget to ring you. 'Oh, didn't I tell you I was going to Julie's for the night?' Kate would say with innocence, as a get-out!

Kate went to Liverpool University where she obtained a law degree, but, like Jan, she has gone into teaching and clearly learned a lot from her mother. She married an Army major called Steve Ocock in August 1997 and today they are based in Swindon where she teaches at a local school.

Lucy married Meirion in 1999 and they went off to the Cayman Islands where he took up a post as a quantity surveyor. They have subsequently moved back to the Clifton area of Bristol, but I suspect they may end up abroad again one day, perhaps Australia.

Two of my most wonderful moments were the occasions of walking down the aisle with Kate and Lucy on my arm to give them away on their wedding days. There were, of course, speeches to make afterwards. I have stood up to talk on hundreds of occasions, including addressing close on 1,000 guests at the Hilton and the Savoy, but it does not matter how many times you have done it, the experience is always a little nerve-wracking. Kate and Lucy simply said to me beforehand, 'Make sure you behave', and I think the wedding guests could see just how much I enjoyed the two occasions. While being part of the centre stage as father to the bride, this time I was not actually 'centre stage'. It was a lovely, warm feeling.

At Lucy's wedding I told a story about how she developed the taste for being a student, what with parties and everything that went with it, after spending a few weekends with Kate at Liverpool University. I politely pointed out to Lucy that she still had to achieve the qualifications to get there. 'You can't just jump off a train and say "I'm here" one day,' I told her. Nonetheless Lucy did get her wish to become a student when she went to Middlesex College, although her choice of a catering course rather surprised me because I did not know she could cook. Still, hadn't I chosen rural science in my own college days?

I explained during the wedding speech how I travelled to London to see Lucy's first-term report, although she quickly pointed out, 'You don't get much done in the first term.' Midway through the second term she told me she was top of her class . . . in theory. Lucy could tell you how to bake a cake brilliantly, but actually doing it was another matter entirely. Just like me, I suppose. I eventually knew she would not be going back because you had to take your own cutlery on the course and one day Jan said, 'Can I have my set of knives back?' Lucy replied, 'No, I've sold them, I'm afraid.'

Lucy went on to do a secretarial course in Oxford, earned very good ratings, and has gone on to do superbly for herself. One day, when I was working as a journalist for the *Express*, I rang to speak to the sports editor, David Emery. After we had finished our conversation he said, 'Do you want to speak to Lucy?' I replied that I did not know a Lucy there. He shocked me by saying she had been working on the desk for five weeks as a PA I knew nothing about it whatsoever and she certainly did not use my name to get in there. Part of Lucy's portfolio was to look after big sporting events and she would suddenly throw into the conversation, 'Oh, I was on the telephone to Kevin Keegan the other day . . .' David told me Lucy was extremely popular, good at her job, always happy and smiling, and got on very well with others at the *Express*.

After a while Lucy had enough of London. With the 1999 Rugby World Cup being staged in Cardiff, she went in to see one of the organisers, Keith Rowlands, and landed herself a job working next to Chris Thau, head of the media office. These days Lucy is a PA to a top firm of solicitors.

She, too, excelled at sport, running the London marathon and completing it in such a good time that she was given kit for the following year. Continuing the sporting excellence in the John household is Anna, an excellent hockey and tennis player. She represented Wales at hockey right up to under-21 level and then played at university level while studying at Sheffield. She ended up in Sheffield because, as a fifteen-year-old, she jumped on a train to attend a four-day educational camp there and loved the city. Anna planned everything herself which, for a teenager of that age, showed fantastic enterprise.

But that is Anna for you. Unknown to me she recently decided to take a year off and spend it travelling around the world. Anna had landed a management job with Marks and Spencer in London and they wanted her to start work immediately. Anna told them she wanted to start the following year, stuck to her guns and got her way. She organised a loan with her bank to pay for the trip abroad and needed the employment letter from Marks and Spencer, which detailed the salary she was coming back to, as proof that she could repay the money. On her return Anna has done marvellously with Marks and Spencer and was recently involved with a big launch of the company's Autograph collection of ladies' fashion clothing. Julien Macdonald was one of the designers involved. Anna and her partner Ted seem to be settled in London and have recently purchased a flat there.

As for David, the youngest of the four, he too is an excellent sportsman, with a wonderful eye for the ball and good movement on his feet. He plays rugby to a good standard, as either a scrum-half or fly-half, and is a very good right-sided footballer. If those around him do not sweat, David does not want to know them. He is a popular young man: I have seen him in action with his mates and he is good company. They take the mickey out of one another, but they also lend each other a tenner if necessary and that is what I call friendship. David, too, went to the Cayman Islands, where he became an integral part of the rugby scene out there. They even wanted him to remain there so David could qualify for the Islands at representative level under residency rules. At the moment he and his mates are playing in the United States for Queen City, in the state of Denver, in the Americans' own version of Super 12.

David is very much like me in as much as he would not really feel comfortable with a job that kept him indoors. He's very intelligent. He can turn his attention to anything – that is perhaps the biggest difference between us – and has done various jobs. He loves using his hands and once did some very impressive stonewalling. But deep down, I suspect the sort of job he would like most is in sales; he would be a good salesman.

I would like to think I have been an influence on the four of them, just as I was influenced by the people around me when I was growing up in Cefneithin. Outside that immediate circle, there is also a small number of individuals who had an effect on me once I had made it as a rugby player – and some of them have nothing to do with rugby. No matter who you are, or how famous you may be, there are always some people who have a major effect on how you go about things. In my case the five I will name are Carwyn James, Rhydwen Williams, Sir Alun Talfan Davies, Eddie Thomas and Cliff Morgan.

Let us start with Carwyn, coach to our Lions team in 1971. My admiration for him, and the scandalous waste of his talent in his Wales homeland, will come across loud and clear in another chapter which details what has gone wrong with Welsh rugby. Suffice it to say here that not only was he a brilliant rugby coach, he was also a brilliant Welshman and a brilliant friend. He had a massive influence upon me in the sense that he was from the same village, the local rugby idol I looked up to. Most other villages have to borrow their idol from somewhere else; Carwyn was there amongst us, right on our own doorstep in Cefneithin.

Carwyn had this knack of being able to talk without appearing to look down on you and I have never seen a better communicator on the game. We were once trying to explain rugby to an Icelandic man who knew only the basic rudiments of the game, yet Carwyn spoke with such clarity and insight that our visitor grasped it at once. Only Carwyn could have managed that.

If Carwyn was rugby through and through, the next person on my list – an elderly gentleman by the name of Rhydwen Williams – could not kick a rugby ball from one end of the carpet to the other in the little back room of his terraced house in Llewellyn Street, Aberdare, high up in the Welsh valleys. Rhydwen was a character from the Welsh Eisteddfod world. In Welsh literacy circles he was as well known and respected as Dylan Thomas, whom he knew well . . . Probably because they were together in their prime!

I used to love my trips up to Aberdare to see Rhydwen because they were like an escape for me. If I arrived feeling down, or under the weather because of a cold, his humour, sense of fun and sheer outrageousness would make me feel 100 per cent better. His wife Margaret, as thin as the cigarettes she loved, would march me into Rhydwen's study, which was piled high with books around the walls. Rhydwen would then have me in hysterics with some of his no-holds-barred comments about people – his wicked smile, his flashing brown eyes and that wonderful delivery of lines lighting up the room.

I met Rhydwen through my father-in-law Sir Alun Talfan Davies who, whether he knows it or not, is another who had a great influence upon me. We forged a great friendship and even though Jan and I have separated, I remain on very amicable terms with Sir Alun and his wife Lady Lyn. Sir Alun had many strings to his bow, with contacts in the legal, literary, media and political professions. Through him I was able to mix in a very different world. At times I felt I was gatecrashing their party, someone coming in with a different attitude and holding different views. Yet these very powerful people still seemed honoured to be in my company, not only because they could suddenly talk about what had gone on in the Wales v. England match the previous Saturday, but because they too seemed genuinely pleased to meet someone so different.

Time and again I have asked Sir Alun for his legal expertise on issues, never more so than when I decided to retire and he told me exactly how to go about doing it. Free of charge, I had access to one of the most brilliant legal eagles in Britain. Players who subsequently retired asked me how to go about it and I was able to pass on my own experience and, in effect, help them use Sir Alun's brilliant advice, albeit second hand.

Next on my list is Eddie Thomas, the former British boxing champion. He is perhaps more famous for being the manager of world featherweight champion Howard Winstone in the 1960s and for leading Ken Buchanan to the world lightweight crown during the 1970s. I spent endless hours in Eddie's company and I cannot remember even ten seconds of boredom. He was one of the great communicators – when Eddie spoke, you listened. The stories he rattled off about going to the United States with Winstone and Buchanan, the underhand side of boxing, the politics involved, the dirty tricks some got up to, left me open-mouthed. Eddie was so well respected within his profession that even the great Muhammad Ali used to ring him for advice. When Ali was once asked, in a television interview, to whom he would send a potential future world heavyweight champion for an apprenticeship, he named Eddie Thomas: 'Let him spend three years with Eddie in the Welsh valleys,' said Ali. Well, Ali never found that pretender to his own throne – but if his wish had been granted it would have been the icing on the cake for Eddie.

I found it so sad that Eddie, having been made a Freeman in his home town of Merthyr, was then slaughtered by a television programme that portrayed him as a money-grabber and a man not to be trusted. Clearly some people in Merthyr were not happy with him – ridiculous, because the work that man did for the town is immeasurable. Yet even in Eddie's final year, when we sat outside in his back garden, there was no bitterness from him as he spoke with such pride about his love for Merthyr and the townsfolk around him. You take as you find and in my view, when you talk about a 24-carat person, Eddie Thomas is that man.

Last, but by no means least, I name another rugby figure in Cliff Morgan – one of my predecessors in the Cardiff, Wales and Lions number 10 jersey, who went on to become a leading figure in the broadcasting world with the BBC. I saw Cliff as the prototype of how a fly-half should play. I recall, as a youngster, being the last in a stampede to get Cliff's autograph after one match. I was unlucky on that occasion. It took until I was playing for the Lions in New Zealand, and Cliff was covering the tour as one of the journalists, for me finally to ask for and get his signature. I may have been the leading points-scorer on the tour, but I was not too proud to do that!

If Cliff has a fault, it is his generosity and willingness to do anything for anybody. Just after I had retired he dropped me a line, a two-paragraph note rather than a letter, to say he had noticed me looking tired after my endless round of functions and dinners. 'Barry, you must learn to occasionally say no,' he wrote. Cliff was very much a sought-after speaker, himself, at these functions and the pressure and workload once led to him going to hospital. At that point I wrote a note back, saying, 'Cliff, you too must learn to say no.' Maybe the pair of us took the hint.

Good old Cliff. During that New Zealand tour he became the only Lion to be injured during one provincial match – and he was fifty yards up above the pitch sitting in the press-box. Apparently, when John Bevan scored a superb try, Cliff stood up to punch the air with delight, but in his excitement he tumbled over his stool and twisted his ankle. So the joke went that one Lion did hobble on to the team bus injured that day – albeit a 1955 Lion rather than one from the class of '71!

TWELVE

WHO WANTS TO BE
A MILLIONAIRE?

If I had one pound for every time people ask me, 'BJ, don't you wish you were playing today with the money on offer?', I probably would be a millionaire instead of merely the millionaire they seem to think I would have become. I have been asked that question so often down the years – and it is always supplemented by the comment: 'Because of course, Barry, if the professional era was around in your day you would have been the first player worth £1 million.'

I know what they are getting at and I agree it would have been nice to have had the money, although I suspect talk of a million might be a bit over the top. But I always provide a two-fold answer and the second part concerns the enjoyment I got out of my rugby, a zest I believe I could not have had playing the modern-day game where tight defensive organisation seems more important than flair and adventure. I always tell people I would not swap my rugby era for any other because it was a wonderful time to play the game – not only because there were so many stars of true world-class ability around, but because the rules meant rugby was more thrilling for players and spectators alike.

In fact I would turn the question on its head and say that instead of me playing today's game, why don't we ask a top modern-day fly-half like Wales's Neil Jenkins or England's Jonny Wilkinson if they would like to have played in my era? They will have seen the '70s videos and listened to the old-timers talk about the old days, so it might just make them think twice. Sure, the money would not have been there like it is today. But I suspect they would have found their rugby more fulfilling and would have loved the challenge of seeing just how good they were, if they really could utilise their skills in a more open game where the name of the game was tries, tries, tries, not kick, kick, kick.

I certainly do not begrudge anyone the money they make out of the professional explosion of the modern game. The only thing that surprises me is that it took until September 1995 for rugby union to kick off the shackles of amateurism. The reason I say that is because I can tell you a little story of how it so nearly happened twenty-one years earlier, when the idea of professional rugby was first mooted and I was the go-between asked to secretly organise it. The multi-million pound financial backing would have come from sports-mad businessmen based in the United States, some of whom were the same ones who had earlier tried to tempt me into American Football as a goal-kicker.

Many of the ideas we put forward then are indeed being implemented by the rugby power-brokers today. We planned a European Cup, very much on the lines of the one that was brought in towards the end of the 1990s. We were also proposing to introduce franchise-owned clubs which could decide their own destinies, in its most basic form part of the blueprint Rob Andrew devised as the way forward for the British game in the year 2000. The big difference, of course, is that it has been easy for Rob – even though he probably thinks it was difficult to get his plan approved – because the game had already turned professional. Back in 1974, the stakes in our case were so huge, with the administrators frowning upon professionalism, that we had to keep everything hush-hush, almost talk in whispers and codes. I have to admit to being amazed that the true story has never been leaked about what we were trying, which would have involved taking the world's greatest players into a breakaway set-up.

To a man, the fifty players I approached were keen on the idea. It fell through in the end because three of the eight franchises we planned – in Cardiff, London, Manchester, Edinburgh, Dublin, Paris, Toulouse and Rome – did not come off. But it was that close. Paperwork and contracts were in place, ready to be signed. We would have called ourselves World Rugby and changed one or two of the rules for the better; who is to say, had our scheme succeeded, how the face of the game would have changed? In the end it took the authorities a further twenty-one years to come out of the Dark Ages.

The invitation to travel to southern California to discuss the revolutionary plan came in the summer of 1974 via a telephone call from a delegation of Americans, led by a man called Mike Trope. Quite coincidentally, I set out on my journey from Heathrow, first stop Chicago, on the same day as Willie-John McBride's British Lions were arriving back at the airport from South Africa. They were going on to celebrations at the nearby Excelsior Hotel and, as most of the 1974 party had been with me in New Zealand three years earlier, and I had two hours to spare, I desperately wanted to go to congratulate them and have a drink with them. The chances were, however, that knowing me, I would have carried on chatting and missed my flight. It was too important a trip for that. My mission was this: the Americans wanted to talk to me about the prospects of rugby going professional with teams owned on a franchise basis, very much on the lines of the NFL American Football League.

The trip itself was not exactly uneventful. Because everything was so secretive I was asked at the last minute to travel out and had to rush from Cardiff to London to get a visa from the American Embassy. There was no time to go home and pack, so Mike took care of my flight and hotel details and then took my collar, chest and leg measurements so he could have some new clothes waiting for me when I arrived. With the nonsense and paraphernalia that went with trying to enter the United States in those days, I guess the inevitable happened as my trip had been arranged in such a rush. When the aeroplane touched down in Chicago, my first point of entry, I was told to remain in my seat. Two big security guards then came on and told me to follow them, which I did, entering a room where three customs officials were waiting.

The customs men wanted to know why I was travelling first class with no luggage and clearly thought I was trying to smuggle something into their country. As they surveyed my passport, and I tried to explain where Cardiff was, I wondered what I had let myself in for. My interrogators were not letting up in their suspicions. To make matters worse, I told them I had a room booked at the Hilton hotel, they checked it out and came back to say the hotel staff had never heard of a Barry John. It was desperation stakes by this point and, as my last throw of the dice, I told them to check the name Mike Trope. Just as I thought I was about to be deported, they returned to say that a room had indeed been booked for me in Mike's name and everything was OK. Which was fine, except that while this was going on, of course, I missed my connection to California and had to find my own way across the United States.

Eventually I did meet up with Mike and his colleagues, who were heavily into American Football. As we discussed their rugby proposal, it became clear they had done their homework, realising, unlike today, that the power base was very much in Europe. The Lions of 1971 had won in New Zealand, the Lions of 1974 had just won in South Africa:

there were some top rugby players around who were becoming as famous as the best soccer stars of the day. We decided a lot of secretive research had to be undertaken, which I agreed to do, and on my return to Wales I drew up a proper report, with the help of my father-in-law, Sir Alun Talfan Davies, QC, to look at the problems we would face, what legal obstacles might be put in our way, how the authorities might react and how we could overcome their objections.

Satisfied with the advice I was given by Sir Alun, the next step was to find out if the players were interested. One by one I privately approached fifty top stars to discuss the idea and I was delighted that they all replied, 'Yes, keep me fully informed please, Barry'. Once the verbal commitment from those players was in place, we could really go for it, although I had to emphasise the need for them to keep everything hush-hush.

The plan was straightforward: eight teams set up on a franchise basis in the cities I have already mentioned. The money would come from American businessmen who reckoned that if the marketing and sales pitch were right, they would make a mint out of the project. Losing the odd million was nothing to these people. The rewards they predicted, on the other hand, from sell-out crowds, television money, sponsorship and other spin-offs, were well worth going for. Make no mistake, they were in it for the money themselves.

Cardiff were regarded as the blue chip in this multi-million-dollar game. This was understandable, such was the success of Welsh rugby at the time. But the other franchises were attractive too. We could not stage matches at traditional rugby venues like Cardiff Arms Park, Twickenham, Murrayfield or Lansdowne Road because the respective home unions would not allow professional games to take place at their grounds. So the next step was to find alternative venues, which we did. The Cardiff team, ostensibly a side representing Wales, would have played at Swansea, whose St Helen's ground was owned by the city council. We discussed Chelsea's Stamford Bridge stadium for the London team; Manchester City's Maine Road home for the Manchester (i.e. north of England) team; either Tynecastle or Easter Road for Edinburgh; and Croak Park, home to Gaelic Football, for the Dublin side. Paris and Toulouse were no problem, as the rugby stadiums were owned by the municipale and we banked on Rome being OK.

We were ready to set up our own Rugby Federation, we talked to the television and sponsorship people and the plan was for the eight teams to play one another in a European League before bumper crowds. It was a really exciting proposal and one which, in my view, was guaranteed to be a success because we had the very best players verbally committed to the plan. We even suggested tinkering with a couple of the rules to make our matches even more of a thrilling spectacle. It went that far, with Cardiff, London, Manchester, Dublin and Paris having franchises in place. In the end there were problem areas with Edinburgh, Rome and Toulouse, which was the one that surprised me most because I assumed they would really go for it in the south of France. We had eight different consortiums ready to pump in $1 million apiece, but the trouble was they each wanted one of Cardiff, London, Manchester, Dublin or Paris. We even tried splitting the other three franchises between the eight groups, but it wasn't to be. In the end we decided that a five-team league simply could not work and the effort that had gone into canvassing everybody for the plan went to waste. But it was close . . . Very close.

Do you know, too, that Mike Trope still owes me $12,500 for my fee in acting as the go-between? I was never paid a penny for the behind-the-scenes work I put in. On one occasion, to discuss the most recent developments in our plan, Mike came to my house in Cardiff and while there used the telephone to negotiate a deal with an American Football wide-receiver called Johnny Rogers. Johnny had won the Heisman Trophy for being the outstanding player at college. Mike confirmed his contract from my study in Radyr – and did not even pay for the phone call!

That said, when I first went to the United States to meet Mike and his business partners, they proved to be fantastic hosts with no expense spared. They had set up a new American Football team called South California and I travelled with them to Tennessee to watch a match against Nashville. The night before the game, I was given the honour of being allowed into the players' room at the hotel as the coach gave his pre-match talk about tactics. On one side of the room were two tables with mountains of food – tons and tons of salad on one, big mounds of steak, chicken and burgers on the other. Modern-day players talk about carbohydrate diets, but these giants of men, weighing a minimum of 230lb and making me look like a little mascot in comparison, would pick up a chicken wing and in three mouthfuls it would be gone! That food did not do them much harm because they were big, quick, athletic and fit.

As Barry John was supposed to be known around the world, the coach introduced me to his players, but there was no response from them. That amazed him, so he went into detail about what I had achieved in my career. Again, no response. 'Listen you lot,' said the coach, 'This man is his sport's equivalent of Namath,' who was the famous American Football quarterback. At that point the message registered and they stood up to give me a standing ovation. I was quite touched by it.

On the flight back, though, I witnessed the ruthless side of professionalism for the first time. I was sitting next to a defensive end called Booker Brown who, mid-flight, was asked to go down the plane to see the owners. I have never seen such a miserable face as his when he walked back to his seat. Booker had been told he was being transferred to Philadelphia Eagles. He had no say in it. The owners did not just own the club, they owned the players too. Once Booker had signed his contract, he was just another asset for the owners to do what they wanted with – even though he told me the last thing he wanted to do was uproot.

So in the end my trip to the United States proved to be unsuccessful in terms of bringing in professional rugby. But I think I can still say I was party to its eventual arrival twenty-one years on because it was Vernon Pugh, QC, as chairman of the International Rugby Board, who made that famous announcement in Paris that the game was going open. Guess what? I encouraged Vernon to stand for election to rugby's governing bodies.

Vernon and I have known each other for years. We come from similar small west Wales village backgrounds, speak Welsh, have the same type of humour and have even holidayed together on the Costa Blanca in Spain. Vernon had impressed me with the way he ran youth rugby in Cardiff and one day, while we were sitting around the poolside, I mentioned that I was disappointed with the quality of the people sitting on the Welsh Rugby Union and suggested he put his name forward. Vernon's initial response was that, as a leading QC, he did not have the time to devote to the task. I encouraged him a second time shortly afterwards and so it didn't surprise me when, a few years on, he did indeed put his name up for election.

Vernon was immediately voted on to the Welsh Rugby Union. With respect to the others, in terms of IQ, management skills, communication and knowledge of how rugby works, he left them standing, in my opinion. I do not think anybody has shot up the ladder so quickly. Vernon is such an exceptional administrator that he was soon nominated as the Welsh representative on the International Rugby Board; he then became chairman of the IRB, a post to which he was re-elected for a further four years in April 2000. After the President of the International Olympic Committee and the President of FIFA, I would say Vernon is up there as the next most powerful man in sport. In fact, I would not be surprised to see him on the International Olympic Committee soon.

The unfortunate thing is that when Vernon made that famous statement in Paris in September 1995, a heap of fresh problems arose. While his words were easily understood on the surface, in my view the massive implications of the whole issue were not looked into deeply enough. The upshot of that was a number of clubs heavily over-budgeting and then almost going to the wall. Sadly, this happened in Wales more than anywhere else. My old club, Llanelli, had to be rescued by the Welsh Rugby Union (who purchased their Stradey Park ground) while Neath were taken over by the WRU. Others who got into a financial mess included Swansea and Bridgend, while lower down the scale there were a host of smaller clubs heavily in the red – everything being a legacy of paying big money to players. Money that those clubs simply did not have. They are still recovering from the financial nightmare today.

What should have happened is that everybody should have gone away to deliberate everything thoroughly for a year, look at the problems associated with professional sport and study potential contract difficulties – not just involving players, but also sponsors, television people and anyone else liable to become involved. When we were chasing our plan in America I spoke to Gordon Taylor, leader of the professional footballers' union, the PFA, to ask about pitfalls of contracts, players' insurance and various other issues. He was only too willing to help me then and his advice should have been canvassed again.

Once the word 'professional' is used, you need proper financial structures and business plans put in place. Suddenly rugby became more than a game. But instead of coming together and discussing everything properly, the leading clubs tried to shoot one another down, each wanting to be top dog, it seemed to me.

The number-one contract that had to be signed, sealed, delivered and made absolutely watertight was with the television people. Without television no sport at the highest level can exist. With the television moguls on board, sponsors are happy, you can strike your commercial and advertising deals, and everything flows from there. Once those firm and binding agreements were in place, then, and only then, should clubs have discussed contracts with players and told them how much money they were to get. Instead clubs, and I repeat, notably in Wales, went out and spent money before knowing for certain that it was coming in. The rugby authorities were still locked into the old television deal from the amateur days and there proved to be no end of problems in trying to strike a new deal to take the game into the professional era, mainly because of pathetic, stupid and unnecessary arguments. The power-brokers, instead of going to bed on amicable terms with the television people, became too high-handed and wanted to show who was boss.

There was so much naïvety among people with no real business background it was almost untrue. But because certain figures were on the committees who ran the game, which in truth had run itself for over 100 years, they felt this gave them power to wield the big stick – and that led to problem after problem.

In the meantime clubs had agreed bumper contracts with their players, with no guarantee of the money coming in. We are not just talking about Manchester United or Arsenal – or in rugby's case Cardiff and Harlequins – when you use the term 'professional' either. This financial madness filtered right down to the grass roots of the game. I know of countless stories in the Welsh fourth and fifth divisions where players were paid hundreds of pounds per game, a ridiculous amount at that level. Greed was the name of the game. Players saw bumper sums of money being thrown about and they wanted a share of it.

I do not blame the players for that, but the clubs needed to be far more sensible in their budgeting. It is no good shelling out hundreds of thousands of pounds on expenditure if you do not have the same amount coming in via the turnstiles, television and sponsorship deals, as those clubs unfortunately found to their cost. It was supposed to be professional, but the way the finances were being handled was just amateurish. Had this sort of thing happened in any other business, the shareholders would have been asking questions and told those at the top to sort it out within a week . . . or else.

Fortunately, after this period of madness, sanity has prevailed again. In the lower divisions clubs are back to just paying a few pints after a game. But the horse definitely bolted and many of those clubs are still playing catch-up with their finances. It is going to be some time before they find themselves on an even keel.

So, going back to what I said at the start of the chapter, yes – it would have been nice to earn the financial rewards open to modern-day players. I remain convinced, however, that while I may have had money in the bank, I most certainly would not have enjoyed my rugby anywhere near as much. The game has changed so dramatically, as a result of law-makers tampering with the rules, and has become so defence-orientated, that I feel a little sorry for today's players. Particularly the fly-half. Everyone is frightened to try those little off-the-cuff things, the moments of panache and genius that spectators love so much, for fear of making mistakes.

OK, I know today's players, and for that matter everybody connected with international teams and the top club sides, feel they are under enormous pressure to deliver the goods. But are those pressures to win really any greater than they were in our day? What I know for certain is that there could be no bigger match than New Zealand v. the Lions in the third Test shoot-out in Wellington, or the France v. Wales winner-takes-the-lot Grand Slam decider the same year. What I also know is that we regularly played before packed crowds in our club matches and those thousands of spectators, who had paid their hard-earned money to watch you play, expected you to justify the expense. How often do you see sell-out gates today? Very rarely.

No, the game was definitely more enjoyable before and I repeat my earlier question – I wonder what response you would get from Neil Jenkins or Jonny Wilkinson if you asked them if they would like the opportunity to have played in the '70s. I guarantee one thing, they would have had more freedom to express themselves – if they were good enough!

The ideal scenario, of course, would have been to earn the money of today and play under our rules and with the free spirit enterprise of the '70s. You see, when I watch matches these days, I reckon every five games out of six are dreary, drab, downright boring affairs. Which brings us on to another issue . . .

THIRTEEN

MY FEARS FOR
THE GAME I LOVE

I have to put my hands up and admit to it – I do have fears and reservations about rugby union and its future, for a whole variety of reasons. To be quite blunt, I can count on the fingers of one hand the number of thrilling international matches I have seen in the past five years or so. The 1999 World Cup final between Australia and France in Cardiff was such a bore that I spent much of the first half signing autographs and chatting to people around me who were equally unimpressed with the game, while shortly into the second half I actually left the stadium. I had had enough and so had many others. Thousands of youngsters are being lost to the game, choosing other interests to pursue instead. That is why it is paramount that rugby's shop-window, and by that I mean the World Cup, other international games, the Super 12 tournament and the European Cup, have to be seen to be thrilling and entertaining. The World Cup tournament that remains freshest in the memory was anything but that, thirty minutes of French second-half semi-final magic against New Zealand apart. In fact if anything, the competition was a rugby turn-off.

Modern-day rugby has to address these problems and I would recommend something radical and revolutionary to shake up the game: make it a thirteen-a-side contest. Yes, I know the administrators will throw up their arms in horror at the suggestion. Taking my advice would, I suppose, mean they were finally accepting that rugby league was right in going down that route those many years ago. But we can't have *that*, can we?, the rugby union power-brokers will be saying to themselves. Because of that, I can see 'political' objections to the game going down the thirteen-a-side route.

Make no mistake, however. Something must give to create more space on the pitch, because today's players are so big, and teams are so well organised defensively, that there is simply no room to move out there. At least my plan could encourage a return of the best rugby ingredients: pace, movement and sleight of hand, instead of the power, commitment, confrontation, physical presence and kicking components that make up the requirements of the modern-day player. It has gone too far in that direction and as a result matches, principally the showpiece ones, have become downright boring.

Rugby always was, and still should be, a game for people of various shapes and sizes – from the dapper little wing who could turn on a sixpence and race away at blistering speed, to the dynamic centre capable of bursting through, to the six-foot-six-inch lock-forward with ball-handling skills, to the burly props holding up the scrum. We used to have different attitudes and training requirements, but we needed each other. It was the very reason the team functioned. I know we are now in an era of cloning, but these days I see rugby players at the highest level who are becoming a combination of 200-metre runners, javelin throwers and pole-vaulters! I apply that criterion from numbers 1 through to 15, too. Everybody looks the same. We have wingers who are as big as second-row forwards, centres who are no different in build to flankers, full-backs who are not that much unlike the big, beefy prop-forwards . . . Even the training routines of, say, a hooker and a fly-half are – the odd subtle difference apart – by and large the same these days. Basically, what I am saying is that there is too much of a muchness out there and the thought of this trend continuing, with the administrators doing nothing about it, frightens me.

I first suggested my thirteen-a-side idea a couple of years ago, when I was doing a question-and-answer session at a sports forum in Wales – mainly to stir up enthusiasm as the evening was turning into a bit of a damp squib. I expected a 'what are you on about?' reaction, with the audience lining up to have a go at me. On the contrary, I was asked to expand further and I regarded that as a terrible indictment of rugby because it meant that, like me, they were not enjoying the game any more.

I explained that as forwards and backs alike get bigger, the space on the pitch gets more and more squeezed, particularly in today's defence-dominated game, and the opportunity for thrilling movements becomes less and less. To rectify this, the two sets of players I would do away with are the flankers – traditionally, in my book, the players with most overall ability in any side. They need to be big and strong to mix it with the forwards; be quick and athletic to get to the breakdown first; and possess ball-handling skills to link support play with the backs. Of course, this would not mean world-class players like Josh Kronfeld and Olivier Magne being lost to the game. They would merely reappear in another position and adjust accordingly, because they are versatile enough and good enough.

Rugby has also become so mediocre because of law-makers trying to resolve a problem by bringing in new rules – yet creating two extra ones instead, because they've not thought through the change properly. Classic examples for me are in the scrum and the line-out. Rugby, by its very nature, is supposed to be a competitive game, thirty players trying to get the better of one another in a hard, bruising, physical encounter. Often we do get mismatches, but the one area where you were always able to compete, at the very least, was at the set-piece. Not any more. How often do you see a scrum taken against the head – and because lifting is allowed in the line-out, we have reached the point where the non-throwing side do not even attempt to jump for the ball any more. They know they are not going to win possession, so they just take up defensive positions instead.

A mixture of the lack of space and daft changes in the laws has created our third major problem: rugby has become so territorial that kicking accurately is the key to any team's game plan. When I go to matches these days, I see youngsters applauding a good kick to touch as if their team has won the game. Nothing wrong with that, except that because of the line-out change I have just discussed, their side is bound to lose possession as the other team have the throw-in. What saddens me most, though, is that youngsters today sometimes seem to identify more with that sort of thing than a winger beating two men on the spot and running in for a try. In my view they should be applauding a flash of magic that makes your pulse race, not something like a kick to touch which I would class as earthy.

I was once labelled a kicking fly-half and when I started playing you could kick direct to touch from any part of the field – even ten yards from the opposition try-line – if you wanted to gain a further five yards. You would concede the throw at the line-out, of course, but at least in those days the set-piece was competitive. It was the Australian Rugby Union that suggested only being able to kick direct to touch from inside your 25-yard line, one of the better rule changes that has been made. A newspaper reporter told me at the time, 'Well Barry, this is the end for you because you won't be able to kick any more.' I told him that, on the contrary, it was the best news I had received in ages. I explained that whereas other fly-halfs were merely big thumpers of the ball, I could put the ball to my boot and, like a good golfer, select exactly how I wanted to kick it – the big thumper, a grubber kick, a little floater into space, a clever chip. Other fly-halfs who were regarded as marvellous rugby players were suddenly getting disastrous reviews, finding themselves being put under pressure in games and at times even hacking the ball behind them! That particular rule-change, by contrast, was music to my ears and I believe the period following it saw youngsters learning how to kick properly.

That was fine for a while, but these days it has gone full circle with the game becoming so territorial that you even see frequent examples of rival full-backs exchanging five or six booming kicks in the same sequence of play in a bid to gain positional advantage. In fact, 90 per cent of an international team's game plan is to get the ball down into the opposition 25 and sort it out from there. The thinking, the panache, the ability to create space from deep, have all gone, I'm afraid. Hence my suggestion of thirteen-a-side to try to bring some of it back. There are recent games which stand out at international level because of the thrilling tries scored – such as the French second-half magic in that World Cup semi-final against the Kiwis. There was also Brian O'Driscoll's three-try wonder show as Ireland beat France in Paris in March 2000 and I particularly loved Wales's 32–31 victory over England at Wembley the previous spring. But by and large these examples are rarities. Let's act, while we still have the chance!

There are other areas the administrators need to tackle as a matter of priority as well, the most important of the lot concerning the tens of thousands of younger players who have simply walked away from the game. At least the English Rugby Football Union is addressing that one at grass-roots level because those in power at Twickenham have spent £100,000 on setting up regional directors who will ask coaches to go around schools and encourage pupils to play and enjoy their rugby. The other home unions need to follow that lead.

What alarmed me perhaps more than anything else, in the past five years, was an article I read in *The Times*. I received a telephone call from a friend asking if I had seen what the newspaper had written about me in that morning's edition. Without blowing any trumpets, to this day I remain in the media spotlight somewhere around the world, so my reply was a flippant, 'Oh no, what have I said this time?' This one, however, was different because my friend went on to explain that the article in question was not on the sports pages, but rather in the education section. Intrigued, I went down to the local newsagent's to buy a copy and as I turned to the education pages I immediately saw a picture of myself staring out of the page. The article was about the decline of sport in schools and to highlight the problem *The Times* had cited my old haunting ground, Gwendraeth Grammar, as an example. This was the school that had produced me, Gareth Davies, Carwyn James and Jonathan Davies, four Wales fly-halfs. Yet the article stated the school was unable to fulfil a Saturday fixture because it could not find fifteen players.

I found that quite staggering and I recall remarking at the time that the PE master must have found the situation embarrassing. Gwendraeth Grammar had produced such a conveyor belt of capped internationals that, in modern-day parlance, it would have been regarded as a sporting academy. At least two senior teams played every weekend and there were the under-15, under-14 and under-13 sides too. The physics master would look after one side, the maths teacher would take charge of another. Sometimes they would drive from places like Llandovery (over an hour away) on their day off just to make sure their team was OK. Yet here was the school with that fantastic rugby pedigree unable to field a side. Not only did that sadden me, it also angered me and I believe questions have to be asked about why it has been allowed to happen. I'm also sure that these problems exist throughout the United Kingdom. Other examples will not be as great, because the history of past names will not be involved, but the principle remains the same.

The penny at last seems to have dropped at government level, to the point where sporting excellence at school, if not as big an issue as education in general, is becoming an important part of any political election manifesto.

I was reading another article in one of the national broadsheets, this time *The Observer*, that was headlined, 'Scandal of the playing-fields that Labour did not rescue'. The story, written by the newspaper's sports news correspondent Denis Campbell, was based on Labour's pre-election pledge to put an end to the controversial Conservative policy of selling off school playing-fields for housing development. Tony Blair has always insisted he wants to protect our sporting heritage, yet the newspaper pointed to the fact that hundreds of playing-fields have still disappeared under bricks and mortar during Labour's time in office, and that in the previous fifteen months alone, more than a hundred had gone. This was despite a clamour from the Football Association and the Rugby Football Union for sell-offs to be halted immediately.

Labour know they simply cannot let this go on. One big change from the Tories' time in office is that any school wishing to raise funds by selling a playing-field to developers must first seek the permission of the Secretary of State for Education. Should he so wish, the Cabinet Minister can block any plan. The fact that he has been given this power indicates that Labour are clearly worried by the whole affair and at least Tony Blair, who does not want Britain to become a nation of couch potatoes, appears to be trying to address the problem of declining sporting standards, from top to bottom.

Three of the areas the authorities have to look at in rugby are cheating, violence and expression of skills – the last of which can only come with enjoyment of playing the game. But let us start with the first one. What is the difference between gamesmanship and cheating? Many people probably think they are the same, but there is a distinct difference. Gamesmanship, certainly at the highest level, is an accepted part of the sport, where you attempt to get one over on your opponent – maybe by cunningly lulling them into encroaching offside, whatever. Cheating, on the other hand, is when you make a deliberate attempt to con the referee.

The most blatant example I have witnessed came at Cardiff Arms Park when the New Zealander Andy Haden dived out of the line-out against Wales in 1978, conning referee Roger Quittenton into awarding a penalty. (Brian McKechnie successfully slotted the kick to give the Kiwis a 13–12 win.)

I was in the press-box, fully seventy yards away from the incident, and the moment I saw Haden go down I got to my feet and shouted, 'Hollywood'. With the Lions, I had seen at first hand how New Zealand react when their script is not going to plan and it most certainly was going wrong for them that day with Wales looking on course for victory. At once I knew this was a piece of acting by Haden: the only thing missing were points for artistic impression! If Haden had conned a Welsh player, fine, that would have been gamesmanship and I could have understood it. But to do it to the referee was unacceptable, totally unforgivable. Then, to compound everything, Haden brought out a book a few years afterwards in which he admitted to the dive. What was the point of that, other than to rub Welsh people's noses in the dirt again, not to mention that of Mr Quittenton, who received some vitriolic hate mail in the press after his wrong decision? You cannot encourage the sort of thing Haden did, because youngsters pick up bad habits as well as good ones.

Violence is another area that needs to be addressed. I watch school games and see players being manhandled and bullied. No one wants to witness that. Sometimes people say to me that I must be disappointed David did not follow in my footsteps as a top rugby player, but I reply that on the contrary, I much preferred to see him – and Kate, Lucy and Anna for that matter – play tennis, hockey and other sports. I did watch David playing in games when he was fourteen and fifteen and from the sidelines I would wince at the ferocity of some of the tackling. But at least that was fair rugby. In other matches I have watched, bullies have gone in to take out certain opposing players early on – and, most alarmingly of the lot, with the full encouragement of their coaches on the touch-line. We have to drive that sort of thing out of rugby. Played properly, the game is physical enough without that type of nonsense making it even worse.

The other area that needs to be addressed is the technical development of young players. I was recently invited to hand out the medals at a mini-rugby (nine-a-side) presentation night. I won't name the club involved, because I do not want to embarrass them; but they were based in mid-Glamorgan and whereas I expected to be there for an hour in the evening, and had made arrangements for dinner, I did not manage to get away until gone 11.30 p.m. I had to telephone to cancel my restaurant booking.

There were awards for the under-8s, under-9s, under-10s, under-11s, under-12s . . . Hey, I was the only person in that room who did not collect a cup or medal that night! You cannot knock winners, but there were so many of them that night I felt it was indecent. This was nothing to do with youngsters developing skills and enjoying the game – it was only about winning, winning and winning. More often than not, too, those games were won by just two of the bigger youngsters who grabbed the ball every time, scored the tries, kicked the goals and never gave their team-mates a look-in. What was the point of the other seven members of the side winning medals when they had hardly touched the ball? Imagine a youngster going home and saying, 'We won. Justin scored the tries, Justin kicked the penalties, Justin took the conversions.' That youngster would probably become disenchanted and want to give up the game – a sad loss to rugby, because as certain players develop physically over the years, they actually turn out to be the most talented of the bunch.

I'm the first to admit that in my school days I scored more than my fair share of tries. But sometimes, as a game loomed, our PE master, Mr Williams, would tell me I was not playing in the first half in order to give others a fair chance. He was absolutely right to do that, too. I have played in these mini-tournaments and the big thing was always to encourage people to enjoy taking part in the game. That is the philosophy they have in football on the continent, at academies like Ajax's in Amsterdam, where they teach and develop skills and do not try to stifle youngsters into becoming one-dimensional. Winning matters, but it can come once those basics are right.

I did not like what I was seeing that night in mid-Glamorgan, where the whole emphasis was put on winning. 'We have not lost at this level for two years,' one of the coaches boasted to me. But did the team really win, or did just two players in that team and the coach win? I could see they were becoming obsessed, but as I had been invited there as the main guest, I did not feel it was my place to butt in with what I felt. Instead I gave a little speech pointing out that this particular team had won tournaments in Wales, England, Scotland and Ireland and should be congratulated. I flippantly went on, 'You'll probably conquer Canada next'. The comment went down like a lead balloon – because they had only hired a jumbo jet and were flying out to Toronto the following weekend! They probably won that tournament too – but I wonder how many of those players will lose interest in rugby because of the pressure put on them to win every match at such a young age.

I have outlined enough reasons there for you to understand why I have my concerns for the future. That said, please do not think everything is doom and gloom, because it is not. I just feel that unless I, and other former players, highlight these problems, we would be doing the game a great disservice. If we point out the pitfalls, maybe the administrators and authorities will act and do something about them. In fact I expect that they will. Deep down I still believe rugby is the best game going and I love it dearly – but there is the central point. Rugby gave me everything I have. I want others coming into the game in the next ten to twenty years to have the same opportunities for fun and excitement. But unless things change for the better, my concern is that those opportunities are not going to be present.

FOURTEEN

WORLD CUPS – THE LOWS AND THE HIGHS

I believe I am probably one of the few people, even among the press corps, who has been to every one of the World Cup tournaments, from the inaugural competition in New Zealand in 1987 through to the event hosted by Wales in 1999. I feel I speak with some knowledge, therefore, when I hold up my hands and come clean in saying that the last tournament in Wales was the biggest shambles of the lot – a disaster off the pitch and a disaster on it with the dull fare of the rugby served up.

While I have made it clear that I would not swap my rugby era for any other, the one thing we former players universally agree upon is that we would love to have played in a World Cup or two. The razzmatazz that goes with the five-week tournament makes the competition so special. Indeed, after the soccer World Cup, which I rank as number one these days, and the Olympics, the rugby World Cup is the third-biggest sporting event on earth.

Wales 1999 should have been the best. Unfortunately, as someone who also saw New Zealand 1987, England 1991 and South Africa 1995 – the lot from the opening ceremony through to the final – I have to say it was without question the worst. The sad thing is that I saw it coming, too. I remember a conversation I had with a huge Afrikaans man (which of them isn't huge?) shortly before leaving Johannesburg after that memorable South African victory over New Zealand in 1995. The game may not have been an out-and-out rugby classic; but the image of Nelson Mandela, wearing François Pienaar's green-and-gold number 6 shirt, presenting the cup to Pienaar himself is one of the images that will never leave my thoughts. As I was packing my bags to leave, this man said to me in that strange South African brogue, 'Listeen maann, after this World Cup you've got a lot of work to do to match it in four years' time in Cardiff.'

Four years sounds a fair way off. But even then, with the experience of three World Cups under my belt and knowing everything the tournament entails from the playing side and administration of matches to organising hotel accommodation and travel, I had bad vibes of 'Has it come too early for Wales?' Unfortunately, as I feared, the words of my Afrikaner friend did indeed come back to haunt us four years on. There were problems with the new Millennium Stadium in Cardiff, venue for the final, which very nearly was not even completed on time. Attendance figures at some of the grounds, notably in Scotland, were dismal owing to stupid prices being charged for tickets. We had a situation in Wales where tickets were double booked so spectators could not get into their seats. The build-up was dreadful in terms of marketing the event, a point acknowledged by Rugby World Cup chairman Leo Williams when the Australian made a fact-finding visit to Cardiff a few months before the tournament was due to start. I even know of people who turned up for the traditional Cup-final dinner on the night the tournament finished – and whose names were *on* the seating plan – only for them to walk away in disgust, barred from going inside the room because they'd not been given their actual tickets. I am sorry to say that as a proud Welshman I found the whole thing embarrassing.

Then, to compound everything, whereas the other tournaments had produced some thrilling matches (notably in South Africa four years previously), Wales 1999 was by and large one big bore. Australia emerged as the eventual winners, not because they were the team with most flair in the tournament, but because they had the best defence and were the most functional. In fact, had it not been for thirty minutes of second-half French magic in the Twickenham semi-final against red-hot favourites New Zealand, the rugby would have been non-rateable. It was that uninspiring. I found the final between Australia and the French, the supposed showpiece match, such a turn-off that I got up from my seat shortly after half-time and left the ground. I could not watch any more.

I realise Rugby World Cup Ltd was able to deliver a handsome profit in excess of £40 million. If profit equals success then this was the most successful tournament yet. In reality it was anything but and the figures mentioned make you wonder just how much of a roaring success the five weeks really could have been had everything been run as professionally and properly as it should have been. It came as no surprise to me when, a week after dictating these words for this book,

Leo Williams went on the record to slam the running of the tournament in his official report. The critical points he made were very similar, but few others have had the guts to stand up and tell the truth.

The one thing I will always remember as a huge plus factor was the fantastic day in Cardiff on 1 October 1999, when Prince Charles opened the tournament. I was privileged to be involved in the opening ceremony, which also featured top artists such as Shirley Bassey, Michael Ball, the opera singer Bryn Terfel and rock group Catatonia. Some of us so-called golden oldies, including Gareth Edwards, J.P.R. Williams and myself, were asked to walk around the pitch at twenty-yard intervals before the opening game (Wales v. Argentina) to commemorate some of the great moments of Welsh rugby. As we did so, many of our tries were shown on giant video screens situated at either end of the stadium.

After a marvellous luncheon hosted by Rugby World Cup Ltd inside one of the Millennium Stadium's plush hospitality suites, we former players were asked to remain behind as the other 200-odd guests who had been dining with us went to take up their seats in the stand. Suddenly, to a man we felt nervous. There were 72,500 people packed inside the Millennium Stadium, not to mention the millions watching on worldwide television, and we had not been out in front of a crowd like that for years. I rarely used to feel butterflies like that when I played, but on this occasion I was on edge – and I did not even have to throw, catch or kick a ball! I'm told Gerald Davies, whom I felt should have been out there with us, was doing the loudspeaker announcements to introduce us and apparently he was brilliant. I have to take the word of other people for that, because the cacophony of noise from the crowd was so great I could not hear a thing. Gareth led us out and I was next in line, followed by JPR. As we turned the first corner from left to right, the noise went off the Richter scale. Gareth turned around to say something to me – I know that because I could see his mouth moving – but I could not make out any of the words! It was one of the most emotional moments I have known and we each needed the big glass of wine we were handed as we went back inside again afterwards.

That was a rare good moment, however, for the overall organisation left an awful lot to be desired. The moment Wales were given the World Cup, the bulldozers and demolition men should have come in to knock down the old Cardiff Arms Park ground and start building the new Millennium Stadium which was replacing it. What we did not need was the Welsh Rugby Union playing extra internationals and domestic cup finals, because the profits made from those games were loose change in the overall scheme of things when it came to funding the building of the stadium. More important than the money was the precious time that was being taken up, the passing weeks and months. I felt that every month lost would quantify to two afterwards. The race against time to get the ground ready for the opening match was blatantly obvious to everyone towards the end, but four years earlier I feared that was going to happen. I told members of the Welsh Rugby Union of my fears, but they responded: 'Barry, what's the matter with you? Today these things can be built in no time.' They seemed to think they were putting up a bungalow or a garage, when in fact this was one of the biggest engineering projects known in Wales.

As time dragged on, the cost of the project rose from £101 million to £121 million. There were rows between the Welsh Rugby Union and Cardiff RFC, who owned part of the land they wanted to develop, and everyone started to get shaky. We needed to utilise every second. Yet memo followed memo, meeting followed meeting, e-mails and faxes winged around the world as those in charge tried to overcome the obstacles – and the one thing that kept passing was time. As the pressure grew, Leo Williams made a trip from Australia to Cardiff to see what was happening for himself, despite the messages of reassurance from the organisers in Wales. When he arrived, literally just a few months before the tournament was due to start, and first set eyes on the building site that was soon to host the final, Williams must have thought a bomb had landed in the Welsh capital.

I understand contingency plans were drawn up to take the final to Twickenham if the Millennium Stadium was not completed on time. Too right. Williams and his colleagues would have been mad not to do that. It would have been an embarrassment for Wales if we had lost the chance to host the final, but one day I suspect we will find out just how close they actually were to implementing those standby plans.

On his trip to Wales, Williams also stressed how surprised he was at the lack of marketing of the tournament, pointing out there was no merchandising to purchase. It was so different from South Africa four years earlier, but what shocked Williams was that this was going on in Wales. Around the world, rugby is known as the national sport of Wales. I was asked to do various things on the commercial side, but no one would give me a guaranteed contract – and I could understand that, because who knew for certain whether the event would go ahead or not in Cardiff? In the end it did proceed as planned, although even on 30 September, the night before the opening game, the contractors

On your marks . . . From the left: Bobby Moore, myself, Roger Taylor, Tony Jacklin, Joe Bugner and Jackie Stewart, at Crystal Palace in the 100 metres during the first *Superstars* contest. I won the event — but my time wouldn't have qualified me for the semi-finals of the women's race in the AAA championships, held at the same venue the following weekend!

The Three Musketeers. Myself,
Gerald Davies and Gareth Edwards.

Two proud Welshmen. With Ian Rush, before a golf tournament.

TOP: I sit back and listen as Gareth makes a point. We had been invited over to Spain to speak about rugby development, the only 'official' time I have been asked for my thoughts by rugby administrators.

ABOVE: Pop star status? Well, they did make a record about me, to the tune of the Welsh song 'Sospan Fach'. This is the sleeve.

You beauty! It's a smile not a grimace (honest!) as I watch my tee-shot soar towards the green.

TOP: Proud man. With Kate, Anna and Lucy.

ABOVE: My nephews, Craig and Scott Quinnell, who have themselves gone on to shine in the red shirt of Wales.

Sporting Excellence. Anna was a top hockey player. Here she is
with me, after being selected for the Wales Under-18 side.
[Courtesy of *Western Mail and Echo*]

TOP: On the buses. No, I'm not making a comeback.
I was participating in a television programme
about the old Cardiff Arms Park.

ABOVE: On the wall. Same programme, but this
time the advertising is on a billboard.

were still working on the stadium. Earlier in the year they'd had to seek permission from the local authority to work through the night, while even today the stadium complex is far from finished.

There were other mistakes in Cardiff, the hub of the tournament. The biggest involved the distribution of tickets. There were many instances of doubling up on seats, where people would turn up to the place allocated on their ticket, only to find someone else had the same spot. This was totally inexcusable for any sporting event, let alone one of this magnitude. Still, at least every game in Wales was a sell-out – unlike in Scotland, where Murrayfield looked deserted for a few matches, some even involving the Scots themselves. What they should have done, of course, was sell the tickets cheaper and give thousands away to schools.

As for the rugby itself, let us just say here that it was the least exciting of the four World Cups. I do not, however, blame the players; I blame the way the modern game has evolved. I have already mentioned that rugby has become so confrontational that the fittest, hardest and certainly the most disciplined teams will, nine times out of ten, emerge as winners – more often than not, in matches not worth remembering. Australia, as victors of the 1999 tournament, sum up my argument perfectly. They came to do a clinical job to lift the cup in the final against France and they did it very well, but from a spectator's point of view the eighty minutes were poor from start to finish.

That was the tournament for you, though. Fiji, Japan and Argentina produced odd moments that would provide walk-on parts for a video compiled about good rugby, but only the French really captured the imagination with that shock semi-final victory over New Zealand. Their second-half performance at Twickenham gave me a lift and proved that, while strength and defence do dominate, there is still room in the modern game for will-o'-the-wisp, native cunning: the ability to do the unexpected. To a certain extent, though, we paid the penalty for that semi-final brilliance because the one thing you can say about the French is that their consistency is in being inconsistent. They could not produce another big performance just a week afterwards – they do not possess the concentration span to do that, and Australia duly proved far too strong in running out 35–12 winners. I had left the ground in boredom way before John Eales was presented with the cup by Her Majesty the Queen. (Ironic that one, for twenty-four hours earlier thousands of Australians had been ranting and raving about wanting to become a republic as they held their referendum vote on the issue. That one, by the way, went in Her Majesty's favour.)

I was not the only one who found that final to be a turgid affair, for even Australians were not exactly thrilled with what they were watching. A couple of Aussies were sitting next to me and before the game I signed autographs for them and we struck up a conversation. We settled down to enjoy the match, but within twenty minutes those Australians, and others, turned around to start talking again. Someone then said, 'Can we have a photograph please, Barry?' Others came forward to ask for more autographs. They simply were not interested in what was going on down below them on the pitch.

For the previous three World Cups, Scottish Equitable and Ian Robertson teamed up to produce a book on each competition and I was asked to name a man of the tournament each time. In 1987 my choice was the New Zealand skipper David Kirk; in 1991 it was the great Australian wing David Campese; and in 1995 who else but the awesome Jonah Lomu? I'm glad I did not have to do it in 1999 for I would have found it extremely difficult to select one individual who had set the world on fire. The sponsors officially named Tim Horan as man of the tournament, but while I have nothing against the selection and agree the Australian centre probably deserved the honour, to me his selection represented what rugby had become – hard, physical and defence dominated. Horan is a talented player. He is solid, he is professional, he does not make many mistakes and, indeed, you can probably build a midfield around him. However, he does not excite or produce that magic ingredient like Campese or Lomu, does he? Youngsters aspire to be a Lomu. I doubt they would aspire to be a Horan.

As for the performance of the host nation, it was a bumpy ride for a while but in the end Graham Henry's Wales side did as well as anyone could have expected, even though they came into the tournament on the back of some super wins over England, France and South Africa. I did not envisage Wales setting the world alight in their opener against Argentina, simply because the pressure surrounding the whole occasion was too great. What concerned me was the naïve option-taking that I saw in their narrow 23–18 win, while the basics of support play had to be worked upon. Wales beat Japan in the next game, but they lost their last pool match and had to rely on the Japanese doing them a favour by keeping Argentina to within 49 points to ensure they topped their group and remained in Cardiff for the quarter-finals.

At least Wales managed to avoid having to go through the quarter-final play-off phase, unlike England, who, after New Zealand had topped their group, had to meet Fiji in an extra match for a place in the last eight. Ireland had to go through the same process. They finished second in their pool to Australia (no real surprise there) but then inexplicably lost to Argentina in their play-off. Wales did go straight through to a last-eight showdown against the Aussies. They did well, without threatening to topple the would-be world champions, going down 24–9. I always felt the Australians were able to step up another gear when necessary in that game.

Not only did Wales have to face fifteen battle-hardened Aussies on the pitch: a glance at the programme suggested the visitors even brought their own prime minister as referee! No, only joking. This Bob Hawke is actually a New Zealander.

The referee did not have a good game, as it happened. He missed a knock-on which led to an Australian try; and he pulled Wales back to award them a penalty at one point, when they were in a great position to go for a try and he should have played advantage. Nonetheless, there was no disgrace in Wales going out to the eventual winners. Objective One in getting that far had been reached. The same with Scotland, who lost 30–18 to New Zealand in their quarter-final match.

England, on the other hand . . . ? The blunt truth for Clive Woodward's men is that they had enough talent to go further. Losing 44–21 in the quarter-finals to South Africa, on that famous day in Paris when Jannie de Beer kicked an incredible five drop-goals, must have come as a bitter pill to swallow. England's style of rugby was never going to set pulses racing, but with their huge pack of forwards and a decent set of half-backs in Matt Dawson and Jonny Wilkinson to keep the ball in front of them, Woodward's men should have proved a big, tough outfit to beat.

The coach did not help matters, though, with his team selection policy, for he seemed totally confused about which fifteen players made up his first choice line-up. When I played there was always one thing I wanted to know – am I in the team as a regular or not? I did not want to have to worry about scanning the next team sheet to see if my name was on it, or dreading the telephone call that would say I was dropped. There is nothing like a settled side to provide confidence and understanding and England should have had one by the time the tournament kicked off. They did not and ultimately that cost them dearly.

OK, Woodward could afford to leave out Martin Johnson or Jason Leonard in the 'lesser' matches, the two forwards knowing full well they would be back in the thick of things for the big games. But there was genuine uncertainty about far too many positions, with players not seeming to know whether they would be in or out. This was highlighted perfectly against South Africa when Woodward had too many players on the substitutes' bench who should have been in his starting line-up – including Wilkinson, who would have grown in stature as the tournament progressed, but who was handled badly. It is vital a fly-half knows the number 10 jersey is his, but Woodward kept fluctuating between Wilkinson and Paul Grayson. Wilkinson was the fall guy against the Springboks when his flair may just have given England the extra dimension they needed.

When players feel the coach is uncertain in his thoughts, his lack of confidence manifests itself in them. Then, when things go wrong on the field, as they did with de Beer's five drop-goals, the players lack the collectiveness and leadership to turn things around. They did not seem to have a definitive game plan and scuttled around the pitch that afternoon in Paris with little real direction. Someone should have grabbed the situation by the scruff of the neck, gathered everyone around and insisted, 'We must get back to plan A.' Oh yes, the forwards grouped together a few times during breaks in play when someone was injured, but you sensed they were gathering for the sake of it. Nothing positive seemed to be conveyed. If it was, it most certainly was not put into action.

Woodward deservedly took real flak afterwards, because to say his team under-performed is an understatement. No one thought England would take apart New Zealand, Australia or even South Africa. But we did expect them to perform well at the very least – to be eliminated having fought together, the players totally shattered having given everything. To me England did not even compete as well as the opposition towards the end of that South Africa game and with the World Cup coming around only once every four years, that represented a real lost opportunity. Woodward's men missed the boat after years of preparation for that moment, having played way below their best.

That said, I believe Woodward has learned from the experience and bounced back superbly. His job was very much on the line and he was expected to be out of work before the start of the first Six Nations campaign in early 2000. Having taken time off to reflect, Clive probably thought he had nothing to lose, so he decided just to go for it. Clive was a very gifted centre himself for England and Leicester and you would have thought he wanted his team to perform in the same exciting manner. It appears he is thinking that way, because after the

World Cup débâcle he drafted in a number of talented young players – particularly among the backs – who produced some thrilling rugby in winning the Six Nations (even if their Grand Slam march was halted in the final game by Scotland).

It was almost a last throw of the dice by Woodward and he was helped by circumstances too. An injury to Martin Johnson meant Matt Dawson took over as skipper and he was a revelation. Jeremy Guscott retired, so Woodward brought young Matt Tindall into the centre and he has been superb. Wilkinson has at last been given the number 10 jersey and, as I suspected, he is growing into the fly-half role. Fate has played a part, but the way Clive has encouraged them has been superb. I know hindsight is a great thing, but I bet he wished he had adopted this more expansive approach with the younger players in the World Cup itself.

If Rugby World Cup '99 was a disaster in my opinion, the 1995 tournament in South Africa was a roaring success on and off the pitch and turned out to be my personal favourite. I travelled out as a BBC commentator with Nigel Starmer-Smith. From the moment we went with our little accreditation forms to the media office at the Newlands ground, Cape Town, to a month afterwards when we left Johannesburg, we were treated with total courtesy and respect. Normally you find that when you put men in official positions at tournaments like this, they become right Mr Jobsworths. Even when you are polite as can be, they will find a reason why you cannot go into certain areas, cannot do this, that or the other. Not in South Africa. 'Yes sir,' they would say – unable, it seemed, to do enough for us. Everything went so smoothly. Then came the rather more important double bonus of seeing the new post-apartheid South Africa and the wonderful rugby with which we were entertained.

Having the advantage of the whole sporting world backing you, rugby nations and non-rugby playing nations, was a distinct advantage to South Africa. It came as no surprise to me when Australia wilted under the pressure in the opening match in Cape Town and the Springboks emerged 27–18 victors. Even the great David Campese was caught up in the tension of the occasion, losing his footing to let South Africa in for one of their two tries. Mr Mandela, who had been down on the pitch beforehand officially opening the tournament, wore a huge beaming smile at the final whistle. He did not stop smiling for the next few weeks, either, for that game set the tempo for the most amazing month to follow. Most matches were sell-outs, even the lesser games being given an incredible sales pitch by the marketing men.

It was the 1995 tournament, of course, where we also first set eyes on a certain young mega-star in the making – welcome to the rugby world from Jonah Lomu. Just before the final in Johannesburg between South Africa and New Zealand, I had to name my man of the tournament, explaining the reasons why, for Ian Robertson's book. I did not have pen and paper on me, but was able to borrow some from Trevor McDonald, who was out there with ITN doing interviews with Nelson Mandela. Trevor had to smile at my request, asking, 'What is the BBC coming to – has it reached the stage of them having to scrounge pen and paper from the opposition?'

Lomu was so far ahead of everyone else in that tournament that he could have had the worst game of his career in the final and it would not have altered my choice one iota. England, and Tony Underwood, must still have nightmares about the way he charged through them for four tries in New Zealand's 45–29 semi-final thrashing of Will Carling's battered side. I have never seen anything like Lomu before. Not only is the man physically massive for a wing, standing at six foot five inches, he is so exceptionally fast with it. People look for flaws, argue that defensively he can be dragged out of position and that he lacks concentration. My retort to that is that if you have a player as good as Lomu in your team, he can lose concentration as often as he likes! Focus on his try-scoring strengths instead: if he is out of the match for a while, his New Zealand team-mates should watch his defensive positioning and say 'Back five yards, Jonah' if necessary. It *is* supposed to be a team game, isn't it?

As it was, Lomu was on the losing side to the Springboks, who won the final 15–12, but he could have sealed the game for New Zealand in the first few minutes. Lomu came off his wing, causing total chaos as he took a pass from Andrew Mehrtens, and he had enough room to go back outside and leave the Springbok full-back André Joubert stranded. Instead, Lomu took Joubert head on, got his legs tangled up and another South African arrived to help bundle him over. After that the South Africans put two men on Lomu every time. As summariser for BBC Radio Five, I remember saying on air that I was amazed the New Zealand centres Frank Bunce and Walter Little did not seem to realise this and miss him out more, using the space Lomu had created elsewhere. Being as powerful as he is, Lomu had to have the two tacklers every time because it was as hard to rip the ball away from him as from a big lock-forward. New Zealand did not use the decoy system enough, however, and they paid the penalty.

I honestly believe that had that final been played another four times, the New Zealanders would have won the lot. On the day, though, they did not read the script right, got their tactics confused, and – like Australia on the first day – got caught up in the emotion of the occasion. I know there were rumours of a New Zealand pre-match meal being tampered with. That is conjecture, although I have to say New Zealand certainly seemed to lack conviction that day: there was a back foot nervousness about them, as if they had question marks over themselves. I have never seen that from a New Zealand side before. When the final whistle was blown, some of the South Africans stood in shock. Then blacks and whites began hugging each other in sheer joy and finally we had that image of Mandela presenting Pienaar with the cup. I know people in Wales go on about 'I was there' moments, and generally it is an overused phrase. But believe me, after what I had seen of apartheid before, that really was an 'I was there' occasion. It was simply monumental.

If the Kiwis failed on that occasion, at least they triumphed on their home soil in 1987 when we didn't really know what to expect from the first tournament in terms of organisation, stadiums and standard of rugby. It was new to everybody. Some of the games were fantastic, the best of the lot being France's unexpected 30–24 semi-final victory over Australia when Serge Blanco scored that memorable last-minute try in the corner. The Aussies were so distraught at losing, with everyone having anticipated a big final shoot-out between themselves and New Zealand, that they did not want to travel for the third-and fourth-place play-off match with Wales. Paul Thorburn's last-minute conversion won that game 22–21 for Wales, but it was a false result because Australia had a player sent off early on and played with fourteen men for most of the time. Yes, Wales got the bronze medal, but I knew we were way behind the leaders of the pack.

Those leaders proved, as expected, to be New Zealand, who easily defeated the French 29–9 in the final. However the real winner was the game of rugby because you could tell, in terms of sponsorship and media coverage, that this tournament was here to remain.

I named David Kirk as man of the tournament in 1987 and four years on, when the four home unions and France hosted the event, I had no hesitation in giving the honour to David Campese. What can you say about Campo? Outrageous runs, entertainer extraordinaire, box-office quality, his sublime skills were evident for everyone to see. Never more so than in the big semi-final shoot-out with New Zealand in Dublin when Campese was brilliant in leading his side through to a 16–6 victory over their great rivals. Not only was Campese player of the tournament, he was also character of the tournament. Only he could come out with lines declaring that England were boring, that their players were plastic – and get away with it.

This caused a fair bit of mirth on my behalf when I was asked to present Campese with the *Daily Express* Overseas Sportsman of the Year award at a lunch at The Hilton in London. I was sharing a table with six of the England players who had been beaten 12–6 in the final, and who did not exactly have Campese top of their Christmas card list after his outspoken comments about them. When I got up to make my presentation speech I said it was a one-horse race; that Campese was definitely the winner; that his performances had left me enthralled. At one point I looked up at the England players still sitting at the table and noticed them wincing. When I went on to say that even the players would acknowledge Campo was the undisputed winner of this award, there was a look of total and utter horror on the faces of those England men! I had a wry smile to myself as I walked down from the stage and back to our table.

When England, and their manager Geoff Cooke, look closely at the video of that final, I suspect they will come to the conclusion that they had enough pressure positions to win the cup. Australia were certainly not at their best, but England foolishly fell into the trap of listening to the people who insisted they had to change their game plan. The strength of that England XV was up front, where Jason Leonard, Brian Moore, Jeff Probyn, Paul Ackford and Wade Dooley formed a formidable front five – supplemented by their excellent back row, with Rob Andrew's boot keeping them going forward. A tight game based around that pack and Andrew's boot had taken England to the final and, despite being labelled dull, they should have stuck with it. Instead, they listened to various media people insisting the style that got England to Twickenham was not going to be good enough to win them the final itself because Australia would gain parity up front.

I knew, however, that you simply cannot change your dance routine at that stage. When you have gone that far, you are there to win the thing by tried and trusted means; and when Cooke and Will Carling, the England captain that day, have quieter moments to themselves, they will probably reflect on what might have been had they stuck to what they knew. England certainly created enough danger positions, but then wasted them by throwing the ball around for the sake of it and losing possession, instead of grinding down the Australians with the forward power play which had taken them to the final.

That 1991 World Cup was the best opportunity we have had yet to see a British nation break the Southern Hemisphere domination of the tournament. Will we see England, Wales, Scotland or, for that matter, Ireland lift the cup one day? An obvious gulf in class is there and the answer to the question is a cautious 'we will have to see'. What I want to see more than anything, however, is the 2003 World Cup in Australia turn out to be a roaring success again, like the first three. I suspect the organisers will put Wales '99 to bed by ignoring what happened here and get on with doing things in a totally different fashion – because when it comes to plus points from the last tournament, they are very few and far between.

FIFTEEN

WALES, OH WAILS –
WHERE IT WENT WRONG

The great Bill Shankly once said, on hearing that other teams were planning to topple Liverpool's domination of British soccer: 'If they want to join us, they will have to come *up* and join us – because we are sure not going back down to them.' Wales, Scotland, Ireland and, to a lesser extent, England would do well to heed the great man's words and apply them to international rugby at the start of the new millennium. While people say we are making progress – indeed Wales and Ireland have done since New Zealanders Graham Henry and Warren Gatland came over as their respective coaches – they sometimes tend to overlook the fact that the Southern Hemisphere élite of New Zealand, Australia and South Africa are also improving at the same time. They don't just stand still you know: they're busy unearthing another Jonah Lomu, John Eales or André Joubert.

There is a saying in sport that the wheel goes around. If that is the case, it is a pretty big wheel for Welsh rugby, because the success days we saw in the 1970s are taking some time to come back around. The sad truth is that the Celtic nations are still a fair way off mixing it with the big guns and if we want to, we are going to have to reach their standards – they are not going to drop down to our level. The point Shanks was making was that it was no good other teams saying they were catching up just because *they* had improved 20 or 30 per cent. By the time they got to the level Liverpool were at, Shankly would have moved his team on to another dimension.

The better modern-day soccer analogy is Manchester United. Other Premiership sides fancy their chances of toppling the Reds, reckoning they will be as good in a couple of years if they can strengthen their side with a couple of key signings. They forget that United also improve themselves by making multi-million pound signings like

Dwight Yorke and Jaap Stam every year. If Manchester United improve just 10 per cent, the gap remains enormous, simply because of the higher level they are already at. That is exactly the situation with Welsh rugby at present, for while things have definitely taken a turn for the better since the appointment of Henry, there is still a very sizeable gap to close.

For me, the international scene can be divided into four 'leagues'. In Division One are the Southern Hemisphere trio, plus England and France when they are at their best. In Division Two are Wales, Scotland, Ireland and perhaps Argentina. In Division Three are the likes of Japan, Italy and Canada, with cannon fodder such as Spain and Portugal on the bottom rung of the ladder. If the teams in the top two divisions played each other and at the end of the sequence of matches you took an average score, there would be a difference of more than twenty-five points. That is the level we have to aspire to – and then higher again.

Yet do you know what the saddest thing of the lot is? In our midst, during the 1970s, Wales had perhaps the most brilliant and most visionary rugby guru in Carwyn James, the Picasso of rugby at the time, sitting right among us. Yet silly pettiness meant Wales ignored his message on the way forward, while the rest of the world – and particularly those Southern Hemisphere nations – lapped up his every word. They got better and better, Wales went into almost immediate rugby decline and things became so bad that we conceded almost 100 points in a Test match against South Africa in 1998.

The Welsh people have some marvellous traits, but one or two pretty awful ones too. Carwyn once said to me, some time after leading the Lions to that 1971 victory in New Zealand, that no matter how successful you are, your rugby philosophy and ideology are not necessarily taken on board in your own country. There can be a terrible jealousy factor in the Welsh psyche, a flaw in our make-up, which is a great pity. In a rugby sense, the most blatant exposé of this flaw was that Carwyn wasn't allowed to contribute and help the game in his own homeland. Tudor James, who used to write a column for the *Sunday Mirror* under the slogan, 'WHAT TUDOR SAYS TODAY OTHERS SAY TOMORROW', once told me that senior figures in Welsh rugby seemed to be scared stiff of Carwyn and the respect he was commanding. He crossed other borders besides rugby, became a sporting icon and was creating what would be dubbed as a manager's power-base in modern-day soccer parlance.

But those of us who knew Carwyn were fully aware that having a power-base would never have entered his thoughts. He wanted nothing more than to sit undemonstratively in the stands with his John Player fags and watch exciting young Welshmen perform in the manner he felt was right for our rugby future.

Carwyn made no bones about the fact that he was a proud Welshman. It is rumoured that he turned down an OBE because he did not believe in such honours. I suppose we will never know the truth of that one, but what is undisputed is that he was an above-board member of the Welsh nationalist political party. He even took on Labour's Jim Griffiths – who, after Aneurin Bevan and Lloyd George, was one of the greatest Welsh politicians in history – in an election for the Llanelli constituency. Jim, the first Secretary of State for Wales and a deputy leader of the Labour Party, had one of the biggest majorities in the United Kingdom and anyone else competing with him on a Welsh nationalist ticket would have lost their deposit. In those days the nationalists did not have the deserved profile they possess today. But Carwyn actually recorded more than 8,000 votes, which must rank as one of the great unwritten triumphs of post-war politics. The electorate did not vote for the Welsh nationalists, they voted for Carwyn. That is how much the public loved him.

Sadly, however, Carwyn felt people picked up on his politics and held it against him, warning that he was using rugby for other purposes. Tudor James once told me he was even visited by one person in authority who urged him to stop writing good articles about Carwyn. Tudor told him in no uncertain terms to get out of his house – and the following Sunday penned his best column yet about Carwyn!

While Carwyn's message was ignored here, in New Zealand they could not get enough of him. Carwyn was such a great communicator that on that Lions tour he had people hanging on his every word as he did countless round-table talks for them on the way forward for rugby. It was, perhaps, the most unselfish thing I have seen, for other coaches would have just shut up shop, fearing they would give away Lions secrets. Carwyn was astute enough, however, to know the New Zealanders could not get it right straight away. They heeded his advice for the future and got it right. Wales chose to ignore the message and then began the decline. We went through a terrible period when youngsters just could not get excited about their rugby. When I grew up I had stars like Cliff Morgan and Ken Jones to look up to. During the 1970s, I would like to think myself, Gareth and Gerald were people the teenagers of that era could respect. Suddenly, in the 1980s and for most of the 1990s, this huge chunk of Welsh youth had no one. There are multiple reasons for Welsh rugby's failure during that period, but without idols to revere, is it any surprise that youngsters went looking elsewhere for their icons? – notably to footballers from Liverpool, Manchester United and Arsenal.

The packed houses for club matches also disappeared. In the old days everyone was so one-eyed that they would applaud me in the red of Wales one week, cheering every successful kick, and boo me the following Saturday if I was playing for Cardiff at Newport, Llanelli or Swansea, willing me to miss every kick. That is how passionately everyone felt about the game, how absorbed they were in it. In fairness, in the past couple of years that has quietly begun to manifest itself again in Wales and we can thank Graham Henry for the way he has gone about the job. The first thing he had to do was understand what being Welsh meant and he picked it up pretty quickly, realising just how important rugby was to the people. Ironically, the next thing Henry had to do was tell the players themselves about their responsibility to the nation – and he had had to learn it himself first! Henry re-established the battling qualities in the Welsh team, the determination of everybody to fight for one another, the ability to close down doors with a solid defence. Basic ingredients in any international side really, but ones which had been missing from the Welsh team.

Before Henry came on the scene we had some pretty lean years, with Welsh fans having just one Triple Crown (1988) to celebrate in recent times – a lucky one with a last-second Paul Thorburn penalty against Ireland – and a Five Nations Championship (1994) when Ieuan Evans's team were easily beaten by England on the day they lifted the title courtesy of having the best points difference. Those were rare successes amid a catalogue of defeats which included the following: 49–6 by New Zealand in 1987; 52–3 and 54–9 by New Zealand in 1988; 63–6 and 38–3 (a record Cardiff defeat) by Australia and 71–8 by New South Wales in 1991; 42–3 by Australia in 1996; 42–7 at home to New Zealand in 1997; 96–13 by South Africa, 60–26 by England and 51–0 by France in 1998.

Current Welsh players, and some of those who have played throughout the past twenty years, have had a go at people like Gareth, Gerald, Mervyn Davies, J.J. Williams and me – those of us who have become established writers or broadcasters on the game – for criticising some of the colourless, passionless, commitmentless and running-around-like-headless-chickens displays they have served up.

But the Welsh supporters want the truth and they are knowledgeable on their rugby. So can you imagine what the reaction would have been had we gone into print to make excuses about the thrashings by saying the refereeing decisions went against Wales, the bounce of the ball was unlucky, or the performance was better than the scoreline suggested? As media analysts employed by newspapers, television and radio, we would not be honouring our contracts by doing that. But most important, I wouldn't feel I was being honourable to myself or the Welsh public.

As a player I knew that if I had a bad game, I would be criticised in the newspapers, and rightly so. It greatly saddens us old-timers to see cricket scores rattled up against Wales; to witness people leaving stadiums with glum faces, clearly hurt and with nothing to smile about. In one of the matches I believe the referee even blew up early to spare Wales further torture. The Southern Hemisphere nations do not want these sorts of results. The magnitude of triumph in a sporting contest is only as good as the respect you have for the opposition. If, when the final whistle goes, you have extracted every ounce from your body, you are physically and mentally shattered and the game has gone down to the wire, then you know you have achieved a victory that is really worthwhile. That is why beating New Zealand, not just once but twice, was the ultimate for me. In some of those aforementioned matches, however, it was more like a training exercise in the end for some of Wales's opponents.

Another thing that did not help the Welsh cause was the attitude among the hierarchy to finishing third in the 1987 World Cup. Through another last-minute Paul Thorburn kick, Wales had beaten an Australia side condemned to fourteen men for seventy-six minutes of the match after David Codey was sent off early on. The Aussies were so distraught at having lost to France in the semi-finals that they did not even want to fly to Rotorua in New Zealand for the third-and fourth-place play-off match. The game was meaningless to them. Yet the result was seen as a sign, according to some, that everything was rosy in the Welsh garden. 'Don't be silly, we are nowhere near being third-best team in the world,' I remember telling Welsh team manager Clive Rowlands, afterwards. Some statistics simply do not tell the truth and that was one of them. Everyone seemed conveniently to forget that we had just been beaten 49–6 by New Zealand in a meaningful match against fifteen players in the semi-finals.

I must say that under the Henry regime I thought the day of the cricket scores against Wales had gone, because he had brought back to the team the basic quality of 'fighting for the cause'. In 1999 the new coach led Wales to ten straight victories, reviving enthusiasm in our game. That is why in the 2000 Six Nations I found the 36–3 thumping by France, and then the embarrassment of losing 46–12 to England at Twickenham, tough defeats to stomach. Certainly against England, Wales seemed to go on to the field with almost an inferiority complex, as if they did not relish the eighty minutes of battle ahead. By the end they were like a rudderless ship and had England taken their chances, the margin of defeat would have been even greater.

That is when fate took a hand. A mixture of the dramatic eligibility row (which meant Henry could not call upon fellow Kiwis Shane Howarth and Brett Sinkinson until they provided documentary proof of Welsh roots) and injuries forced the Welsh coach to change his team. He brought in the twenty-two-year-old Llanelli full-back Matt Cardey, who had an outstanding début against Scotland, and the Scarlets' young fly-half Stephen Jones, who was named man of the match. Then Cardey was injured playing for his club side, so Henry had to bring in another youngster, Cardiff number 15 Rhys Williams, who proceeded to have an even better début against Ireland than Cardey did against the Scots!

To Wales's credit, they fought back with victories in those remaining games and with other youngsters also in the frame like flying left-wing Shane Williams and flanker Nathan Budgett, who looks a wonderful prospect, things are looking up again. Shane is a terrific talent, with startling pace and the ability to finish moves, although the one fear I have for him is that with an abundance of 16-stone plus wingers about, opposition coaches are liable to tell them just to run straight through the young Welshman. Tackling is not Shane's greatest strength and it is vital that Wales vary their tactics, particularly from defensive set-pieces, by sometimes bringing Shane inside and temporarily putting bulkier backs on the wing. What concerns me about Wales is the ageing front row, but at least the youngsters I have mentioned offer hope. Without going overboard, there is evidence to suggest we can keep improving and reach the next World Cup in reasonable nick – although, as I have already pointed out, that does not necessarily mean we can catch the Southern Hemisphere trio, since they will keep improving too.

Ireland also have reason for optimism, having in the last couple of years encouraged, rather than insisted, that their top stars play their rugby in Ireland itself. The plan seems to have worked: we've seen Ulster winning the European Cup, Munster reaching the final too and

Leinster developing into a more than useful side. Perhaps Ireland's weakness, which is a lack of numbers in terms of players, is actually being turned into their very strength. Because of the dearth in numbers they have provinces, rather than club sides. That means their players are mixing with the best in Europe on a regular enough basis to prepare them for international rugby and turn Ireland into a dangerous XV. I do like the look of some of their young backs, notably young Brian O'Driscoll in the centre. His three-try performance in the Six Nations victory over France was one of the best individual displays I have seen in rugby. Very few players possess what I dub box-office quality – the ability to fill a stadium with their presence alone – and O'Driscoll is not in that category quite yet, but he will be soon. His pace, side-stepping, positive running and ability to seize upon a mistake and run in for a try make him a truly outstanding prospect. It is unfair to tag young O'Driscoll with the label of the 'new Mike Gibson', which is happening in Ireland. Gibson was a one-off, among the greatest rugby players I have played with or seen. O'Driscoll has miles to go yet before the comparison can even be made. That said, I do look forward to seeing him play over the next few years and I expect him to thrill crowds throughout the world.

Scotland do not have an abundance of young talent coming through and losing to Italy in the opening Six Nations match did nothing to help their morale. That sort of thing is embarrassing. It makes you the butt of jokes. But they bounced back at the end of the 2000 campaign to beat England at Murrayfield, ending the Grand Slam charge of Clive Woodward's men, and one of the main reasons for that upset was the presence of Ian McGeechan as coach. 'Will the players play for the coach?'– that is a question administrators have to ask before appointing someone to take charge of an international team. In McGeechan's case, the answer is always an unreserved 'yes' and the way the Scots stopped England in their tracks was evidence of that. What the Scots need is for Gregor Townsend to be more consistent in the centre and Chris Paterson, with whom I have been very impressed, to maintain his progress as a full-back of real potential.

Realistically, though, if anyone is going to break the Southern Hemisphere grip on the World Cup, England or France are going to have to be the ones to do it. The English annoy you with their arrogance at times and nothing angered me more than their move to negotiate their own television deal for international rugby. When Wales were dominant in the 1970s we would never have gone off on our own to do deals for the Five Nations. Then again, we probably have to accept that England are in a unique position simply because they are England, holding the aces with the massive money and business conglomerates they can call upon in London. England know we need them because without their presence in the Six Nations, and without matches against their clubs, there is simply not the same amount of money on the table for the Celtic nations.

I'm impressed with the way England, who noted they had lost 25,000 young players in the last five years, spotted the flaw and have gone about improving their structure from the top right down to grass-roots level. The moves they have made will ensure that they have real strength in depth in the future. While it might hurt Wales to be left behind, it could also work in our favour: if seeing England soaring away from us is not a big enough kick in the backside to get our own structure right, then *nothing* will be.

Even though England blew the Grand Slam, there is little doubt they will form the bulk of the Lions side to take on Australia in the summer of 2001. Whereas during the 1970s Wales supplied most of the Lions XV, these days England have taken over the mantle. You look at Clive Woodward's side and you think, how can we improve England with players from the Celtic nations? That will be the philosophy of the Lions' management. In Lawrence Dallaglio, Neil Back and Richard Hill, England have a wonderful back row and their half-back pairing of Matt Dawson and Jonny Wilkinson is head-and-shoulders above any other. In players like Perry, Cohen, Tindall and Healey, England have a proliferation of other talented young backs likely to make their mark in Australia.

I think we can put the Grand Slam defeat by the Scots at Murrayfield down to a bad day at the office, one which people like Dawson and Wilkinson (who will control the tactics in Australia) need to learn from. In atrocious weather conditions, like those we saw that Sunday, you get nowhere playing seventy-yard rugby. Get the ball in the opposition territory and play from there. Dawson and Wilkinson will be aware, or certainly should be aware, that they should have employed those tactics and I doubt they will make the same mistake again. What impresses me about England is that they have abnormal strength in depth: Woodward can put any reserve into any position, knowing that particular individual will not let the side down. Based on this, if you were going to put your money on anyone from the Northern Hemisphere winning the next World Cup, then England look the best bet.

That said, while we talk of Southern Hemisphere dominance of the competition, it should be pointed out that France have reached two finals and England one – so it is not as if the Big Three have had it totally their own way and the rest of us are simply there to make up the numbers. In fact, when you talk about great World Cup matches, France's famous semi-final victories over Australia in 1987 and New Zealand in 1999 rank right up there with the best of them. The French have proved that on their day they can beat the best. Doing it two matches in a row is what has proved beyond them to date.

Realistically you still have to say that either Australia or New Zealand, closely pushed by South Africa, will win Down Under in 2003. But I'll tell you something: while the Southern Hemisphere sides keep winning the World Cup, they aren't half envious of our own Six Nations competition. Packed houses, terrific social occasion – I know it took Graham Henry aback when he took charge of his first match in the competition, against Scotland at Murrayfield in 1999, and saw tens of thousands of Welsh fans in Edinburgh. The fervour for the tournament hit Henry straight in the face like a rugby culture shock. I know of players who have won Welsh caps, but do not regard them as 'real' because they were not gained in either the Five Nations or the new Six Nations tournament. Playing in those matches seems to give international caps an authenticity.

Southern Hemisphere domination of the world game? In terms of World Cup results, yes . . . But while Australia, New Zealand and South Africa have their own Tri-Nations competition, they would love the glamour we have had to ourselves down the years with our special little annual tournament.

SIXTEEN

BOOT MONEY, 'KIDNAPPED', RUGBY ON THE RATES, MERV'S FAG

Jimmy Greaves once called football 'a funny old game'. Well, the same applies to rugby. Despite the high-intensity pressure that went with being a top sportsman, there were many lighter, shall we call them off-the-wall moments, during my career that gave me plenty of laughs. Here is a small selection to share with you.

I was able to bow out of rugby as European Player of the Year, an honour I picked up at an awards ceremony in the Royal Hotel, Cardiff, after my last international match for Wales against France. The function will be easily remembered by two Welsh fans – because it ended with a loss of conjugal rights for them and very nearly a couple of divorces too. The French sports newspaper *L'Equipe* had organised the bash and asked me to attend as soon as our game had finished. I was hardly going to turn down their request, for there was lots of wine and champagne on offer – just my scene. So I showered quickly and went up to the first floor of the hotel to receive my award, while my Welsh colleagues went back to the team hotel 600 yards away for the traditional after-match dinner.

After a hard game of international rugby, while you may look fit, in actual fact you are physically and mentally drained. So when *L'Equipe* supplied me with two huge jeroboams of champagne to take back to share with my Welsh team-mates, I quickly discovered I had no strength left to carry them. Down the stairs came Barry John, arms almost reaching the floor because these great big things were so heavy.

At one point I stopped to pretend to sign autographs for the Welsh fans still milling around the hotel, when in reality I just wanted to rest my arms.

I was never going to be able to carry them 600 yards up the road to the team hotel, so I enlisted the help of two burly looking Welsh fans. They were in their mid-twenties and married. Between us we got these things up to the room I shared with Gareth Edwards and, feeling my two helpers had performed beyond the call of duty, I asked Gareth to take them to the team room for some souvenirs and signed photographs. After changing into my dinner jacket for the team dinner, I sauntered down, handed the two the key to our bedroom and said, 'If you want any drinks, have them from the mini-bar on Gareth and me. Thanks for your help again.'

Well, this pair must have thought Christmas had come early. Not only were they in Edwards and John's room, there was free booze on offer too – and they drank the lot. I spent the night at home and when I returned the following morning it was as if a bomb had hit the room. Bottles and cans were strewn everywhere. There was a sting in the tail, however, for when the pair arrived home in the valleys at nine in the morning and told their wives what had happened . . . Well, let's just say they were not believed. Would you accept that reason? The story the two told could not have been more honest or correct, yet the wives thought they must have been up to hanky-panky and insisted that the pair must have rehearsed this daft story on the way home. Off they were packed to the spare room and bang went their conjugal rights, with divorces looming.

I had left my home phone number, should they require tickets in the future, and four days afterwards the telephone rang. 'We're in a pickle, Barry,' I was told. 'Put the wife on the phone,' I said. 'I'll explain exactly what happened and how grateful I am to the two of you.' That is what I did, only for the angry female voice on the other end of the line to bellow, 'You're another friend who is in on the act. Do you think I'm stupid or something?' and down the phone was slammed.

Of course, valley towns being what they are, this story soon went the rounds and my two new 'pals' were slaughtered. 'Close pal, Barry, is he?' others chortled; 'or is it Gareth who you know best?' I soon received another telephone call, this one out of desperation. 'You couldn't come up, could you?' I was asked. Well, I had no option but to go to rescue the situation. It was only when I walked through the door of the local social club and strode over to shake the hands of the two 'innocents' that the wives finally accepted they were telling the truth. Full marital and other rights were restored – but it was a close one for a while. I bet those two weren't in a hurry to help any more rugby players for a while.

Anyone who went to that aforementioned Wales v. France match and looked up at the balcony of the city centre-based Wales team hotel just two hours before kick-off would have spotted a pair of boots hanging over the rails. These were there for a very good reason – to dry out a sponsor's logo I had just painted on. My boots had been supplied by a firm called G.T. Law, size nine, custom made for me with a very soft leather which was so comfortable it felt more like putting on a glove than pulling on a rugby boot. Therefore, when I returned from the 1971 Lions tour and Adidas and Puma wanted to pay me to wear their boots, there was only one solution.

I could not put myself, the Welsh team and the Welsh public at risk by breaking-in new boots during an international, so I grabbed my old ones and, depending on whose turn it was, painted on either the Adidas or Puma logo on the morning of the game. Out they then went on the balcony to dry. Trouble is, for that last game against France, it rained very heavily and the logo became rather 'disfigured' as the paint started to run. There was a lovely photograph of myself kicking the ball in the newspapers the following day with the Puma logo prominent – only about an inch below where it should have been!

An Italian delegation got in touch just before I retired and asked to meet me about a possible move abroad. Rugby was not prominent in Italy at the time and they wanted their growing club game to be given a boost by landing a big-name signing. Apparently, a few ex-pats who had set up home on the Mediterranean had suggested my name. We met one Tuesday morning in the foyer of a Cardiff hotel and over coffee and biscuits the Italians enthusiastically outlined their proposal to me, offering a sizeable amount of lire based on appearances, points scored and win bonuses. Because of the amateur status of rugby in those days, they would set me up with a full-time job, but that was only a cover.

The Italians explained that my presence was vital because they did not get big crowds, had no sponsors and little in the way of incoming revenue. Which prompted the following question from me: 'So how are you going to pay me this money, then?' Without blinking, the Italians' lead man replied, 'Oh, don't worry about that. We've been to the local council . . . And we've asked them to put up the rates!'

A few thousand extra lire per household to pay for Barry John? Ten out of ten for imagination, but needless to say the move never materialised.

Speaking of Italian lire, I was due to play for Llanelli against Neath during Rag Week at college. On the morning of the match a Scarlets committee man received a telephone call. The voice at the other end of the line said, 'We've kidnapped Barry and if we don't get a ransom he won't be turning up for the game.' My captors, of course, were no one more sinister than my fellow students who were just trying to raise some money for the college. I'm not sure Llanelli saw the funny side and I was not laughing either when I heard they felt the 'ransom' fee was too much and were refusing to pay it. How much were my mates charging for my release? The grand sum of £25 – and Llanelli felt I was not worth that!

After two or three more telephone calls, during which time Llanelli realised they had nobody else to wear the number 10 jersey, they agreed to cough up and I was duly transported to the game. A few years ago I re-told the story in a brochure produced as part of some Llanelli celebrations. Only, when I got down to the nitty-gritty of the ransom fee involved, I decided to convert it to lire. I hadn't the foggiest how much 25 million lire was in pounds, shillings and pence, but I knew it sounded a whole lot better than £25.

During my trip to the United States to discuss the setting up of a professional rugby circus, my hosts took me to an American Football match in Nashville where we were given miniature American footballs, the size of a small coffee pot, as souvenirs. After the match had finished (at around 2 a.m., because the searing heat meant the game couldn't kick-off until 10 p.m.) we went down to pitch level to have a good look at the stadium. I had not kicked a ball in anger for two years, but I couldn't resist a little pot at goal – even though it was going to be a lot harder to kick this little thing than a normal-sized rugby ball.

Anyway, I caught the miniature football beautifully and over it sailed from forty yards out, right through the middle of the posts. A couple of people helping to clean the stadium looked on in total amazement and one eventually broke the silence to say in his deep American drawl, 'Hey buddy, have you done this sort of thing before?'

If only he knew.

We were playing Scotland at Cardiff Arms Park and began assembling for the customary pre-match team photograph on the Cardiff club ground next door. The routine on these occasions was always the same: jog a few laps of the pitch, throw the ball around a few times and then our coach Clive Rowlands would bellow for us to fall in and get the picture done. We gathered, as normal, on two benches – big forwards, like our marvellous number 8 Mervyn Davies, at the back; the smaller ones at the front. 'No smiling please,' the photographer would say, at which point we always deliberately burst out laughing. Click, click, click, job done. Up we would get for a final warm-up and back into the dressing-room we would go.

Only this time the photographer called Clive over and said we needed to take another picture. 'And this time tell Merv to take the fag out of his mouth,' he said. There we were, fifteen minutes to kick-off, and Merv the Swerve was running around smoking a cigarette! Clive, being the good man-manager that he was, did not get heavy. He just said, calmly, 'Merv, if you've got to smoke, make sure the cigarette is behind your back when the picture is taken!' I have never seen a print of that original photograph, but someone, somewhere, has got a cracker in his dark room.

My great friend Clem Thomas, himself a former Wales and Lions player who then became a rugby writer for *The Observer*, stood for election in Swansea as a Parliamentary Liberal candidate. Trouble was that Clem could be a bit impulsive at times and during a Wales tour to New Zealand, which Clem was covering as a journalist, he went around the squad during our refuelling stop in Tel Aviv to ask them to sign a postcard. Everyone, including Clem, had had a few drinks on the flight and was tired, but luckily I still had my wits about me when Clem approached me, put the postcard in my hand, and barked 'Sign this'.

On the front was a picture of Yasser Arafat, leader of the Palestine Liberation Organisation. Considering we were in Israel, I found this a bit odd, so I turned the postcard over and studied the address. It was made out to 'Caio Evans, HMP Swansea'. I said, 'Hang on a minute, Clem,' and tore it up in front of him. He went purple and looked so angry I thought he was going to throttle me. Caio Evans, I should point out, was the leader of the Free Wales Army – and Clem was sending him a postcard with Yasser Arafat on the front, from Israel, signed by the entire Welsh rugby team! Caio and the Free Wales Army were getting a few column inches at the time, but if this one had got out . . .

The following day, when we had landed in New Zealand, I went up to Clem and asked, 'Do you remember last night?' He had had so much to drink he did not. 'Listen, you silly man,' I went on, 'You're going to be running for Parliament and you do something like this.' When I told him exactly what had happened, Clem put his head in his hands and said, 'What can I get you to drink, Barry?'

When John Dawes retired from the Welsh captaincy, my name was heavily linked with the post. 'This is the true crowning of the King,' declared the newspapers. I did not want the extra responsibilities of captaincy and I telephoned our manager, Clive Rowlands, one night to express my concerns. He replied, 'Don't worry, we haven't even considered you, Barry!'

The comment did not take me aback as such, but I did smile to myself. Anyway, as I used to tell people, 'What does the title captain matter – because I've been running the show for years anyway.'

I was asked to pose for a portrait for the National Library of Wales in Aberystwyth, a great honour indeed as some of the major figures in Britain had their faces up on the wall there, including Prince Charles. My artist was a man called David Griffiths and when I walked into his studio I was immediately mesmerised by the great sketches he had done of so many famous people, most of them royalty, professors, doctors of philosophy and hugely qualified and successful individuals.

David was a lovely man. After four or five sessions he opened up more and we got on extremely well. Then one day he came out with a classic. 'Do you realise, Barry, that you're the first non-academic man we've had here?' As I stared at him open-mouthed, David's face getting redder and redder, he quickly said, 'Oops, I didn't mean that like that!'

Danny Blanchflower, the Tottenham double-winning captain in 1961, told me a lovely tale about his side's victory in the FA Cup final over Leicester. Before the match the two sides were introduced to the Queen, the Leicester players sporting spanking new tracksuit tops bearing their individual names. Spurs, on the other hand, were kitted out in plain old white shirts, blue shorts, and white socks.

The Queen went down the Leicester line and then it was Tottenham's turn, Danny introducing her to his team-mates. When, at the end, Her Majesty commented on Leicester's posh tracksuit tops and asked why the Tottenham players did not have their names emblazoned on their shirts, quick as a flash, in front of 100,000 people, Danny replied in his mischievous Irish way, 'Well, you see Ma'am, our players know one another!'

SEVENTEEN

THE GREATEST NAMES
THE GREATEST

Picking your fantasy team is a subject that gets debates and arguments going in pubs and clubs throughout the land. Everyone has their own personal preference for certain positions, everyone thinks their side is better than that of their friends. The only thing that you can guarantee is that no two people will come up with exactly the same line-up. I have called upon more than thirty years of experience as a player and rugby observer from the press-box and commentary gantry to name what I believe is the definitive Dream Team. As you have to set your parameters somewhere, I have excluded anyone from before my own playing days – thus ruling out world-class stars like Cliff Morgan from the 1950s. But after much soul-searching, and some near impossible choices, I have come up with a XV which, in my opinion, you would struggle to better. In fact, I would back my line-up to beat any side Mars or the other planets could produce!

In most positions I am totally spoilt for choice, starting with full-back, where the scintillating French pair of Pierre Villepreux and Serge Blanco were wonderful, as were the South African André Joubert (dubbed the Rolls-Royce of the position) and Scotland's Andy Irvine. I first set eyes on Blanco playing for France B against Wales B at Aberavon. He scored brilliant tries and was so head-and-shoulders above everyone else on the pitch that it seemed he was running on five star petrol while the rest were on three star. I had never seen one person stand out quite as blatantly on a rugby pitch.

But even Blanco misses out to my choice of **J.P.R. Williams**. I know people will accuse me of bias because he was a team-mate of mine, but JPR really did epitomise everything required in a full-back . . . and more. He was a great tackler, he was solid under the high ball, he made devastating bursts into the line, and he possessed great pace, strength and positional sense. Knowing that JPR was behind me gave me the freedom to express myself on the field, because if I made a mistake I knew he would be there to cover. With other full-backs, there would have been an element of risk involved. Not with JPR. He was the rock who let nobody through. When we looked around and saw him wearing the number 15 jersey, it gave us an enormous feeling of confidence which went right through the spine of the team. You could not keep JPR out of the action either. If he had been quiet for ten minutes, next thing he would be running like Geronimo, with that famous headband of his and hair flowing, with ball in hand and crossing for a try. The crowd loved him and you could see why.

If JPR's breaks into the line were not trouble enough for the opposition, imagine him being flanked on either side with any two wings out of the following three – Gerald Davies, David Campese and Jonah Lomu. This is probably my toughest choice of the lot. Who do I omit from that trio? If I left the selection to someone else, I'd more than willingly take the one he chose to leave out. This is without even considering other great wings like David Duckham, John Bevan and the New Zealander Bryan Williams.

Well, I simply cannot ignore **Lomu**. Big, powerful, exceptionally quick, the New Zealander at his best is like a rampaging and unstoppable rhinoceros. His rugby league equivalent is probably that wonderful Australian Mal Meninga – another who had phenomenal pace and natural ability, but who was so big and awe-inspiring with it. Lomu, like Meninga, is almost worth two or three men to his side because of the options he brings. Name him in your line-up and the 'sold out' notices go up at once. It is bizarre to think that Lomu has yet to gain a World Cup-winner's medal, but there is no doubt he was the star of the 1995 and 1999 tournaments. He is still young enough to dominate the 2003 competition and possibly the one beyond that.

So if Lomu is on the left, is it Gerald or Campo on the right? You can almost throw a coin for this one. I will plump for **Davies** in the end, simply because I had first-hand knowledge of his try-scoring exploits in so many big games. Anyone can have a good game, maybe even a good season. But Gerald sustained it game after game, week after week, season after season with some truly amazing tries. His defence was pretty special, too. People often overlook the countless tackles he used to put in.

It is strange to think Campese, one of the greatest rugby talents I have seen, cannot make my starting line-up. He may have got under a few people's skin (particularly the English) with his outspoken comments, but he always delivered and he was five-star entertainment. Not a bad bloke to have as first-choice substitute, eh?

In the centre I have always felt the Australian partnership of Tim Horan and Jason Little was effective; Jeremy Guscott was magical for a decade with England and the Lions; while John Dawes, because he was not the most charismatic of players, was underrated. His qualities would appeal to the rugby connoisseur more than the man on the terrace, but he was very much a players' player. I have plumped, though, for the great Irishman **Mike Gibson** and the French star **Maso**. Gibson, like Gareth Edwards, is a complete rugby footballer: terrific natural ability, fast hands, deceptive pace and tough as old boots too. Knowing a player of Gibson's class was on my right shoulder with the Lions was a dream come true for me.

If Gibson is the best centre I have seen, Maso is a close second best. The darling of the French crowds, he was silky and skilful and had the most classical of passes. He knew exactly when to release the ball, confounding opponents who could not get near him. He had the knack of making the game look *so* easy.

I'm also spoilt for choice at fly-half, but on this occasion I have no hesitation in coming down in favour of one man: **Hugo Porta**. My selection of the Argentinian may surprise a few people, but Carwyn James and I were fortunate enough to be sitting next to one another in the stands when Porta produced two of the most virtuoso performances I have seen from a rugby player. The first occasion was for Argentina against Wales at Cardiff Arms Park in 1976, when only a last-gasp penalty prevented Porta from giving the South Americans a shock victory. His display that day was perfection. Porta took the right options every time, but his execution of them, whether a kick, pass or darting run, I rated at eleven out of ten on each occasion. I have seen ballet critics go over the top in drooling at certain performances on the stage. This was the rugby equivalent of that.

Carwyn and I also saw Porta play for the South African Barbarians against the 1980 British Lions at Kings Park, Durban. Same again – his performance was amazing. Porta did not play for a very good international side in Argentina; but that day, in a star-studded South African Barbarians line-up, you could see he was instantly at home in such exalted company and stood out among them. Imagine how good he would have been had he played regularly in a top team.

A few years ago, fifteen players were inducted into rugby's first Hall of Fame at a dinner in London. It was not a team as such, but rather a selection of fifteen individuals. Four fly-halfs were honoured, including myself, Cliff Morgan and the great Australian Mark Ella. The fourth was none other than Porta, chosen by a group of top rugby analysts from throughout the world. He gets my nod too.

When it comes to Porta's scrum-half partner you could easily pick from an abundance of New Zealand players, for number 9 is a position in which they have been consistently strong over the last three decades. Chris Laidlaw and Sid Going are two who particularly stand out – short, stocky, very strong and effective. In contrast there was the devastating acceleration and athleticism of the Springbok Dawie de Villiers, strengths shared by the more recent South African first choice, Joost van der Westhuizen. But I have to go for the master himself, **Gareth Edwards**. To a man, I suspect the others I have mentioned would bow in agreement with my choice too.

I thought I knew Gareth's game inside out from the years we were paired together for club, country and the Lions. But it was only when I sat in the stands after retiring that I grasped just how good he really was. Perhaps before I had been too close and didn't realise just how powerful Gareth was, how he could dump big forwards on their backsides in tackles. Gareth was the darling of the forwards who used to tell me that when the going got tough, they would look down at him – literally too, because he was a lot smaller than them – and take confidence because they knew he could turn bad ball into good. He was so strong he could hold off three opposing forwards until his own team-mates gathered around again. These are not qualities you will see defined in the standard textbook of scrum-half play. They are qualities Gareth created through his own play, his own personal pages, if you like. He is in my side, no question.

The best back-row combination I have seen was the South African trio of Jan Ellis, Tommy Bedford and Piet Greyling on the Lions tour in 1968. Bedford was a number 8 master, Greyling was destructive, while Ellis was like a panther – so quick that if you hesitated over a decision for one millionth of a second he would pounce on you. However, I will go for three individuals who, if they were put together, would have the edge over even that phenomenal Springbok trio.

At number 8 **Mervyn Davies** gets the nod ahead of great New Zealanders like Zinzan Brooke, Wayne Shelford and before them Brian Lochore. Merv's gangly frame tended to make you forget just how tough and strong he was. He could go the full distance in any sort of weather conditions and regardless of what sort of game plan was needed. Merv was as effective in a dour slog in the mud in Dublin as he was in the sunshine of Transvaal. He had almost an in-built radar which would tell him where the ball would go next. Merv would decide no one was covering a certain square area of the pitch, so he would trot over there – and next thing you knew he would be underneath a high ball. It happened too often to be regarded as laziness. Merv was simply brilliant at reading the game.

Open-side flanker is, after the wings, perhaps my toughest call. I loved watching our own John Taylor dart around the field; the great Irishman Fergus Slattery; the New Zealanders Graham Mourie and Josh Kronfeld; that blond-haired French flier Jean-Pierre Rives. In more recent times Neil Back and Olivier Magne have been dynamic in the position. I'm a great believer in fast flankers who can get around the field, rather than just big strong men: the players I have mentioned were always up with the action, possessing great hands to keep movements going too. However, imagine those qualities allied to size, too, and you have a flanker with an extra dimension. The player who had the lot rolled into one was **Ian Kirkpatrick**, a true world-class forward in any era. Beating a New Zealand side with a man of his stature in it in 1971 simply made our Lions victory even sweeter.

On the blind side I will pick another big man who possessed pace, power and great hands and who knew the game inside out. Step forward Australian 1991 World Cup-winner **Willie Ofahengaue**, who edges out rivals like Jean Claude Skrela of France, the Scots' great white shark John Jeffrey, Derek Quinnell and Mike Teague. Ofahengaue was arguably the most influential forward in that victorious Australian side. Known throughout the game simply as Willie O, he brought new standards to the number 6 position and would blend perfectly with Davies and Kirkpatrick.

In the second row I unhesitatingly name two more greats from Down Under in **Colin Meads** and **John Eales**. I rated the English pair of Wade Dooley and Paul Ackford highly – each better than Bill Beaumont, who was a better captain than player – while I always liked the New Zealand stalwart Ian Jones and the 1974 Lions skipper Willie-John McBride. But Meads was comfortably the most complete tight-five forward the world has seen. He was a big powerful lock, yet was never actually the biggest man on the field at any given time in the physical sense. In stature, however, he was feet ahead of everyone else. Great in the line-out, technically excellent, his handling skills would have done justice to a world-class centre. He was also a great captain of New Zealand.

Speaking of great skippers, the same can be said of Eales, very much Australia's talisman when he lifted the World Cup in 1999 (the second time he has won the trophy). I wonder whether Australia would have emerged victorious on either occasion had Eales not been there. He plays the modern game, which entails a more loose variety of forward play in rugby, but I have no doubt that Eales, like Meads a brilliant athlete, could have slotted into any era and become a big star.

On to the front row and at hooker I would be happy with any one of Peter Wheeler, Jon Pullin, Bobby Windsor or the giant Aussie Phil Kearns. In the end, though, it comes down to a straight choice between Keith Wood – easily the number one in the world at present, and Sean Fitzpatrick. Wood is comfortable popping up anywhere on the field and can even side-step while running at pace. But because he was at the top for such a period of time, I have to come down in favour of **Fitzpatrick**. You could argue it was easier for him because he was part of an outstanding New Zealand pack, but I do not accept that. Fitzpatrick, as captain, was the man who made that pack tick in the first place. You do not remain number one in New Zealand if you are not at your very best and he managed it year after year. Strong in the scrum, great athlete in the loose, he was the modern-day hooker men like Wood probably aspired to be.

Packing down next to Fitzpatrick I plump for the New Zealander **Ken Gray** on the loose-head and my fellow Welshman **Graham Price** as tight-head. Gray was the first awesome front-row forward that I came up against. It was hard enough as it was against the New Zealand pack, but he was half like a prop, half like a second row – so it was as if they had a tight five-and-a-half! Pricey was the best in his position for a decade and to hold down that tag as a prop-forward is the equivalent of a fly-half being the very best for fifteen to twenty years. There are no easy games in the front row. There are not even any easy training sessions. It is hard, gruelling, physical work; but Pricey managed to retain his form, appetite and technique. His speed from standing starts at line-outs, where he would gather the ball from the number 8 and peel away to run at the opposition, was quite startling – a pace any other athlete of similar weight would have found difficult to match.

My philosophy as a player was that if I broke through and, by fluke, one of the front five forwards was up in support, there was no point in me passing the ball. I guessed they would only botch it up, so I might as well kick ahead and everyone could chase the ball. With Gray and Price, as with the other members of my front five, I would happily give them the ball, knowing they would carry on the move in style.

So that is my line-up. A great mix of awesome forward power allied to stunning pace and running ability from the back line. Meads is my captain, Carwyn James is the coach and I will have the honour of managing the team – so I can just sit back in the stands, enjoy the rugby they serve up and go to the cocktail parties afterwards.

Yes, that really is fantasy rugby for me.

BARRY JOHN'S FANTASY XV

J.P.R. Williams (Wales); G. Davies (Wales), Maso (France), Gibson (Ireland), Lomu (New Zealand); Porta (Argentina), Edwards (Wales); M. Davies (Wales), Kirkpatrick (New Zealand), Ofahengaue (Australia), Eales (Australia), Meads (New Zealand, capt.), Price (Wales), Fitzpatrick (New Zealand), Gray (New Zealand).

EIGHTEEN

THE FUTURE

'You've taken plenty out of the game – but you've never given anything back.' If I have heard that comment once down the years, I have heard it a thousand times. Particularly when people have had five or six pints, lose their inhibitions and begin jabbing the top of my shoulder blade.

They want to know why I have never coached a side, why I don't sit on rugby committees and basically why I have never been involved off the pitch since quitting as a player at the age of twenty-seven. I try to explain that I could never have done it in the past because I had effectively turned myself into a professional and that rugby union was an amateur game. The only thing I was able to do was give my views on the game either through writing or broadcasting.

'Yes, but you're paid for that – you're still not giving anything back to rugby,' comes the counter-charge. To which I then counter back myself, 'Don't you think that playing from the age of twelve to twenty-seven, winning with Wales and the Lions and giving people lots of joy, was giving something to the game?'

If I had taken one of the big-money offers to go to rugby league, there would have been no problem. Straight away people would have understood that the rugby union authorities simply would not have allowed me, as a professional, to be involved in their sport in any capacity. However, what the public could not fully comprehend was that by allowing my name to be used to endorse boots and sports clothing, I had commercialised and professionalised myself anyway.

I was asked to coach teams in an unofficial capacity a few times, but I always had politely to decline the offers, explaining the reason why. The moment I stepped on to the training pitch I would have professionalised the entire team and they would have been in hot water. Big time.

Of course, with rugby union subsequently going professional, that situation has since changed. But the only 'official' thing I have been asked to do, funnily enough, was in northern Spain: John Toshack, managing the local soccer club at the time, invited a few of us out to speak at a rugby development forum. Tosh is a rugby nut and once he was able to tell the organisers he had secured the services of Barry John and Gareth Edwards, the place was packed out.

There was one occasion at the beginning of the 1990s when my old Wales mate Jeff Young, who was the WRU's coaching director, asked me to help out the under-21s side who were training at Sophia Gardens in Cardiff. I know Jeff really well and he said, 'Look Barry, just come and talk to them and let them hear your views. They'll really listen to you'. I did spend forty minutes with the backs, but it was more on an informal basis – a favour to a friend, if you like.

The next question people invariably ask is: 'Do you regret not being asked to be involved more?' My answer to that is that you can only be frustrated about something if you know you could have done it. I knew I couldn't have done it – end of story. If I'm totally honest, I was always privately glad that the rules forbade me.

Number one, I could never have been a rugby committee man. Still couldn't: I'm too impatient for that. You have to accept democratic decisions, but you sometimes get twelve people around a table discussing an issue over a great period of time – an issue two or three of those committee men know next to nothing about. Yet you get them blocking the sensible route just because they vote with their mate. No thanks. That's not democracy, it's plain daft. I used to chair business board meetings and I always tried to make them quick and to the point. I feel some rugby officials, whom I term 'professional committee men', talk for the sake of it. Nonetheless, I'm often approached for my advice on how things should be done and I willingly offer it. Often I'll then notice my thoughts have been implemented, but I deliberately remain low-key about everything.

As for being a coach, maybe I could have been a consultant rather than someone in a tracksuit, encouraging young players, offering guidance and advice. It does make me laugh, though, when I see clubs employ backs coaches and forwards coaches. Hey, the game is not about seven backs and eight forwards - it is about three units of five. If you need a specialist coach, it is for the middle five; made up of three of back row forwards and the two half backs. They are the hub of the team, the Rolls-Royce, the creative engine driving the side on.

I'm too old to become a coach these days. Yes, I know there are plenty out there who are older than me, but they've done the job for years. I can't be expected to start from scratch in my mid-fifties. No, I tell people if they wanted an input from me over the past twenty-five years, they only had to read my *Daily Express* column where I always endeavoured to put forward constructive views on the game, the style of rugby played and other aspects.

In fact I would argue that through my newspaper column and broadcasting experience with the BBC, I have made a bigger contribution to rugby than most coaches in tracksuits!

So, what does my future hold? Well . . .

I have a dream. In my own little pleasure land it involves the racecourse and, should one or two horses oblige in the next few years, they might find one of my own being put in the stalls next to them in the near future. The dream involves owning a racehorse called Caring and Sharing – my motto in this world since I was brought up those many years ago in Cefneithin.

I used to go racing as often as possible, although my visits to the track have dropped off in the past four years. I have always loved the sport, though, and a few years back I was co-owner of a two-year-old called British Lion. Twelve of us, including Gareth Edwards, David Duckham and myself, got involved in the venture. The horse was trained by Ian Balding, a rugby nut who just happened to be the Queen's trainer (well, nothing but the best for us . . .). British Lion won a few times, although I don't recall making any money out of the project. By the same token I never received any bills either. The horse just about paid for himself.

It was a fabulous experience to go and watch British Lion. I saw his first race at Wolverhampton and in one of his next outings, at Chepstow, Gareth and I made the mistake of walking into the enclosure to wish Ian Balding and the jockey for the day the best of luck. Oops! Two-year-olds, as anyone who follows racing will know, are highly-strung animals. The moment Gareth and I strode out towards Ian, the place erupted. The crowd's rugby favourites were suddenly right there in front of them – trouble was, the horses were not impressed with the sudden burst of noise and these thoroughbreds starting bucking up in the air, making their jockeys scared stiff. Gareth and I went over to help, trying our best to hold down British Lion. Well, that was it. He was a 7–1 shot before that moment; suddenly, because people realised we were involved with the horse, everyone filed towards the bookmakers to put a bet on him and within minutes British Lion was installed as favourite at 6–4. The punters lost their money – and ten minutes afterwards Gareth and I were not so popular!

Although that was just a brief flirtation with being a racehorse owner, it gave me enough of a taste to harbour ambitions to do it on my own one day. Maybe, in years to come, those of you who follow the racing pages will note the name Caring and Sharing in the 2.40 at Ascot, see the name B. John next to the horse and know just who that owner is.

Until that moment happens, the future for me will be . . . Well, very much like the past twenty-five to thirty years have been. I have worked project by project in recent times, by and large making up my own timetable, the sort of working pattern tens of thousands of others would love to have. That is the way I see it carrying on. Basically the future changes very little, as far as I'm concerned. Even when Forward Trust and Bowring employed me, I never worked the conventional office hours of 9 a.m. to 5 p.m. If I needed time off to go on tour with Wales or the Lions there was never any interference, because the firms felt I was still representing them and the publicity was good for them. If I wanted to go off and play golf, I could do so without having to ask permission.

I have not been involved with a specific company for the past three years, now. The one thing I miss above anything else is easy access to secretarial duties: people to plan my affairs, sort out which invitations I accept and which I don't, send signed photographs to fans and all that sort of thing. In the past not only did secretaries do me a huge favour by sorting out the mound of administration, I think it also broke up the monotony of their normal working day. I suppose one or two of them would argue they even used to run *me*. More a case of the tail wagging the dog!

To this day I still receive personal invitations which even millionaires could not buy. Simply through being a famous rugby player, that is bound to happen. I'm synonymous with certain things, just as George Best and David Beckham are in football. I will be known for a few generations yet and if it is not exactly a case of trading on my name, it is inevitable it will have a bearing on what I do. As a result *Wales on Sunday* approached me before the start of the 1999 World Cup to ask me to become a rugby columnist for them. After a quarter of a century with the *Daily Express*, and an amicable parting of the ways, I thought my journalistic days were over. I did not fancy getting out my umbrella with the holes in it and getting wet as I travelled hundreds of miles up and down Britain to watch matches. But, with the vast majority of games that I see these days being in Cardiff, I decided to give it a go. I have thoroughly enjoyed doing my column, too, particularly as I now write for a Welsh nation rather than a UK audience.

I have other projects ongoing as well; but the one thing I want to make clear is that while my pensions will kick in soon, I am not just waiting for the day to retire. The calendar may tell me when I'm officially at retirement age, but that doesn't mean I will pack everything in. No one will know when to give Barry John a gold watch: there are still many things he wants to do. My friends always tell me, because of the lovely existence I have led, that I have been retired for the past twenty-five-odd years anyway!

I suppose one day it would do me good to join a company again on my own terms. As Jan once said, I'm a bit of a gypsy – and maybe having to go in to work at ten in the morning for maybe two or three days a week would give me a regimentation, a conformity, that maybe I need. But by and large I will continue to set my own agenda, as I have done throughout my working life. It has been a bit of a roller-coaster ride, but the ups have definitely outweighed the downs. I have always recognised my mistakes, but I have made a point never to dwell upon them. Rather than reflect upon the regrets I had about quitting at my peak, I prefer to consider how lucky I was to appear in teams with so many great players for Llanelli, Cardiff, Wales and the Lions. It was the best era to play rugby, I had wonderful times; and through my deeds on the pitch I was able to meet some very famous and fascinating people from other fields.

Sport, in a nutshell, has given me an outlook and definition money cannot buy. Maybe, if I am fortunate, the next step will have been achieved when you hear the television commentators saying, '. . . And it's Caring and Sharing, owned by Mr Barry John, in the lead with two fences to go . . .'

A lovely little prospect for me and something I will definitely aim towards. After that it will be something else I'm capable of achieving, but with an obstacle there to ensure it is not easy. Just as it has always been, I suppose.

NINETEEN

WHAT THEY SAY ABOUT THE KING

WILL CARLING (England rugby captain 59 times, 1988–96)
Unfortunately I do not remember watching Barry John play in person, but I have a host of memories of seeing him on videotapes. Among the sheer brilliance, what always struck me was that he managed to achieve everything he did without looking as though he even broke sweat. He was so relaxed, so nonchalant, it was almost as if he could take it or leave it. I just hope, for the rest of us mere ordinary players, that it was slightly more strenuous than it appeared . . . Otherwise us gasping, sweaty also-rans were not even playing on the same planet.

JONAH LOMU (New Zealand superstar)
My agent, Phil Kingsley-Jones, is Welsh and several times he has played videos for me of the great Wales team when Barry John was in his heyday. I watch Barry's skills time and again in awe and wonderment. No wonder they called him 'The King' over in Great Britain. In fact, watching the old tapes of Barry and Gareth Edwards had a bearing upon me actually taking up rugby in the first place.

Barry seemed to have this uncanny knack of making opponents look as if they were not there. One minute you see them standing in front of him, the next he has broken clear with ball in hand, racing for the try-line – and this is done, it appears, in such an effortless manner that Barry does not seem to break sweat. Everyone else, by the same token, is straining like mad.

If Barry were playing today, it would be interesting to see how he would cope with the packed defences of modern-day rugby. But it is unfair to compare world heavyweight boxing champions of different eras and the same applies to rugby. The one thing I will say is that Barry had this priceless knack of making the game look easy, thus creating time for himself. If he could do that in the 1960s and 1970s, I'm sure he could have done it today. He was one of that rare breed who possessed true rugby genius.

GARETH EDWARDS (former scrum-half partner, 53 Wales caps)
I think it is fair to say, after years of rooming together for Cardiff, Wales and the Lions, that I know Barry as well as anybody in rugby. Hey, when he broke his collar bone in South Africa I was the one buttoning his shirts and helping to put his trousers on him! So how would I describe Barry? Gregarious, fun, good conversationalist, happy-go-lucky. With him, every day was Christmas. What I mean by that is that he enjoyed each day as much as the previous one. The one thing I will say against him, however, is that he fancied himself as a bit of a singer – and, having heard his voice in the shower, I'm still not quite sure where he got that one from!

Barry was such a contrast to me as a personality. Before matches I was full of nervous energy; Barry was far more relaxed. In fact, if he could have persuaded them to put back the kick-off until after he had finished his leisurely lunch, he would have done. He simply took everything calmly in his stride, but once he stepped out beyond that white line the man was immense. There was no stopping him.

Like Barry, I recall the origination of the 'You throw it . . . I'll catch it' line very well. The one point I would like to make, however, is that Barry had already been capped. This was my first Welsh trial, the biggest day of my career – so no wonder I wanted to practise for it. Although it was a one-liner from Barry, it gave me terrific confidence to know there was somebody behind me who really was that good. That said, he did drop a few passes. Very occasionally. Then again, when I threw out poor passes Barry had this terrific knack of picking the ball up cleanly and making me look good.

It was a huge disappointment for me when Barry retired, aged just twenty-seven, because, while I respected his decision, I felt he was packing it in too early and that a part of me was lost that day too. I tried to talk Barry out of it, but to no avail. That was one of the great things about Barry: he was so decisive. Once he had agreed upon a chosen path, nothing was going to change his thoughts.

BILL McLAREN (BBC TV and radio commentator)
I count myself extremely fortunate and privileged to have been commentating during the golden era in which Barry John was at the height of his powers. I had never seen a player like him before, nor one

since for that matter. He did not seem to run, but rather ghost through defences, possessing this uncanny knack of creating space for himself and others. Barry was frail looking and it often seemed he was about to be flattened on the pitch. At times you kind of worried for him, in a way, because he seemed almost dream-like in his mannerisms. But Barry had this knack of being able to step up another gear in pace and that half-a-yard was enough to take him away from any would-be tackler. The only time I can remember him being caught was for the Lions in South Africa when the big Springbok flanker Jan Ellis collared him. The very fact that one incident stands out so easily as the exception to the norm speaks volumes.

I am honoured to be able to say I worked with Barry, after he quit, in our BBC role as commentator and summariser. He had this ability to use his own experiences as a player to help the TV viewer or radio listener understand exactly what was going on down there on the pitch. That is the true art of summarising. Barry mastered it as well as he did the actual playing of the game.

GERALD DAVIES (Wales wing, 46 caps)

I have known Barry since school days and when we began playing rugby together, and I always felt he reflected the mood of the time. It was the '60s, the era of flower power, everyone so easy-going, a sense of freedom and youthfulness, a bit of rebellion too. That lot was Barry to a tee. He had that rebellious streak in him on the rugby field: 'I do what I want and I'm allowed to do what I want.' More often than not he did, too.

Even his body language on the pitch portrayed a languid, almost couldn't-care-less attitude. In reality, nothing could be further from the truth because Barry had a strong competitive edge to him, an inner steel to win. He just made the game look so easy. Whereas everyone else was running around at the rate of knots, Barry was always calm and collected, never flustered.

Norman Mair, the rugby writer for *The Scotsman*, once came up with a classic line about Barry: 'I was always relieved to see Barry walk through the door to after-match dinners – rather than just materialise through the wall.' He saw Barry as ghost-like on the pitch in the way he ran through teams, so he was glad to see that in person, he was just a normal human being!

Well, as normal as Barry John could be, anyway.

JOHN INVERDALE (BBC Radio Five presenter)

Barry John is the player whose posters were up on my bedroom wall – although he was eventually superseded by that great Scottish full-back Andy Irvine! You could not help but marvel at Barry's skills and many years on I was fortunate enough to sit next to him on countless big rugby occasions for the BBC when I discovered his insight into the game and its tactics was unsurpassed.

As someone who still tries to run around the rugby field in his forties, I find it extraordinary that Barry could give up the game he loves when he was twenty-seven and with the rugby world at his feet. But having said that, the Barry John legend remains intact. Who is to say if he had kept going, had a bad injury, played on and lost that touch of magic, whether the legend would be the same today? What I do know is that Barry was a rugby genius and will always be remembered that way.

BARRY'S FACTS AND FIGURES

FOR WALES

3-12-66	*v* Australia (Cardiff) Lost 11–14
4-2-67	*v* Scotland (Murrayfield) Lost 5–11
11-11-67	*v* New Zealand (Cardiff) Lost 6–13 (drop-goal)
20-1-68	*v* England (Twickenham) Drew 11–11 (drop-goal)
3-2-68	*v* Scotland (Cardiff) Won 5–0
9-3-68	*v* Ireland (Dublin) Lost 6–9
23-3-68	*v* France (Cardiff) Lost 9–14
1-2-69	*v* Scotland (Murrayfield) Won 17–3 (try)
8-3-69	*v* Ireland (Cardiff) Won 24–11 (drop-goal)
22-3-69	*v* France (Paris) Drew 8–8
12-4-69	*v* England (Cardiff) Won 30–9 (try, drop-goal)
31-5-69	*v* New Zealand Lost 0–19
14-5-69	*v* New Zealand (Auckland) Lost 12–33
21-6-69	*v* Australia (Sydney) Won 19–16
24-1-70	*v* South Africa (Cardiff) Drew 6–6

7-2-70	*v* Scotland (Cardiff) Won 18–9
28-2-70	*v* England (Twickenham) Won 17–13 (try, drop-goal)
14-3-70	*v* Ireland (Dublin) Lost 0–14
16-1-71	*v* England (Cardiff) Won 22–6 (2 drop-goals)
6-2-71	*v* Scotland (Murrayfield) Won 19–18 (try, pen, con)
13-3-71	*v* Ireland (Cardiff) Won 23–9 (2 pens, con, drop-goal)
27-3-71	*v* France (Paris) Won 9–5 (try, pen)
15-1-72	*v* England (Twickenham) Won 12–3 (2 pens, con)
5-2-72	*v* Scotland (Cardiff) Won 35–12 (3 pens, 3 cons)
25-3-72	*v* France (Cardiff) Won 20–6 (4 pens)

TOTAL 25 CAPS, 90 POINTS

FOR BRITISH LIONS

1968 TOUR TO SOUTH AFRICA

22-5-68   *v* Western Province (Cape Town) Won 10–6

25-5-68   *v* South-West Districts (Mossel Bay) Won 24–6

1-6-68   *v* Natal (Durban) Won 17–5

8-6-68   *v* SOUTH AFRICA (Pretoria) Lost 20–25
                   (injured with broken collar bone early on)

TOTAL 4 MATCHES

1971 TOUR TO AUSTRALIA AND NEW ZEALAND

15-5-71   *v* New South Wales (Sydney) Won 14–12 (2 pens, con)

22-5-71   *v* Counties/Thames Valley (Pukekohe) Won 25–3
                   (3 pens, 2 cons, drop-goal)

29-5-71   *v* Waikato (Hamilton) Won 35–14 (try, pen, con, drop-goal)

2-6-71   *v* NZ Maoris (Auckland) Won 23–12 (6 pens, con)

5-6-71   *v* Wellington (Wellington) Won 47–9 (try, 2 pens, 5 cons)

12-6-71   *v* Otago (Dunedin) Won 21–9 (pen, 3 cons, drop-goal)

26-6-71   *v* NEW ZEALAND (Dunedin) Won 9–3 (2 pens)

30-6-71   *v* Southland (Invercargill) Won 25–3 (5 cons)

6-7-71   *v* NZ Universities (Wellington) Won 27–6
                   (try, 3 pens, 3 cons, drop-goal)

10-7-71   *v* NEW ZEALAND (Christchurch) Lost 12–22 (pen, drop-goal)

14-7-71   *v* Wairarapa/Bush (Masterton) Won 27–6 (2 tries, 2 cons)

17-7-71   *v* Hawkes Bay (Napier) Won 25–6 (2 pens, 2 cons, drop-goal)

24-7-71   *v* Auckland (Auckland) Won 19–12 (3 pens, 2 cons)

31-7-71   *v* NEW ZEALAND (Wellington) Won 13–3 (try, 2 cons, drop-goal)

7-8-71   *v* North Auckland (Whangarei) Won 11–5 (con)

10-8-71   *v* Bay of Plenty (Tauranga) Won 20–14 (drop-goal)

14-8-71   *v* NEW ZEALAND (Auckland) Drew 14–14 (2 pens, con)

TOTAL 17 MATCHES, 188 POINTS

FOR LLANELLI

1963–64   5 matches, 5 points

1964–65   21 matches, 57 points

1965–66   33 matches, 69 points

1966–67   27 matches, 68 points

TOTAL 86 MATCHES, 199 POINTS
(including 25 drop-goals)

FOR CARDIFF

1967–68   28 matches, 61 points

1968–69   14 matches, 40 points

1969–70   15 matches, 28 points

1970–71   22 matches, 114 points

1971–72   14 matches, 120 points

TOTAL 93 MATCHES, 363 POINTS
(including 24 tries, 30 drop-goals)

N.B. Try upgraded from three points to four points in 1971–72 season

BARRY'S BIG MOMENTS

His 188 points for Lions in 1971 set a new individual record

His 90 points for Wales in international matches surpassed the previous best mark of 88 set by Jack Bancroft in 1914

His 35 points in 1971–72 Five Nations Championship set a new record for Wales

Won 2–1 with the Lions in New Zealand in 1971

Won Five Nations Championship and Triple Crown in 1969; share of Championship in 1970; Championship, Triple Crown and Grand Slam in 1971; Championship in 1972

Named Welsh Player of the Year, 1971

Named European Player of the Year, 1972

Named one of five New Zealand Almanack Players of the Year, 1971

Named Man of the Tournament in 1969 Snelling Sevens after record 36-point haul for Cardiff in tournament

One of 15 original players named in the International Rugby Hall of Fame.